Apple Pro Training Series
DVD Studio Pro 4

Martin Sitter/Adrian Ramseier

Apple
Certified

Apple Pro Training Series: DVD Studio Pro 4
Martin Sitter/Adrian Ramseier
Copyright © 2006 by all4DVD and Martin Sitter

Published by Peachpit Press. For information on Peachpit Press books, contact:

Peachpit Press
1249 Eighth Street
Berkeley, CA 94710
(510) 524-2178
Fax: (510) 524-2221
http://www.peachpit.com
To report errors, please send a note to errata@peachpit.com.
Peachpit Press is a division of Pearson Education.

Contributing Writer: Matt Geller
Menu Design: Darcy Dahl, Paul Kyle, Yan Shvalb, Martin Sitter
Editors: Geta Carlson, Serena Herr, Kristin Kalning, Nancy Peterson
Production Editor: Amy Hassos Parker, Specialized Composition, Inc.
Technical Editor: Matt Geller, Jonathan Eric Tyrrell
Technical Reviewers: Stephen Kanter, Steve Martin
Copy Editors: Darren Meiss
Compositing: Specialized Composition, Inc.
Indexer: Jack Lewis
DVD Production: Evan Pricco, Victor Gavenda
Cover Design: Frances Baca
Cover Illustration: Tolleson Design; images © Getty Images, Inc.

ISBN 0-321-33482-5
9 8 7 6 5 4 3 2 1
Printed and bound in the United States of America

To freedom of speech, and the right to ask questions. —M.S.

*To all those who want to tell their stories, share memories and music,
and use this technology to bring people together. —A.R.*

Acknowledgments

Martin Sitter Thank you Serena Herr, for keeping the bubble floating between the lines. A warm thank-you to Patty Montesion for ensuring that proper education is out there. Thanks also to Brian Schmidt, Don Steele, Margaret Tinsley, Phil Jackson, Jessica Steigerwald, Bill Forester, Vidas Neverauskas, David Dvorin, Victor Alexander, and all of my other friends at Apple. Deep respect goes to Mark Stope and Sli-fi.com, as well as the team at macProVideo.com, for suffering through endless delays while I finished this unexpected project.

And finally, I'd like to acknowledge my peers, the other Apple Lead trainers: Adam Green, Steve Martin, Abba Shapiro, Damian Allen, Mary Plummer, and Diana Weynand. See y'all at the next show.

Adrian Ramseier First and foremost, I am grateful to my wife and business partner, Judith Ramseier, for guiding this book along its path, and my kids, Jessica and Pascal, for having patience with me.

The all4DVD team: Darcy Dahl, Chad Fahs, Paul Kyle, Frank Rohmer, Ernie Schaeffer, and Yan Shvalb all made valuable contributions to the first edition, and much of their work is showcased again here.

The Apple team: Patty Montesion for the opportunity to write this book; Matt Geller for his excellent written and technical contributions; Stephen Kanter and Steve Martin for their technical review; and Kirk Paulsen for his writing contributions.

The Peachpit Press team: Serena Herr and Kristin Kalning for managing this project, Geta Carlson for developmental editing, Darren Meiss for copy editing and proofing.

And grateful thanks to Oliver Stauffer from Switzerland Tourism (www.switzerland.com) for the terrific Swiss footage, and to Carol Amore for providing her gorgeous Tiger footage.

Contents at a Glance

Table of Contents

Swiss Project: Creating a Simple DVD

Tiger Project: Creating a Complex DVD

Black Box Project: Advanced Authoring Techniques

Getting Started

Welcome to the official Apple Pro training course for DVD Studio Pro 4, Apple's powerful DVD authoring application. The goal of this book is to provide a complete guide to authoring DVDs using DVD Studio Pro 4.

In addition, this book includes lessons on how to use other Apple applications designed to work with DVD Studio Pro, such as Compressor, which prepares video and audio media for use in a DVD project, and Final Cut Pro, Apple's groundbreaking non-linear digital video editor. In Appendix A you'll learn how to create a motion menu with a soundtrack in Final Cut Pro and export it directly into DVD Studio Pro.

Whether you're a professional DVD author or are just getting your feet wet, DVD Studio Pro can do it all. So let's get started.

The Methodology

This book is a hands-on course that demonstrates, with practical lessons, the best ways to author a project with DVD Studio Pro. Since there are different ways to accomplish the same task, the book focuses on the methods preferred by professional DVD creators. Each lesson is designed to help you start authoring projects in DVD Studio Pro at a professional level as quickly as possible. Once you have worked through a lesson, you can continue on to the next exercise, which builds on the knowledge and the project you just completed.

Course Structure

During the course of this book you will create four DVDs. To get you started, the first project is a simple DVD for a tiger documentary, with a movie, slideshow, and two basic menus. Next, over the course of the following five chapters, you will build a more sophisticated DVD on Swiss tourism and learn the basic functions of DVD Studio Pro. The two DVD projects that follow, Tiger and Black Box, are successively more complex, but both build on the basic techniques and structure introduced in the first project. Finally, there are two lessons that focus on specific advanced authoring techniques. As you progress through each lesson, you will learn how to access more intermediate and advanced features, as well as how to customize DVD Studio Pro to suit your working style.

Organizing the course around four DVD projects instead of one requires you to repeat, and thereby reinforce, the same basic tasks on every DVD. As each project reinforces the previous one, it also introduces powerful new tools and features that enhance the look and sound of the DVD, or speed up the authoring process. By the time you finish the fourth project, you will know how to build a full-featured DVD with multiple video angles, subtitles, motion menus, and alternate streams of audio for foreign languages, audio commentary, or even 5.1 channel Dolby Surround Sound.

The lessons are broken down as follows:

Lesson	Project	Level
Lessons 1–2	TigerBasic	Basic
Lessons 3–9	Swiss	Basic/intermediate
Lessons 10–13	Tiger	Intermediate
Lessons 14–18	Black Box	Intermediate/advanced
Lessons 19–20	Advanced Techniques	Advanced
Appendix A	Create a Motion Menu in Final Cut Pro	Intermediate/advanced
Appendix B	Bit Budgeting	Intermediate/advanced

Copying the Lesson Files

Apple Pro Training Series: DVD Studio Pro 4 comes with a DVD that contains all of the files you need to complete each lesson. The disc is prepared in a way that allows you to watch, on any DVD player, the DVD projects you will ultimately create when doing the lessons (the Swiss PAL project is not included). So before copying the lesson files to your hard drive, take a moment now to tour the projects you're going to create.

Touring the Projects You Will Create

1 Insert the *Apple Pro Training Series: DVD Studio Pro 4* DVD into the DVD drive of your computer (or any DVD player).

Your DVD Player application will launch automatically, and a menu will appear showing three of the four projects you will create.

2 Click through the interfaces of the projects to familiarize yourself with them.

3 Quit your DVD Player application. You will now see the icon for the DVD, titled *APTS_DVD-SP4*, on your Desktop. You can access the book's media and project files from there.

Installing the DVD Studio Pro 4 Lesson and Media Files

The *Apple Pro Training Series: DVD Studio Pro 4* DVD includes a DSP Book Files folder, which contains a Media folder, a Lessons folder, and two folders called My_Projects and Appendix A. These folders in turn contain the media, project, and other files you will need to complete this course. To work through the lessons in this book, you'll need to copy these files onto your hard drive. After the media files have been copied to your hard drive, they can be easily accessed for use in the lessons.

> **NOTE ▸** You will also see a VIDEO_TS folder and an AUDIO_TS folder on the DVD. These contain the files for the demonstration you just played above. Do not load the VIDEO_TS or AUDIO_TS files onto your hard drive.

1 Insert the *Apple Pro Training Series: DVD Studio Pro 4* DVD into the DVD drive of your computer, if you haven't already.

2 Drag the DSP4 Book Files folder to your hard drive. The folder contains about 3 GB of media, so it will take some minutes to copy.

It is important to keep the Media and Lessons folders together on your hard drive within the single DSP Book Files folder, and not to move them after you have begun working through the lessons. Moving the media or lesson files could result in broken links and project file errors.

As you work through the lessons, you will be asked to come back to this folder location to import the media necessary for the four DVD projects. In other words, remember where you parked your files.

Reconnecting Media

When you move the media and lesson files from the APTS_DSP4 disk to your hard drive, you may lose the links between the project files and the media files.

The easiest way to avoid broken links is to save your project file after each lesson and reopen it when you start the next lesson, thus using the same file as you work progressively through the project. This is the method we assume you'll use.

If you choose to skip a lesson, however, you'll need to use the project Start file from the disk, and you may need to establish valid links between the project file and the media files you copied to your hard drive.

Reconnecting your media is a fairly simple task. When you open a project with media that has become disconnected, you are presented with a screen that asks you to reconnect the media files. Follow these steps to reconnect your media:

1 When the Missing Files window appears, click the asset you want to reconnect. In some cases, this will open the Relinking File window. If it does not, go to step 2.

2 Click the Locate button.

3 Find the file on your hard drive.

4 Click Relink.

Once you relink one asset (that is, one track), DVD Studio Pro will automatically detect all other media files in the track at once. You'll have to repeat these steps for the menus and graphic files, pointing DVD Studio Pro to each of those folders when it prompts you for the folder's location.

System Requirements

Before you begin to use DVD Studio Pro 4, make sure that your computer meets the minimum requirements for working with the application. Many of the frequently used preview and encoding functions rely on adequate system performance to work properly. For up-to-date information on system requirements, see Apple's Web site at www.apple.com/dvdstudiopro.

Resources

Apple Pro Training Series: DVD Studio Pro 4 is not intended to be a comprehensive reference manual and is not a replacement for documentation included with the application. For more information about DVD Studio Pro features and troubleshooting advice, refer to the following resources:

▶ *DVD Studio Pro 4 for Macintosh: Visual QuickPro Guide,* by Martin Sitter (Peachpit Press)

▶ DVD Studio Pro 4 Help guide, which is accessed through the Help menu in DVD Studio Pro

▶ Apple's DVD Studio Pro Web site: www.apple.com/dvdstudiopro

About the Apple Pro Training Series

Apple Pro Training Series: DVD Studio Pro 4 is part of the official training series for Apple Pro applications developed by experts in the field. It is both a self-paced learning tool and the curriculum of the Apple Pro Training and Certification Program.

The lessons in this book are designed to let you learn at your own pace. Although each lesson provides step-by-step instructions for creating specific projects, there is room for exploration and experimentation. You can follow the book from start to finish, or you can dive into the sections and lessons that interest you most. If you are new to DVD authoring or to DVD Studio Pro, however, we recommend that you complete the first nine lessons in sequence before jumping ahead to later lessons.

Apple Pro Certification Program

The Apple Pro Training and Certification Programs are designed to keep you at the forefront of Apple's digital media technology while giving you a competitive edge in today's ever-changing job market. Whether you are an editor, graphic designer, sound designer, special effects artist, or teacher, these training tools are meant to help you expand your skills.

Upon completing the course material in this book, you can become an Apple Pro by taking the certification exam at an Apple Authorized Training Center. Certification is offered in Final Cut Pro 4, DVD Studio Pro, Shake 3, and Logic 6. Successful certification as an Apple Pro gives you official recognition of your knowledge of Apple's professional applications while allowing you to market yourself to employers and clients as a skilled, pro-level user of Apple products.

To find an Authorized Training Center near you, go to www.apple.com/software/pro/training.

For those who prefer to learn in an instructor-led setting, Apple also offers training courses at Apple Authorized Training Centers across the world. These courses, which use the Apple Pro Training Series books as their curriculum, are taught by Apple Certified Trainers, and they balance concepts and lectures with hands-on labs and exercises. Apple Authorized Training Centers for Pro projects have been carefully selected and have met Apple's highest standards in all areas, including facilities, instructors, course delivery, and infrastructure. The goal of the program is to offer Apple customers, from beginners to the most seasoned professionals, the highest quality training experience.

Tiger Basic Project: Using the Basic Configuration

Matt Geller is a Chicago-based systems integrator, consult-
ant, and all-around technology therapist specializing in dig-
ital video postproduction installations. In addition to his
work as a video editor and motion graphics artist, Matt is a
certified instructor for Apple, Boris, and Discreet, and is a
courseware author and technical editor for Apple. He helped
form the Chicago Final Cut Pro Users Group and served as
its treasurer for three years. You can find out more about
Matt at http://thetechtherapist.com.

1

Lesson Files	Lessons > 01_TigerBasic_Finished.dspproj
Media	Media > TigerBasic folder
Time	This lesson takes approximately 60 minutes to complete.
Goals	Learn the six steps of DVD authoring
	Learn about the DVD-Video Specification
	Learn what assets can be used for DVDs
	Work with the Basic view
	Assemble a simple DVD project
	Use the Palette window
	Create a basic menu
	Create a slideshow with audio
	Burn a disc

Preparing Your First DVD Project

Welcome to the world of DVD authoring! As an interactive medium, DVD-Video gives you, the DVD author, a unique opportunity to plan and create an experience for the user. The experience you create includes not only things to see and hear, but also choices for users to make along the way. Apple DVD Studio Pro 4 provides elegant, simple, and powerful tools to help you create this user experience.

In the first lesson in this course, you'll learn some fundamental facts about the scope and limitations of what a DVD-Video disc can be. Then you'll jump right into the DVD Studio Pro interface and author an entire disc. By the end of this lesson, you'll have a fully burned disc that's ready for viewing. So fire up that Mac and let's go!

DVD Creation Process

DVD authoring involves six steps:

1. Planning your user experience by means of a storyboard.

 A *storyboard* is a visual diagram that shows main elements of your project and how they are linked.

2. Creating your assets, which are the actual media files that will form the content of the disc.

 Video, audio, and image files are all examples of assets. These assets can either be created using content creation software, such as Apple's Final Cut Pro or Logic, or Adobe Photoshop, or pulled directly into the computer from other sources, such as videotape, an audio CD, or a digital still camera.

3. Importing your assets into DVD Studio Pro.

4. Assembling these assets into items that make up a DVD-Video disc.

 Disc items are containers that hold assets. Examples of items are menus, tracks, and slideshows.

5. Linking these items to form the user experience.

 This step involves referring to your storyboard to ensure that the experience flows correctly—and creating menus, submenus, and, most important, buttons that link up every item on the disc and guide the user through the experience.

6. Building and formatting the disc.

 In this step, the computer takes all your authoring work and creates the files that wind up on the disc itself.

Those of you who are already familiar with the authoring process may be thinking, "Hey, what about encoding?" Encoding is the process of converting your assets from whatever file format they're in to the file format necessary for DVD authoring. Unique to DVD Studio Pro is the choice you have when you do your encoding.

Traditionally, encoding is done between steps 2 and 3, and is accomplished most efficiently with programs such as Compressor and A.Pack. These two additional programs, which come with DVD Studio Pro, will be covered in depth later in this book.

You also have the choice of importing assets directly into DVD Studio Pro without changing the nature of the assets at all. If you choose this method, you have two further choices. You can choose to let DVD Studio Pro encode your assets in the background as you work, or you can encode just before step 6, in a process called *encode on build*. The best part of choosing the second of these two in-program encoding methods is that all the lonely, computer-only, time-intensive parts of the process are relegated to the final step, and we authors can go outside and play.

The DVD-Video Specification

Although DVD-Video is not nearly as flexible as other interactive formats, such as museum kiosks or Web sites, DVD-Video does include many unique features. These features are defined as part of a list of technical guidelines referred to as the *DVD-Video specification*. There's lots of gobbledygook in this specification, so let's just concentrate on the cool stuff:

DVD-Video discs can contain up to 99 tracks of content. Each track can include up to 9 streams of video, 8 streams of audio, 32 subtitles, and multiple languages, all of which makes DVDs ideal for multinational and multicultural experiences. The user can switch between the multiple video, audio, and subtitle streams at any time. Tracks can have *chapter markers*, which allow the user to navigate directly to specific places on the track. You can also control the playback of a track's chapter markers via *stories*, which essentially function as playlists for the content between chapter markers.

DVDs have an item called a *slideshow*, which can contain up to 99 still images that advance either automatically or manually, with or without music playing in the background.

Menus are the main interactive item of a DVD, and you can have tens of thousands of them on a disc! Menus can contain up to 36 buttons to link up your disc items.

If this isn't enough, you can also write *scripts* that customize the user experience even further by instructing the DVD-playing device to do specific tasks based on user input or environmental conditions.

Even with all these features, the DVD creation process is rather simple, in part because the specification is rigid and limited. Theoretically, every set-top DVD player should be able to play any DVD that is created according to this specification, without the need for special plug-ins or other software. The uniformity in DVD discs and players ensures universal compatibility.

Finally, DVD Studio Pro allows access to every corner of the DVD-Video specification, and it even has a few tricks up its sleeve that allow you to enhance the user experience beyond the limits of the specification, without violating any specification rules.

DVD-Video File Formats

A requirement of DVD-Video is that the assets it contains must be encoded into very specific file formats. The DVD specification calls for the following, and only the following, file formats when authoring a disc:

► Video files must be in MPEG-2 (Motion Picture Experts Group, version 2) or, less commonly, MPEG-1 formats.

► Audio files must be in PCM (Pulse Code Modulated, also known as AIFF and WAV files), AC-3 (Dolby Digital), or MP2 (MPEG1-Layer 2. Yep, that's an audio file format) formats. Alternatively, audio files may also be in DTS (Digital Theater System) format.

► Still images must be in MPEG-2 still image format.

These limited choices for encoded asset file formats are all that the DVD-Video specification allows. However, file format flexibility is one place where DVD Studio Pro really shines. Working together with the magic of Quick-Time, DVD Studio Pro allows you to import any of the following file formats listed, and will encode them into the file formats we just listed:

► Video—MPEG-2, MPEG-1, QuickTime (all codecs supported)

► Audio—AC-3, PCM (AIFF and WAV), MP2, MP3

► Images—TIFF, PCT, JPEG, BMP, TGA, PSD (Photoshop)

DVD Studio Pro also accepts the following file formats for automating the creation of subtitle streams and chapter markers:

► Subtitle—STL, SON, SCR, TXT

► Markers—TXT

With the flexibility that DVD Studio Pro gives you to import any QuickTime movie file, a multitude of audio formats, and a number of different still image formats, you can move from the content creation process into the authoring process without pause.

The DVD-Video Disc

The DVD-Video specification was created by an assembly of manufacturers and content distributors known as the DVD Forum. One of the greatest accomplishments of this group was creating a list of disc formats so confusing that it boggles the mind. We won't go there. We're interested in just two of the many (try 38) formats that exist.

DVD-5 This is a single-sided, single-layered disc that can hold 4.7 GB of data. We can burn these discs on our Macs today. All Mac SuperDrives burn onto a physical disc called DVD-R (pronounced "DVD dash R"). More recently, we also have the ability, via third-party burners, to burn onto a physical disc called DVD+R ("DVD plus R"). There are small differences between the -R and +R formats, although it seems that -R discs are compatible with a broader range of DVD players, and -R discs are the only ones to use in a Mac SuperDrive. A DVD-5 disc can hold roughly 1 to 2 hours of video content.

DVD-9 This is a single-sided, dual-layered disc that can hold 8.54 GB of data. This is the disc that you get when you rent a DVD movie from your local video store. We'll soon be able to burn these discs on our Macs, but most authors currently working with this format create the content of the disc in DVD Studio Pro and send it to a disc replicator for mass manufacturing. A DVD-9 disc can hold roughly 2 to 4 hours of video content.

Accessing Features of DVD-Video

A DVD-Video disc uses a remote control device to activate the interactive features of a DVD and operate the player. Whether the user uses a software player in a computer or a hardware player in his or her living room, all of the remote control buttons are essentially the same, although the names may differ slightly between players.

For example, the usual playback control buttons, such as Play, Stop, Forward, and Reverse, are universal. Also, keys for Menu and Title are required to return to a previous menu or to jump to the top menu of a disc. To allow users to

navigate through buttons on DVD menus, all remotes have Up, Down, Left, Right, and Enter buttons. There are also buttons for choosing between alternate video, audio, and subtitle streams of the particular track that is playing. The names for these buttons may differ, but they are usually Angle for video streams, Audio for audio streams, and Subtitle for subtitle streams. You can cycle through the available streams by pressing the corresponding button as many times as is required to choose the desired stream.

As you author your disc, pay careful attention to how the user will navigate through the experience with his or her remote control. In DVD Studio Pro, you can set each of the remote control's features either for the entire disc or for individual disc items, such as tracks and menus. Best of all, you can test how the different buttons function using DVD Studio Pro's Simulator. The Simulator allows you to preview the actual functionality of the disc when it is finished, and it includes a remote control to approximate the functions of a DVD player. The Simulator is an important feature that you will be using often to test your progress as you create the various items for your DVD.

Exploring the Interface

OK, enough background information. It's time to make a DVD! Let's launch the application and dig right in.

1 Launch DVD Studio Pro by double-clicking its application icon in the Applications folder of your hard drive.

TIP Since we'll be using DVD Studio Pro so often during the course of this book, it's a good idea to place its icon in your Dock (if it's not already there). After the program has launched, click and hold on its icon in the Dock, and choose Keep In Dock from the contextual menu that pops up.

If this is your first time launching DVD Studio Pro, you will encounter a dialog that asks you to choose the application configuration, which is the way that DVD Studio Pro displays its interface.

If you were adventurous enough to launch DVD Studio Pro for the first time before cracking open this book, the interface should open to whatever configuration you last selected. We want to start in the Basic configuration, to explore the interface in its most essential form.

2 In the Choose Application Configuration dialog, click the Basic button, make sure the NTSC radio button is selected, and click OK.

If you've launched the application before and are now seeing the main interface, choose Window > Configurations > Basic, or press F1.

The Basic view should open with the project window, which currently has "Untitled" in its title bar. The Palette is in the upper right, and the Inspector (which currently states "Disc" in its title bar) is in the lower right.

The Project Window

The project window is the main interface of DVD Studio Pro. It has a convenient toolbar at the very top, which lists often-used one-click tools.

Just below the toolbar are four tabs:

▶ Menu—Where you create and edit the menus of your DVDs

▶ Slideshow—Where you create and edit slideshows

▶ Viewer—Allows you to view moving and still items, such as tracks and slideshows

▶ Graphical—Shows a graphical representation of all the items of the DVD, and how they link up together

The Palette

The Palette has six tabs. The first three—Templates, Styles, and Shapes—contain thumbnail links to assets that have been created for you by the folks at Apple.

▶ The Templates tab contains entire prebuilt menus, complete with placeholders for still or moving images (called *drop zones*), buttons, and beautiful text and graphics.

▶ The Styles tab contains prebuilt styles for text, buttons, drop zones, and menu layouts.

▶ The Shapes tab contains a plethora of physical shape files that can be used to create drop zones or buttons.

The next three tabs—Audio, Stills, and Video—contain thumbnail links to assets.

▶ The Audio tab contains links to assets in your Music folder.

▶ The Stills tab contains links to assets in your Pictures folder.

▶ The Video tab contains links to your Movies folder.

In these tabs, you can also create links to folders anywhere on your hard drive or your network in order to bring in assets to your current project.

The important thing to remember about the Palette is that it's a window of possibilities. What we see in the Palette are links to actual assets outside of your project, and you will drag and drop them from the Palette into your project window in order to add them to your current project.

The Inspector

Just below the Palette, you'll find the Inspector. The Inspector is a chameleon of sorts. It reflects the properties of whatever is currently selected in your project, and its title bar tells you what asset or element it is currently "reporting" on. For instance, if you're working on a button, the Inspector will bear the title "Button"; if you're working on the disc as a whole, the Inspector will show the word "Disc" in its title bar; and so on. You use the Inspector to change the properties of items and elements. The Inspector is, in fact, the most-used window in the interface.

If you're an iDVD user, DVD Studio Pro's overall window configuration should seem similar to what you're accustomed to in Apple's consumer-level application. The project window is similar to iDVD's main window; the Palette window is similar to the Themes area in iDVD's Customize drawer; and the Inspector is similar to the Settings area.

Creating a Simple DVD in Basic View

Now that you've launched the application, selected Basic view, and gotten a quick tour of the interface, you're ready to begin authoring your disc. First, you'll need to bring some assets into your project. In this first exercise, you'll create new links in the Audio, Stills, and Video tabs of the Palette in order to display and use the assets needed to create the disc.

1 Go to the Palette window and click the Video tab.

2 Click the Add (+) button in the top-left corner of the Palette to select a new folder that contains the video assets you want to add to the project.

3 Navigate to the Media folder located in the DSP4 Book Files folder on your hard drive.

4 Locate the Media > TigerBasic > TigerBasic_Assets > Tiger_Video folder, and click Add to place the folder in the video list in the Palette.

NOTE ▶ If you can't find the DSP4 Book Files folder, make sure you have installed the Media files for this book properly. For details, see "Introduction: Getting Started."

Once the folder is added to the Palette, you should be able to see a thumbnail image of the **TigerMovie1** video file in the list at the bottom of the Palette. This thumbnail represents the first frame of the video.

Now let's add some audio assets.

5 Click the Audio tab in the Palette.

6 Click the Add (+) button to select a folder with the audio assets you require.

7 Select the Media > TigerBasic > TigerBasic_Assets > Tiger_Audio folder and click Add.

After you have selected this folder, the one file in that folder, **TigerAudio**, is displayed in the Audio palette.

Now let's add some still image assets, which you can use later for a slideshow.

8 Click the Stills tab in the Palette.

9 Click the Add (+) button to select a folder with the image assets you require.

10 Select the Media > TigerBasic > TigerBasic_Assets > Tiger_Stills folder and click Add.

The thumbnails for the seven JPEG images in the Tiger_Stills folder are displayed at the bottom of the Palette.

11 Choose File > Save or press Cmd-S to save your project.

TIP You should save your project every few minutes.

12 Type the name *TigerBasic_DVD* in the Save As field in the dialog, but don't click Save just yet.

13 Click the disclosure triangle to the right of the Save As field.

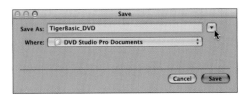

Clicking open the disclosure triangle reveals all the features of the Save window.

DVD Studio pro automatically appends a .dspproj extension to all project files, so that they can be identified by the operating system. By default, you will not see this extension added to the filename because the Hide Extension box is selected in the lower-left corner of the Save dialog. We'll leave this as it is.

14 Navigate to DSP4 Book Files > My_Projects.

15 Click Save, and your new **TigerBasic_DVD** project is saved in the My_Projects folder.

Creating a Menu

The disc you are creating is simple. It has one main track, which will play the **TigerMovie1** asset you just linked to in the Palette. You will also create a slideshow with all the still images you linked to. To allow your users to navigate between the track and slideshow, you will create a main menu with buttons that link to the track and slideshow.

The main menu is the first item that a user will encounter when playing the disc, and it should be eye-catching and easy to navigate. Although you can create your menus from scratch for more advanced projects, it is much quicker and easier to use menu templates, which construct the layout and design of a menu for you automatically. For the TigerBasic project, you'll need to make only slight modifications to the template to customize your menu.

The layout of templates also provides a simple navigation flow for projects that are too small for a storyboard. (You'll get some practice with storyboards later in this book.)

Applying an Apple Menu Template

DVD Studio Pro ships with many high-quality menu templates for you to use. In this next exercise, you will select and add one of these templates in order to create the main menu for your project.

1 Click the Templates tab in the Palette.

2 Double-click the first template thumbnail, Brush Cover.

When the template is applied, the Menu Editor of the project window looks like this:

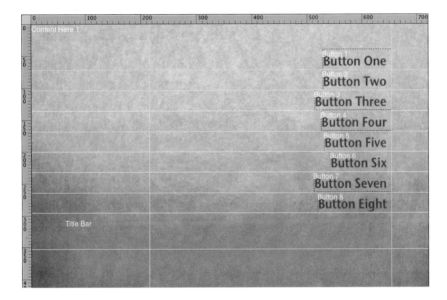

NOTE ► Menu templates may take a while to load, depending on the speed of your computer and the template you choose.

3 Choose File > Save to save your project.

Modifying an Apple Template

Applying a template was pretty easy, don't you think? However, looking at the template, it may not seem like much. That's because this particular menu template is a motion menu. Let's take a quick look at it in motion to see all of its cool features.

1 At the bottom right of the Menu Editor, click the Motion button (the circle with a small figure in it).

Suddenly, a brush stroke makes its way across the screen, from right to left, revealing a text field. At the end of the motion animation, a gray area with an arrow icon in it appears in the upper-left of the screen. Both of these elements are called *drop zones*.

The drop zone in the upper left indicates by its gray area and arrow icon that an asset can be "dropped" into its "zone" in order to create a fade effect. The purpose of the drop zone at the bottom of the menu is to eventually reveal the text. The placeholder text currently says, "TITLE INFORMATION HERE," but not for long. Let's change that text to the title of our disc.

2 Once you see the text revealed by the brush stroke, click once directly on the text, then wait a moment and click it again to highlight the text.

3 Type *Tigers—Tracking a Legend* for the title.

4 Click away from the text box, somewhere close by on the menu's surface, to deselect it.

5 Holding down the Option key, drag and drop the text box down to create a copy of it just below the original.

As you drag the new text box down, automatic yellow alignment guides will indicate how the new text field is lining up with elements around it on the menu. Use them to make sure the copied text box is exactly below the original one.

6 Click this new text box a second time to highlight its text.

7 Type *www.wildlifeworlds.com.*

8 Press Cmd-A to select all of the text you just typed, and then click the Show Fonts icon at the top of the Menu Editor.

9 Use the Font window to change the size of the text to 18 point.

10 Close the Font window.

OK, you've customized the text. Now you need to actually "drop" something into that drop zone in the upper left of the screen.

11 In the Inspector, click the Stills tab.

12 Scroll through the thumbnail list of the seven photos you recently linked, and find the fifth photo, the one with the tiger peeking out from the grass.

13 Select this photo and drag it to the drop zone in the upper left of the menu, but *don't let go of the mouse.*

In a moment, the Drop palette will appear. As you hold down the mouse button, the Drop palette reveals a context-sensitive menu for dropping assets or menu elements onto the menu. An essential part of the DVD Studio Pro interface, the Drop palette saves you a lot of time.

The Drop palette takes a moment to come onto the screen, which gives you an opportunity to practice developing your patience (let's call this *Drop Patience*).

14 Make sure your pointer is located inside the first selection in the Drop palette, which is Set Asset. Then let go of the mouse button.

The image of the tiger now ominously reveals itself when the drop zone fades onto the screen.

Finally, let's tackle this template's default buttons, which appear as the eight little areas in the upper-right corner of the screen. The buttons that come with this template are too numerous for our purposes, and besides, they're a little boring. Let's get rid of them in one swoop.

15 Hold down the Command key, and drag a selection rectangle around all eight buttons. (Be careful to select just the buttons and not anything else on the menu. This is best accomplished by starting at the upper right of the buttons and dragging to the bottom left.)

As you select each button, handles appear around the boundaries of the buttons to indicate that they are selected.

16 Press Delete to remove all the buttons.

Your menu should now look like this:

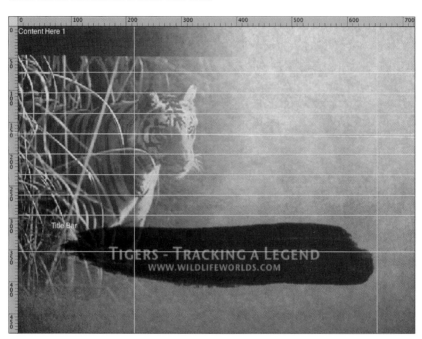

17 Choose File > Save to save your project.

Creating Custom Buttons

Now that you've gotten rid of all the buttons that came with this template, you'll need to create your own. In this exercise, you'll import some beautiful shape-based buttons from the Palette. The new buttons contain their own drop zones. You'll drop some assets into these drop zones to make them even more dynamic.

1 In the lower right of the Menu Editor, click the Hide Guides button to hide all the yellow guides onscreen.

NOTE ▶ It's usually best to keep the guides on so that you can easily align menu elements. For the rest of this lesson, however, we want to position our buttons more freely and also clear up the look of the workspace.

2 In the Palette, click the Styles tab, then the Apple button, and finally the Buttons button to see all the available button styles.

3 Click and drag the Brush Small 1 button onto the top right of the menu. Hold the mouse button down and wait for the Drop palette to appear.

4 Select Create Button, Set Style (the first selection) in the Drop palette.

The new button is called Button 1 in your menu, as you can see in the upper-left corner of the button's boundary.

5 Back in the Palette, click and drag the Brush Small 2 button onto the menu, just to the left and below where you placed your first button, and hold down the mouse button.

The Drop palette appears.

6 Select Create Button, Set Style from the Drop palette.

The new button, called Button 2, appears in your menu.

7 Click the word "Button" at the bottom of Button 1, then click it again and rename it *Play Movie.*

8 Click the word "Button" at the bottom of Button 2, and rename it *Slideshow* using the method described in step 7.

As you place elements like these onto the menu, you need to be aware of the *overscan area* of a television image. Simply put, there is more area to a television image than you can see on the average television set. The overscan area can be compared to the area of a tablecloth that falls off a table's edge.

Fortunately, DVD Studio Pro has two overlays to make sure that all parts of the menu will be seen on a television: the *action safe area* for general images, and the *title safe area* for text. Let's turn on the title safe area to make sure your newly placed buttons will show up properly when viewed on a television set.

9 From the Settings pop-up menu in the upper-right corner of the Menu Editor, choose Title Safe Area.

An outline forms around the menu, indicating where it is safe to display text and any important elements of a menu.

10 Reposition the Play Movie button by simply clicking in its center and dragging it, so that it is within the title safe area.

11 Click the lower-left corner of the Slideshow button outline, and drag it up and to the right to reduce the size to about 60%.

12 Move the Slideshow button up and to the right.

Your new menu template should now look similar to the one shown here:

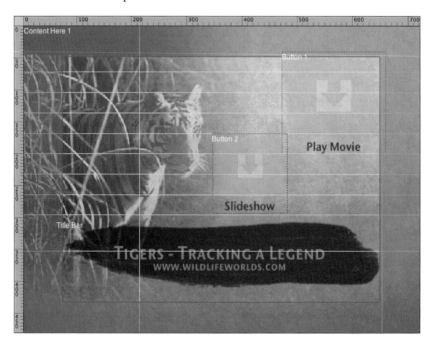

13 Choose File > Save to save your changes.

The new look for your menu is complete. Notice how different the customized menu is from that of the original template.

Connecting Assets to the Menu

You've imported assets and built a menu with the right title text and customized buttons. The next step is to connect all the assets to the menu buttons.

Creating a Track

1 In the Palette, click the Video tab.

2 Drag the **TigerMovie1** thumbnail from the list below onto the Play Movie button in the Menu Editor.

3 When the Drop palette appears, select Set Asset and Create Track, Connect to Track.

Your button is now linked to a newly created video track, which will play when this button is activated. Also, your video's thumbnail image is dropped into the button. Finally, when the movie finishes playing in its track, the disc will jump back to the main menu. That's four authoring steps that the Drop palette has automatically executed for you!

4 Choose File > Save to save your changes.

Creating a Slideshow

You've got **TigerMovie1** linked up. Now it's time to get the slideshow working and hook up the audio.

1 In the Palette, click the Stills tab.

2 From the list of folders in the Stills tab, drag the Tiger_Stills folder onto the Slideshow button in the Menu Editor.

3 When the Drop palette appears, select Set Asset and Create Slideshow, Connect to Slideshow.

With one drag, the Slideshow button is now linked to a newly created slideshow. When the user selects and activates the Slideshow button, your DVD will play all seven of the images in the TigerStills folder.

Notice that the first image of the seven is used for the thumbnail image of the button. Additionally, when the slideshow finishes playing, the disc will jump back to the main menu. The Drop palette has again automatically executed four steps for you.

4 Click the Slideshow tab in the project window to display the Slideshow Editor.

All slideshow images are now displayed in the Slideshow Editor.

Next, let's add some music to play while the slides are being displayed. To add audio to the slideshow, you simply drag and drop your audio file from the Audio palette onto the Overall Audio File area in the Slideshow Editor.

5 In the Palette, click the Audio tab.

6 Drag the audio file named **TigerAudio** onto the little speaker well at the top of the Slideshow Editor.

This audio file is set to play as background music for the slides in your slideshow.

7 Move your pointer over the speaker well, and wait a moment.

A tooltip appears, showing you the contents of the speaker well.

Tooltips abound in DVD Studio Pro, just as in most of the other Apple Pro applications. If you can't remember the function of a button in the interface, or if you're just curious about the contents of an element, simply pause your pointer over it for a moment. The little yellow box that appears will usually tell you what you need to know.

8 Go back to the Menu Editor by clicking the Menu tab.

9 Choose File > Save to save your changes.

Simulating a Disc

It's time to test our disc! The Simulator allows you to test the project as if it were playing in a DVD player. This is an important feature, because it's critical to be able to test a project before burning it to a disc.

1 Click the Simulate icon in the toolbar.

The Simulator opens. You can now test the functionality of your DVD project as if you were watching it on a DVD player.

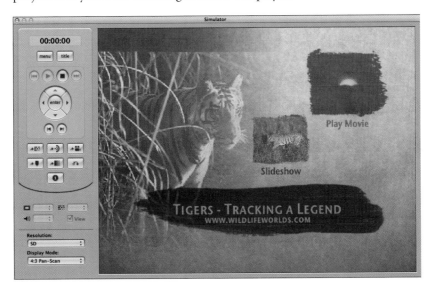

2 Select the Play Movie button in the main menu using the remote control buttons on the left side of the Simulator window.

3 Watch the movie.

When it's done, the main menu should appear again.

4 Select the Slideshow button, this time by clicking it with your mouse, and watch the slideshow.

When the slideshow is done, the DVD should jump back to the main menu.

Now that you've taken a look at your disc's basic functionality, it might seem that the main menu is a bit quiet. Let's add the same audio file that we are using in the slideshow to the main menu. This way, users can listen to music as they decide what to do next.

5 Close the Simulator by clicking the close button in the upper-left corner of the window. (Dismiss the Log window that appears automatically.)

6 In the Palette, click the Audio tab.

7 Drag the audio file named **TigerAudio** onto an empty space on your menu.

The Drop palette appears.

8 Select Set Audio.

9 Click the Simulate icon again.

Your menu now has audio. Navigate through the disc again to see that everything is linking correctly.

Building a Project and Burning a Disc

After you have tested your project with the Simulator and are satisfied with the results, you can go ahead and build the project and burn it to a DVD, or place it in a folder on your hard drive for later viewing and duplication. *Building* a project is the process that DVD Studio Pro undergoes as it combines the various assets and other elements into a finished DVD that can be viewed with a DVD player. In Lesson 9 you'll learn more about outputting a project. For now, we'll use the Burn button in the toolbar, which is identical in function to the Burn button in iDVD.

> **NOTE** ▶ You don't need to proceed with this final exercise, but if you are interested in seeing what your finished project looks like on an actual DVD player and are willing to burn a disc to do so, by all means forge ahead!

1 Click the Burn icon on the toolbar.

2 When prompted by the interface, insert a blank DVD-R into your Apple SuperDrive or external DVD burner.

3 Watch as the elements in your project are encoded, joined together, and output to a disc.

4 Choose File > Save to save your project.

Congratulations! You've created a fully functional, nice-looking DVD with navigation, and you've learned the basics of DVD authoring in the process.

Lesson Review

1. All Video files on a finished DVD-Video disc must be in what format?

2. What is the main function of the Inspector?

3. True or false: The Built-in Apple Templates cannot be modified in the Menu Editor.

4. How do you play a motion menu in the Menu editor?

5. How do you create a copy of a menu element?

6. Tue or False: You can add audio to a Slideshow.

Answers

1. MPEG-2 Video. In fact, every image asset, including still images, get transformed into MPEG-2 when the final disc is compiled.

2. It updates to show you the unique properties of any item selected in the workspace.

3. False. You can change button positions, text, and even the images in Drop Zones.

4. Click the Motion button in the bottom right corner of the menu editor.

5. Hold Option and drag the menu element to a different part of the Menu editor.

6. True. However, the audio does not play seamlessly under the slideshow and if you skip from slide to slide using the remote control's Next and Previous chapter buttons, you also skip forwards and backwards in the audio stream.

Keyboard Shortcuts

Cmd-N	Create new project
Cmd-S	Save project
Cmd-P	Burn
Cmd-Z	Undo

2

Lesson Files Lessons > 02_TigerBasic_Start
(or My_Projects > TigerBasic_DVD)

Lessons > 02_Tiger_Basic_Finished

Media Media > TigerBasic folder

Time This lesson takes approximately 45 minutes to complete.

Goals Expand the interface to its Extended and Advanced window configurations

Take a tour of the seven tabs found in the interface

Create customized window configurations and toolbar settings

Tweak a current project to enhance the user experience

Learn how to create simple chapter markers to aid user navigation

Use button transitions to easily transition from menu buttons to other disc items

Lesson 2

Exploring the Full Interface

In the first lesson, we hit the ground running and authored a fully functional DVD. Already the power of DVD Studio Pro should be evident, especially for those of us who have authored in iDVD or other programs. But we haven't even scratched the surface of DVD Studio Pro, especially its capability to give you access to all the important features of DVD-Video listed in the DVD-Video specification.

In this next lesson, you'll open up the full interface of DVD Studio Pro, using the project that you created in Lesson 1, **TigerBasic_DVD**, as the vehicle for your exploration of the interface. After touring the interface, you'll make subtle tweaks and adjustments to the project that wouldn't have been possible in DVD Studio Pro's Basic window configuration.

Opening the Project

Let's begin by opening the project you created in Lesson 1.

1 Launch DVD Studio Pro.

2 Choose File > Open Recent > **TigerBasic_DVD** (from your Lessons > My_Projects folder).

If you did not complete the last lesson or would like to start with a finished version of the last lesson, choose File > Open, navigate to your Lessons folder, and select **02_TigerBasic_Start**. You should now see your project in the Basic window configuration.

Exploring Window Configurations

You are currently viewing your project in DVD Studio Pro's Basic window configuration, which supplied you with everything you needed to create your first project, but now it's time to break out of the nest and see all there is to see in this interface.

1 Press F2 on your keyboard.

Extended window configuration

NOTE ▸ For PowerBook users, you'll have to press the FN key in the bottom left of the keyboard as you press your F2 key, or (depending on you preferences settings) you'll just increase your screen brightness!

Wow! Don't get overwhelmed; it's just the full interface staring back at you. This is called the Extended window configuration.

The Palette and Inspector have moved further to the right, and the project window has split into three main areas, called *quadrants*. Arrayed in these quadrants are 11 different tabs, which allow you to author every aspect of your disc. You'll notice the familiar Menu, Viewer, and Graphical tabs in the quadrant to the upper right, and the Slideshow tab in the lower quadrant, but all the other tabs are brand new. Not to worry, we'll cover all of them in a moment.

2 Press F3.

Advanced window configuration

This configuration (Advanced) is pretty much the same as the Extended configuration, except that the project window is now split into four quadrants, and the 11 tabs have been redistributed among them.

3 Press F2 again to go back to the Extended window configuration.

A Quick Tour of the Extended Window Configuration Tabs
Let's take a quick tour of the other tabs that you now see in the interface.

1 Direct your attention to the Assets tab, in the upper-left quadrant of the project window.

The Assets tab is the repository of all the assets that are currently imported into your project. This is where you will normally import externally created assets into the project for use in making the disc's items. In fact, from now on in this book, we'll use this tab to do most of our importing.

It's important to differentiate between the Assets tab and the Palette. As you learned in Lesson 1, the Palette is a window of possibilities. It contains links to numerous places on your hard drive that contain both assets and menu elements that you can choose to add to your project. However, the Assets tab contains the assets that you intend to use in the project at hand. When you create a new project, the Assets tab will always be blank, begging to be filled with imported goodies, but the Palette will always have its current links.

Note that the Assets tab currently holds all of the assets that we originally linked to from the Palette. But now these assets are currently being used in the project. You can see the template assets for the main menu, contained in the Templates folder; the still images **TigerPhoto_01–07**, currently in the slideshow; the audio file **TigerAudio.aif**, used in the slideshow and main menu; and the movie file **TigerMovie1** (video and audio), used in your main track. Notice that all assets are currently in use, as indicated by the checkmarks in the In Use column. In addition, all assets except for the movie file have a green dot in the Status column, indicating they are ready for the disc to be built.

NOTE ► In traditional DVD-Video authoring, video assets are pre-encoded into the limited video and audio formats accepted in the specification *before* they are imported into the authoring program. During the encoding process, they are split into separate video and audio files, which are called *elementary streams*. The video portion usually gets encoded into an MPEG-2 file, and the audio portion is usually stripped into an uncompressed PCM file, such as AIFF or WAV, and perhaps further encoded into a Dolby Digital file (AC-3).

In the case of your current project, you have imported an unencoded QuickTime file. DVD Studio Pro deals with imported QuickTime files in a special way. The QuickTime file is symbolically split into its video and audio portions in the Assets tab, as if it was already encoded. Then, however, DVD Studio Pro places an amber dot in the Status column of the Assets tab to alert you that the asset has not been encoded. This allows you to continue to work with the asset as you author the disc, and then either encode on build (just before creating the disc files) or encode in the background as you work.

2 Click any of the assets in the Assets tab.

Note that the Inspector, in the bottom right of the screen, changes to display the properties of each asset as you click it. The title bar name of the Inspector also changes to reflect the nature of the asset.

3 Now direct your attention to the Track tab, in the lower quadrant of the project window.

The Track tab enables you to view the content of your tracks in a timeline. This is called the Track Editor. As per the specification, you can add and view the video (blue), audio (green), and subtitle (amber) streams for each track you create. You will add and edit chapter markers, create and position alternate video angles and audio streams, and create subtitles all from this tab in the interface.

In the single track of our project, you see the video portion of the **TigerMovie1** file placed in the first video stream (V1) and the audio portion in the first audio stream (A1). In the last lesson, you didn't see the Track tab in the Basic window configuration. Even so, the video and audio portions of **TigerMovie1** were placed in their appropriate streams automatically when you dragged this movie from the Palette onto the button in the main menu and selected Set Asset and Create Track.

4 Click the Story tab in the lower quadrant of the project window.

Although not too exciting to look at now, the Story tab allows you to create custom viewings of your tracks by stitching together different portions of content using chapter markers. We'll explore stories in depth in Lesson 12.

5 Click the Script tab in the lower quadrant of the project window.

In Lessons 13 and 20, you'll learn how to create a set of instructions—a script—for how to play your DVD using user and environmental data to customize the experience.

6 In the upper-right quadrant of the project window, click the Connections tab. (If this tab is empty, click in the blank part of the Assets tab to deselect all assets.)

You use the Connections tab to make sure that all buttons and disc actions are connected to the correct disc items, and that the buttons on the user's remote will direct the user to the correct location on the disc. We'll explore this tab further in Lesson 13.

7 In the upper-left quadrant of the project window, click the Log tab.

The Log tab is the super-geek author's dream. It will display all kinds of gobbledygook for the advanced author to track the workings of the virtual DVD player in the Simulator. It also reports on the status of encoding, building, formatting, and burning discs. We'll look at the Log in depth in Lesson 9.

8 In the upper-left quadrant of the project window, click the Outline tab.

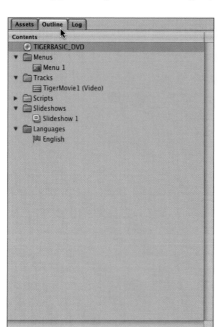

The Outline is a list of the current disc items, starting with an icon of the disc itself, and is separated by colored folders into five categories: Menus, Tracks, Scripts, Slideshows, and Languages. By default, a DVD Studio Pro project will always contain one menu (which is initially set to be the first item that "plays," or first play), one track, and a default language (in our case, English). Our disc contains one more item, a slideshow.

The Outline tab and its cousin, the Assets tab, work together to let you create disc items quickly using the magic of drag and drop. More on this in Lesson 3.

9 Click any of the disc items (Menu 1, TigerMovie1 (Video), Slideshow 1, or English) in the Outline tab.

In the lower right of the screen, notice that the Inspector changes each time to display the properties of that disc item. Its title bar name changes to display the category of the item you clicked—for example, Button or Disc.

This is the end of your brief tour. The Extended and Advanced configurations you have just glanced at, as well as the original Basic configuration, are all default configurations that come with DVD Studio Pro. But you can configure the windows as you see fit, controlling the number of quadrants in your project window, as well as distributing the tabs into any of the quadrants, or displaying the tabs as their own windows. We'll do this next, and then save our own custom window configuration.

Creating Custom Window Configurations

Now we'll make some adjustments to the position and order of the project window's tabs, and the size of its quadrants, in order to customize and enhance our workspace.

1 In the lower quadrant, click the Slideshow tab.

This tab looks a bit cramped down here. Let's reposition it next to some other tabs in the upper-right quadrant.

2 Click the Slideshow tab itself, and then drag it up to the tabs in the upper-right quadrant of the project window, releasing the mouse button when you see a light blue rectangle surrounding the tabs.

3 Click the Slideshow tab again and drag it from left to right, placing it to the right of the Viewer tab and the left of the Graphical tab.

Here's the magic: You can reposition any tab into any quadrant. Furthermore, any tab can form its own window if you drag it out of the project window entirely. This is perfect if you are lucky enough to have multiple displays attached to your Mac.

Now let's change the size of the quadrants.

4 Position your pointer between two of the quadrants, and click and drag to resize them.

5 Position your pointer between all three quadrants, and click and drag to resize all three at once.

Once you have gotten your quadrants the right size, it's time to further customize the window configuration by customizing the toolbar.

Customizing the Toolbar

The series of icons that you see at the top of your project window is called the *toolbar*. As in many Mac OS X applications, the DVD Studio Pro toolbar is a handy way to invoke commands you use often.

DVD Studio Pro allows complete customization of the toolbar. Let's change the toolbar's look to complement our newly created window arrangement.

1 Ctrl-click the toolbar and then choose Customize Toolbar from the contextual menu.

The toolbar button pane drops down below the toolbar, showing the many buttons, indicators, spacers, and separators available to you.

2 Remove three of the less-used buttons by dragging their icons out of the toolbar. From left to right, remove Add Language, Burn, and Format.

TIP ▶ As in any Mac OS X application that has a toolbar, buttons are removed by simply dragging them off the toolbar and letting go of the mouse button. They will disappear in a whimsical puff of smoke.

3 Remove the flexible space that you see between the Build/Format button and the Disc Meter bar.

Your toolbar should now look like this:

4 From your list of tools in the drop-down pane, click and drag a Separator line to add it between the Disc Meter and the Palette button.

5 Add the Show Fonts and Show Colors buttons between the separator you just added and the Palette button.

6 Click Done in the bottom right of the toolbar button pane.

Now your toolbar has a custom look, with oft-used features of the software easily within reach.

NOTE ▶ Depending on your screen size, some of the buttons you add may push the Inspector and Palette buttons off the toolbar. If this happens, you will see a double arrow symbol at the end of the toolbar. When you click the double arrow, DVD Studio Pro displays a list of the rest of your toolbar button choices.

Saving Your Custom Window Configuration

Once you have your window configuration fully customized, it's time to save it so that you can use it in the future. Saving window configurations allows you to preserve all of your quadrants, tabs, and toolbar icons in exactly the way that you prefer.

1 Choose Window > Manage Configurations.

The Configurations window appears, with the three default configurations listed.

2 Click the plus (+) button to create your custom configuration.

A new configuration appears, named Untitled.

3 Double-click the name and rename it *My Configuration*.

4 From the Key pop-up menu to the right, choose F4.

5 Click Apply.

Now your configuration, with its customized toolbar, is saved, and a new keyboard command, F4, is assigned to it. Let's check this out to be sure.

6 Choose Window > Configurations.

You now see your new configuration, with its keyboard command, listed in the menu.

Customizing the window configurations in the software allows you to shape the interface to work most efficiently with your intuition and workflow.

Adjusting the Project

Now that we've taken the time to explore and customize the full interface of the program, let's tweak some of the properties of our current project in order to enhance the user's experience. In the process, you'll get some practice with the tools you've just been introduced to.

Creating Simple Chapter Markers

Let's start by using the Track tab to set some chapter markers. Chapter markers allow the user to quickly navigate through a movie.

1 Click the Track tab in the project window.

2 Click somewhere along the timeline ruler in the Track Editor.

A green playhead jumps to that location, and the Viewer tab will automatically open in the upper-right quadrant to show you the frame of video you clicked.

3 While watching the timecode indicator directly above the timeline ruler, drag the playhead as close to 00:00:35:17 as possible.

You will see the image of a tiger's face in the Viewer.

4 Press M on the keyboard.

A chapter marker, named Chapter 2, appears at the place you marked in the timeline. A new thumbnail image appears in the video stream of the track, and the Inspector, at right, changes to reflect the properties of this new chapter marker.

At this point, we could use the Inspector to change the name and properties of the marker, but since we are creating this marker just for viewer convenience, we'll leave it as its standard name, Chapter 2.

NOTE ▶ Why Chapter 2? If you look at the track, there is always a Chapter 1 chapter marker placed at the beginning of the first video stream. This is a default feature of DVD Studio Pro and also part of the DVD-Video specification. All tracks must have at least one chapter marker at the very beginning of the track. Just try to select that Chapter 1 marker and delete it. I dare you. It can't be done! DVD Studio Pro doesn't allow you to create a track that does not have this mandatory feature.

5 Select the timecode text in the duration field above.

6 Type *11007* into the box, and press Return.

7 The playhead will automatically jump to 00:01:10:07.

8 Press M on the keyboard.

Another chapter marker, Chapter 3, appears at this point.

You have now set some bona fide chapter markers for this track. We'll test them out in a moment when we simulate the disc.

Creating Button Transitions

Button transitions, new to DVD Studio Pro 4, are one of the ways that the program nibbles at the edges of the DVD-Video specification in order to create an experience beyond the traditional. Ask anyone who has created custom button transitions "by hand" using other authoring programs, and they will tell you how long and difficult the process is. But with this new feature it's a breeze. In a few easy steps, we'll set each of the buttons in our main menu to transition into the item that they are linked to.

1 Click the Menu tab in the project window.

Our main menu appears, with its two buttons.

2 Click the Play Movie button.

The Inspector updates to show us the properties of this button.

3 In the Button Inspector, click the Transition tab.

4 From the Transition pop-up menu, choose Melt.

5 Click the Preview button next to the Transition pop-up menu.

The center picture shows you a miniature movie of the transition, which is a melting effect that transitions the menu to the track.

Cool, huh? We will see the full effect when we simulate the disc in a moment.

6 Back in the Menu tab, click the Slideshow button.

Note that the Inspector now displays the properties of the Slideshow button, and since the Transition tab is still active in the Inspector, we see no transition set for this button.

7 From the Transition pop-up menu, choose Page Flip.

8 Click the Preview button to watch this transition.

This transition will create a turning-page effect to transition from the main menu into the slideshow.

9 Select File > Save to save your project.

TIP It's always a good thing to save before you start to simulate your disc.

Simulating the Disc to View the Tweaks

Now let's simulate our tricked-out disc to see the new tweaks.

1 In the toolbar, click the Simulate button.

2 Click the Slideshow button.

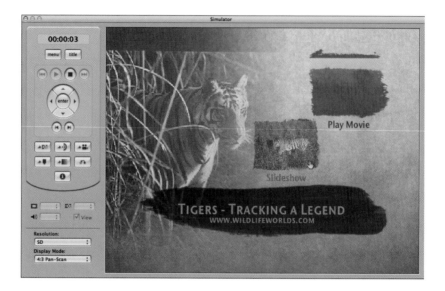

Watch the transition into the slideshow.

3 Let the slideshow play out, and you will return to the main menu.

4 Click the Play Movie button.

The Melt transition takes us subtly into the track.

5 While the track is playing, click the Simulator's Chapter Skip Forward and Chapter Skip Reverse buttons.

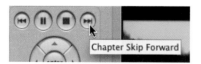

Your movie will jump to the chapter markers that you set in the track earlier.

6 Close the Simulator window.

7 Click the Log tab in the project window.

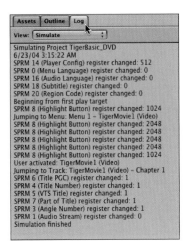

The log displays a geeky list of all the things that happened with our virtual DVD player in the Simulator.

8 Press Cmd-S to save the project.

Burning the Tweaked Disc (Optional)

If you'd like to burn a copy of this modified project, follow these simple steps:

1 Press Cmd-Option-B to start the burn process.

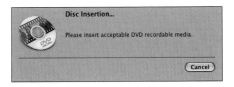

2 Follow the onscreen instructions to burn the disc.

You can watch the Log tab to see the progress of your burn session.

And there we are! Now that you have a simple project under your belt and a comprehensive overview of DVD Studio Pro's interface, you are well on your way to becoming an accomplished author.

Lesson Review

1. Which key do you press to launch the Extended window configuration?
2. True or false: DVD Studio Pro Allows you to customize the look of the Toolbar.
3. How do you create a chapter marker?
4. True or false: Transitions can only be assigned to menus, and not to buttons inside those menus.

Answers

1. The F2 Key. F1 launches the Basic Window Configuration, and F3 launches the Advanced Window Configuration.
2. True. In fact, you can customize almost every aspect of the workspace, from the number and size of quadrants, to the arrangement of tabs inside the individual quadrants.
3. Move the playhead to the place in the track where you want the chapter marker, and them press the "M" key on your keyboard.
4. False. Separate transitions can be applied to every button on the menu.

Keyboard Shortcuts

Window Configurations

F1	Basic configuration
F2	Extended configuration (three quadrants in the project window)
F3	Advanced configuration (four quadrants)
F4–F12	Other custom configurations

Tabs

Cmd-0	Viewer tab
Cmd-1	Assets tab
Cmd-2	Connections tab
Cmd-3	Log tab
Cmd-4	Menu tab
Cmd-5	Outline tab
Cmd-Option-5	Graphical tab
Cmd-6	Script tab
Cmd-7	Slideshow tab
Cmd-8	Story tab
Cmd-9	Track tab

Keyboard Shortcuts

Timeline Navigation

Shift-Z	Fit timeline to window
M	Set marker
Down arrow, Shift-M, Ctrl–right arrow	Next marker
Up arrow, Option-M, Ctrl–left arrow	Previous marker

Other Windows

Cmd-Option-I	Show/Hide Inspector
Cmd-Option-P	Show/Hide Palette
Cmd-T	Show/Hide Font window
Cmd-Shift-C	Show/Hide Colors window

Swiss Project:
Creating a Simple DVD

Adrian Ramseier is the founder and principal of All4DVD, an award-winning DVD authoring and production house that also specializes in training and curriculum development. Located in Irvine, California, All4DVD's team of noted instructors have extensive experience in video editing and DVD authoring. They have created DVDs for clients including Sony Pictures, BMW Motorcycle, Road Stunt Awards, and Reuters. Adrian is the author of *Apple Pro Training Series: DVD Studio Pro 2*. He can be reached at www.all4DVD.com.

3

Lesson Files	None
Media	Media > Swiss folder
Time	This lesson takes approximately 45 minutes to complete.
Goals	Storyboard your DVD
	Set DVD Studio Pro preferences
	Use encoding preferences
	Create a single-play DVD
	Import video and audio tracks
	Manage assets in the Assets tab
	Set chapter markers for faster navigation
	Set first-play action
	Simulate your DVD

Setting Up a Simple DVD

In the next four lessons, you will create a simple DVD for Swiss tourism that contains a promotional movie and a slideshow designed to attract visitors to Switzerland. As befits its European subject matter, the Swiss Tourism project uses the PAL video format, which is the standard in Europe and many countries around the world.

The Swiss Tourism project is a good example of a corporate-style DVD that is relatively simple to put together. It builds on the features that are commonly used in iDVD and at the same time introduces some exciting capabilities of DVD Studio Pro, such as flexible drop zones. As you step through the various exercises, you'll learn how to build one of the most common types of DVD on the market.

This lesson focuses on the first step in this process—creating a single-play DVD that contains only a video track and its associated audio. You will set the DVD to play automatically when it is put into a DVD player. To allow users to skip through the video, you will also set chapter markers by importing them from a list.

Storyboarding Your DVD

Before beginning any new DVD project, even simple projects with only a few assets, you should plan out the way you want the buttons and links to work by creating a *storyboard*. A storyboard is like a road map that simplifies the creative process. It reduces the possibility of mistakes and alerts you to problems you may have while authoring, such as missing media or graphics. We'll go over the process of creating a generic storyboard here, and then go on to create the storyboard for the Swiss Tourism DVD.

The best way to create a storyboard is to make a visual diagram, almost like a flowchart. Your diagram illustrates the navigation path the viewer will follow, from menu to menu, and from button to track or slideshow.

Start your storyboarding process by listing all of the media you want to include, as well as any special elements you might require, such as subtitles or alternate tracks of audio and video. Think about how many menus you will need to link these elements together.

Then begin to draw the chart. Each element in your DVD—menu, video track, slideshow, and so on—gets its own box.

Most DVDs have at least one main menu containing buttons that link to the other project elements. Consider how many buttons you should put in a menu. Although you can have as many as 36 buttons per menu, that would not create a good user experience.

You can handle the need to offer additional choices by adding submenus and creating buttons in the main menu to link to the submenus. Draw squares in each menu or submenu to represent buttons. Then draw a line from each button to the box that represents the element it links to. When you are done, you should have a simple diagram, much like a family tree, that shows how each element is linked, either to a menu, submenu, or another element.

Creating the Swiss Storyboard Using the Graphical Tab

In DVD Studio Pro, the most convenient way to create your storyboard is by using the Graphical view. (In fact, you'll be using the Graphical view throughout this book for various projects.) You can even print the contents of the Graphical tab, or save it as a PDF file, so that you can present the project's structure to your clients and collaborators.

Let's go ahead now and use the Graphical tab to generate the storyboard for the Swiss Tourism project. Our DVD will contain one video track (including markers), one audio track, and a slideshow. The video track will contain markers that can be accessed by the remote control's Next Chapter and Previous Chapter buttons, or by a submenu that contains buttons linked to each chapter. You'll need the following elements for this project:

▶ An intro menu

▶ A main menu

▶ A chapter index menu

▶ A video track

▶ A slideshow

1 If it is not open already, launch DVD Studio Pro by double-clicking the DVD Studio Pro icon in your Dock or Applications folder.

2 Change to Extended view by pressing F2.

3 Click the Graphical tab to activate the Graphical view.

Menu 1 and Track 1 are already there in the Graphical View.

NOTE ▸ One track is required for a DVD to be legal, according to the DVD specifications.

4 Select Menu 1 and rename it *SwissIntroMenu*. This will be an intro menu that transitions to the main menu.

5 Click Add Menu in your toolbar and name the new menu *SwissMainMenu*.

This will be the main menu, with button links to the chapter index sub-menu, the video track, and the slideshow.

6 Click Add Menu in your toolbar again to add another menu, and name it *ChapterIndexMenu*. This will be the chapter index submenu.

7 Select Track 1 and name it *SwissMovie*. This will be the video track.

8 Click Add Slideshow in your toolbar and name the new slideshow *Swiss Slideshow*. This will be the slideshow.

At this point, you have set up the basic structure of your Swiss DVD.

In order to connect all your elements with arrows indicating how the menus will function, you would need to create all the buttons and connections with the appropriate links. That is beyond the scope of this lesson. For now, you've achieved a basic overview of your project. It's a lot easier to print the Graphical tab and use a pencil to sketch the desired navigation in your storyboard.

9 Choose File > Print Graphical View.

If you don't have a printer connected when the print dialog opens there
are options that will allow you to "print" the file as a PDF, which you can
open in Apple Preview or Adobe Acrobat.

10 Choose File > Save to save your project. Save your project as *Swiss_DVD*, and
place it in the My_Projects folder that you copied to your hard drive in the
Getting Started chapter. Click Save.

If you didn't create a My_Projects folder, create one now and put it at the same level as your Lessons and Media folders. See "Introduction: Getting Started" for more details.

NOTE ▶ A file extension of .dspproj is automatically created by DVD Studio Pro. If you have selected the Hide Extensions option in the Finder Preferences, this extension won't be visible, but it will still be added to the filename.

11 In the Outline Tab, click the Disc icon.

As you can see, the disc is automatically named SWISS_DVD. This name is also updated in the Disc Inspector.

Once you output your DVD, this name will appear on it. For example, when you place the disc in the DVD-ROM drive of a computer, the name of the disc that appears on the Desktop will be SWISS_DVD.

12 To complete your storyboard, use a pencil to draw the desired connections on your printout of the Graphical tab. Use the image below as a guide. Notice that the main menu connects to all three of the submenus, and the chapter index menu provides an additional connection to the video track. Notice also that each submenu connects back to the main menu.

This step helps tremendously to give you a feeling for how a DVD works. Each element in your DVD project needs to be linked to another element. For example, if an element, such as a track, does not have an end jump link (an assigned element that the user returns to when the current item finishes playing), it will freeze on the last frame played. If you want to get back to the menu, the only way to achieve this would be by clicking the Menu button on the remote control.

Previewing the Finished Project with Apple's DVD Player

The Apple DVD Player can be used to play back the contents of a DVD's VIDEO_TS folder in order to test the project prior to formatting, or burning, it to disk. The Swiss PAL project is not included on the NTSC build of this book's companion DVD. However, you can still watch the final build of the Swiss project using the Apple DVD Player.

To help you fully understand storyboards, as well as familiarize you with the DVD you are about to create, it might be helpful to examine the storyboard as you navigate through an example of the completed Swiss Tourism DVD.

Opening the Swiss Project in DVD Player

1 Navigate to the Applications folder on your hard drive, and find the icon of the DVD Player program. Double-click the icon to launch the DVD Player application.

 TIP You can drag the icon of the DVD Player program from the Application folder to the Dock to make it easily accessible for future projects.

2 Click the Stop button on your DVD Player controller.

3 Choose File > Open DVD Media (Command-O).

4 Navigate to the Media > Swiss > Swiss_builds > VIDEO_TS folder in the
DSP4 Book Files folder, that you copied to your hard drive, to open the
Swiss PAL project.

5 Click the Play button on the DVD Player's onscreen remote control to
begin playing the project.

Exploring the DVD

The first thing that appears is the SwissIntroMenu that leads to the
SwissMainMenu.

1 Click the down arrow navigation button on the remote control.

The Chapter Index button lights up with a yellow highlight, indicating that you have selected it.

2 Move the cursor to the Slideshow button.

Now it is highlighted, and the other two buttons remain white. In this menu, yellow highlights are used to indicate a button in its selected state, and white indicates a button in its normal, unselected state.

3 Click the Slideshow button.

Notice that the button changes color for a split second before the slideshow starts playing. The red color indicates that a button is in its activated state.

A 1-minute slideshow with multiple transitions will play. When it is finished, the screen will return to the main menu.

4 Press the up arrow on your keyboard once to select the Chapter Index button.

Now you know three ways to navigate with DVD Player: clicking the remote control arrow buttons on the onscreen remote, moving and clicking the mouse, and using the arrow keys on the keyboard.

5 Press Return.

The Enter button on the remote control presses down, as though pressed by remote control. Pressing Return, clicking the Enter button on the remote control, and clicking a button with the mouse will all activate a button.

The Chapter Index submenu will appear. Using any method, navigate to one of the buttons and activate it. It will jump directly to a chapter marker and begin to play from that point.

6 Click the Next Chapter button (the button to the right of the Stop button) on the remote.

The disc will jump to the next chapter marker. Now you know there are two ways to jump to a chapter marker: using the remote control and using the buttons from a chapter submenu.

7 Click the Menu button on your remote control.

The disc returns to the main menu.

8 Click SwissMovie.

The disc will play SwissMovie from the beginning.

9 Watch the movie to familiarize yourself with the content.

10 Click the Next Chapter button on the remote control to jump to another chapter marker.

11 When you have familiarized yourself with the Swiss DVD, click the Stop button on the remote control.

12 Press Cmd-Q to quit DVD Player.

13 Examine the storyboard in the beginning of this lesson.

It should now seem very familiar to you, having navigated the DVD. Now you can draw lines from the elements in your printout to the proper places.

You have seen the blueprint for the Swiss Tourism DVD, and you have seen the finished product. It's time to begin authoring it yourself with DVD Studio Pro.

Identifying Source Video Settings

Before starting a DVD project, you must choose the video standard for your DVD depending on the source material you have (NTSC for North America and Japan; PAL for Europe and just about everywhere else), and set your preferences in DVD Studio Pro to encode and output your video in the correct

format. As you collect and prepare your video, audio, and graphic assets for import into DVD Studio Pro, it is important to know how the footage was originally recorded. If it isn't in the same format you intend to use for your DVD, it must be converted prior to encoding and importing it.

The difference between PAL and NTSC is primarily in the frame rate and size. PAL runs at 25 frames per second (fps), and its frame size is 720 × 576 pixels. NTSC runs at approximately 30 fps, and its frame size is 720 × 480 pixels. The video for the Swiss Tourism DVD was shot with a PAL Betacam camera, and because this project is intended for the PAL market, you will not need to do any conversion. However, you will need to change the encoding settings in the Preferences window, as explained next.

Setting DVD Studio Pro Preferences

Before beginning a DVD project, you may need to modify the default settings of DVD Studio Pro to meet the requirements of your project. In the following exercise, you will open up the Preferences window and learn about the most essential preferences in DVD Studio Pro. Because the Swiss project is in PAL, you will also change the default encoding setting from NTSC to PAL.

1 Choose DVD Studio Pro > Preferences.

The Preferences pane opens. This pane lists preferences that apply to the
overall DVD project.

The Preferences window lists several panes, each containing settings for
specific areas of DVD Studio Pro.

2 Click the Menu icon to view an example of a Preferences pane.

By clicking the Menu icon, you can access the preferences for menus. The default Motion Duration for any motion elements in your menu is 30 seconds. Buttons are automatically assigned from left to right. The default for Final Rendering is your graphics card (this is "Hardware based"). You can also choose the Drop Palette Delay and the Video Background Color for your menu.

3 Click the Project icon. Select the Pal button.

Because this project is PAL, it is important to let DVD Studio Pro know that all assets used in the project will be PAL assets.

Although the settings you define in the Preferences window apply to all of the projects that you create, you can override most of the settings for individual projects. For example, you may use the Inspector window to change settings for elements of the project you are currently working on, while the more global preferences you set in the Preferences window remain the same. (Remember to set your preferences back to NTSC when you've finished working in PAL.)

4 Click OK.

Setting Up Disc Properties

Now that you have learned how to get around in the DVD Studio Pro work-space and how to adjust your preferences, you can begin to assemble a simple DVD project. Putting together a simple DVD will introduce you to methods for working in the application. You will see how easy it is to create a working DVD title in DVD Studio Pro with one video track and an associated audio track.

The first step is to set up disc properties, including the navigation on the remote control.

1 Change to Extended view by pressing F2.

2 At the top of the Outline tab, click once on the disc icon to select it.

3 Go to the Inspector window, which will display the name "Disc" in its window title bar. The Inspector window displays only properties for the currently selected project element.

 The Inspector window appears in the lower right of the screen.

 If the Inspector window does not display global properties for your disc, and "Disc" does not appear in its title bar, click once on the disc icon at the top of the Outline tab (in the upper-left corner of the screen).

 TIP ▸ If the Inspector window isn't visible, choose View > Show Inspector, or use the Cmd-Option-I keyboard shortcut.

4 Near the top of the Inspector window, click the PAL radio button.

Setting the Remote Control

By default, DVD Studio Pro sets the Menu button on the remote control to Menu 1. Menu 1 is now SwissIntroMenu, as you renamed this menu at the beginning of the lesson. Since you are using the SwissMovie track only in this exercise, you should set the remote control Title and Menu buttons to go to the SwissMovie track.

1 Click the Title pop-up menu, and choose Tracks and Stories > SwissMovie > [Track].

2 Click the Menu pop-up menu and again choose the SwissMovie track.

Now if the user presses the Menu or Title buttons on his or her remote, the SwissMovie track will start playing again.

Setting the First-Play Action

The first-play action is used to specify what is displayed when the disc starts playing for the first time after it is inserted into a DVD player. Since the first play is automatically set to Menu 1 when you begin a project, you will need to change this assignment to suit the project you have created. In the following exercise, you will change this property to SwissMovie in the Inspector window for the disc.

1 At the top of the Outline tab, click once on the SWISS_DVD disc icon to select it, and then go to the Disc Inspector window.

2 At the top of the Disc Inspector window, locate the First Play pop-up menu and choose Tracks and Stories > SwissMovie > [Track].

You have now changed the First Play option from Menu 1 to SwissMovie. If a user puts the disc into his or her DVD player or DVD-ROM drive, the SwissMovie will play automatically.

Importing Video and Audio Files

DVD Studio Pro offers you two methods for importing and managing assets:

▶ The Palette window

▶ The Import function of the Assets tab

The Palette window, which is similar to the iDVD Palette window, is basically a file browser. You can use it to select the folders that contain the assets you want to make available to all of your projects. The Palette method is helpful if you need to use the same assets in several projects, such as logos and other identity elements.

The second method for importing assets—the Import function in the Assets tab—is highly recommended if you intend to use your media for only one project. Using the Assets tab, you can organize your media in a way that is very similar to using bins in Final Cut Pro's Browser window.

The difference between the Assets tab and the Palette window is that the Assets tab lists media that have actually been added to your project, whereas the Palette window lists media that are available to be added to your project.

In the following steps, you will import an audio file and a video file, and organize them in the Assets tab.

1 Find the Assets tab in the top-left corner of the DVD Studio Pro interface.

2 At the top of the Assets tab, click the Import button.

3 Navigate to Media > Swiss using your file browser.

4 Open the Swiss_Assets folder and navigate to the Tracks folder.

5 Select **SwissMovie.m2v** and **SwissMovie.AC3** from the Tracks folder.

You can select more than one file sequentially by holding down the Command key and clicking each file, one at a time.

6 Click Import to bring the files into DVD Studio Pro.

The video and audio files will show up in the Assets tab. As you do this, DVD Studio Pro creates a parsing file that contains all the information about the MPEG2 video assets. This process takes a little while, depending on the size of the assets. You will see a "P:" and a progress bar in the Status column of the asset. As soon as the progress bar reaches 100%, a green ready symbol will indicate that the parsing file has been created and the asset is now ready to be used.

7 In the Assets tab, create a folder by clicking the New Folder button.

8 Type *SwissMovie* for the name of your folder and press Return.

9 Drag both **SwissMovie.m2v** and **SwissMovie.AC3** into the SwissMovie folder.

NOTE ▶ Organizing your media is easy when you're working with just two assets. Later on in this project, you will bring in other assets such as menu graphics and slideshows, which you will organize into the appropriate folders.

10 Drag **SwissMovie.m2v** from the Assets tab onto the Outline tab, and continue to hold the mouse button down.

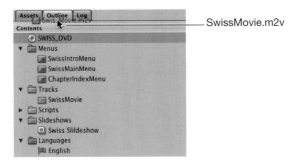

This will activate the Outline tab, which is now accessible to you.

11 Continue dragging **SwissMovie.m2v** down onto the SwissMovie icon in the Outline tab, and release the mouse button.

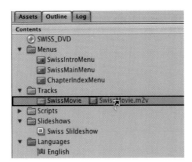

This step causes a few things to happen automatically. The audio is automatically assigned to the track (as long as the audio file's name before its extension is the same as our video file name before its extension). In addition, the movie becomes available in the Track Editor timeline along with any markers that may have been set in Final Cut Pro. However, for this video you will set markers manually, as explained next.

SwissMovie.m2v

NOTE ▶ The Find Matching Audio When Dragging option is the standard setting in the Track pane of the DVD Studio Pro Preferences window. Therefore, your audio will automatically be added to the track with your video—as long as both files have identical names before their filename extensions.

Setting Chapter Markers

In the following exercises, you will learn how to navigate through the Track Editor and set two chapter markers to permit faster navigation through your video track. Typically, chapter markers will already be set at a specific spot in Final Cut Pro (or Final Cut Express or iMovie) and exported to DVD Studio Pro. In this exercise, you will learn how to set these chapter markers in DVD Studio Pro using three different methods. Also you will learn how to move your playhead in the Track Editor.

Resizing the Track Editor

Before you begin working with tracks and adding markers, you may want to adjust the Track Editor window and its timeline to make them easier to view.

1 If the Track Editor is not already open, click the Track tab to open it.

2 Choose the SwissMovie video from the View pop-up menu.

3 Click the clip in the timeline to select it. Then press Shift-Z to resize the video and audio tracks to fit the entire timeline into the Track Editor.

You can also use the Track Editor zoom controls, located in the lower-left corner of the Track tab, to resize the track contained in the timeline. Adjust the slider controls until the window looks like the one shown here.

Track Editor zoom controls

Notice that there is already a marker named Chapter 1 at the beginning of the track. DVD Studio Pro automatically creates a start marker for every track, which is a requirement of the DVD specifications.

TIP ▶ For future projects, chapter marker naming conventions can be changed in the Track pane of the DVD Studio Pro Preferences.

Importing Marker Lists from a Text File

You will now import some markers from a text list. A text list is a convenient way to quickly add markers in DVD Studio Pro. The list you import should be a plain text file (TextEdit or another ASCII file without formatting applied). Once you've imported the markers, you'll use them to view the Swiss Tourism movie in the Track Editor.

If you want to set up your own chapter marker list, use Apple's TextEdit application and just type in the timecode, set a tab as a delimiter, and type the name of the chapter marker. The result is a file that looks similar to the **Swiss_Markers.txt** file. Once you import this file, chapter markers will be set at the timecode specified, and these markers will be named according to the text you have entered.

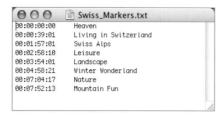

TIP ▶ If you determine the chapter markers based on the timecode in Final Cut Pro, your asset-based timecode typically starts at 01:00:00:00. It is recommended to use a zero-based timecode to set up your chapter marker list, but you can easily change the settings in DVD Studio Pro. Choose View > Timescale > Asset-Based to switch your timescale to asset-based timecode.

1 Ctrl-click in the dark gray marker area of the Track Editor, and choose Import Marker List from the shortcut menu.

Marker area

2 Navigate to the Swiss_Docs folder inside the Media > Swiss folder, and select the text file called **Swiss_Markers.txt**.

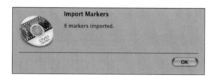

3 Click Import to import the text file with the marker names and the timecode, then click OK.

DVD Studio Pro displays a message that states how many markers were imported. Your new markers should appear automatically in the timeline.

4 In the Track Editor, press the down arrow key on your keyboard to move the playhead to the next chapter marker.

TIP You can also use Shift-M or Ctrl–right arrow to get to the next chapter marker. To move the playhead to the previous chapter marker, you can use Option-M or Ctrl–left arrow.

5 Navigate to the marker called Living in Switzerland, and press the space-
 bar to play this section in your Viewer window.

6 Press the spacebar again to stop playing the track in your Viewer window.

7 Check out the other chapter markers you have created by pressing
 Ctrl–right arrow and pressing the spacebar to start and stop playback.

Creating Chapter Markers Manually

At this point, you need to manually add two more chapter markers. The posi-
tions of these two chapter markers will be 00:06:13:05 for the marker named
Wintersports and 00:08:08:03 for the marker named Explore the Mountains.
You will move to the correct marker positions for these chapters using two dif-
ferent techniques.

1 Press Ctrl–right arrow to move the playhead to the Winter Wonderland chapter marker in the Track Editor timeline.

2 Click the playhead and drag it to the approximate location where you want to place a new chapter point—at about 00:06:13:05.

You can view the current timecode to the left of the Start field in the Track tab (directly above the timeline).

Playhead

If you want to move the playhead one frame at a time, use the right and left arrow keys on your keyboard, and find the exact frame for your marker.

3 Press the right arrow or left arrow key to navigate to the exact position for this chapter marker, represented by the timecode numbers 00:06:13:05.

4 When you arrive at the exact position for your marker, press M on your keyboard, which sets a new chapter marker.

When you place a new marker, a thumbnail image of the frame is created in the timeline track.

5 Name the new chapter marker *Wintersports* in the Name field at the top of the Marker Inspector window.

Properties for the marker you have created should be displayed in the Inspector window. If you accidentally deselect your marker, you can easily select it again by clicking its purple pointer above the timeline.

Now let's use the second method for locating the spot for the next marker—entering the marker position in the current timecode field.

6 Select all the text in the current timecode field, enter *080803*, and press Return.

When you enter a new time in the timecode field, DVD Studio Pro adds the appropriate colon separators—08:08:03—and moves the playhead to that position.

7 Press M once to create a new chapter marker.

8 Name the chapter marker *Explore the Mountains* in the Marker Inspector window.

Simulating Your Project

Before you build or burn your project, you should check your disc's navigation. Using the Simulator, which works like a DVD player, you can make sure that all of your button connections and other project elements interact correctly.

In this exercise, you will use the Simulator to test that your video and chapter markers function properly.

> **NOTE ▶** You will be using the Simulator throughout this book. It is an extremely helpful feature to quickly test what you have created in DVD Studio Pro. However, since the Simulator uses assets that have not yet been converted into the final DVD format, loading an asset or jumping to links on a disc may take longer than it will when the disc is finally built.

1 Click the Simulate icon in your toolbar to automatically test your project.

The keyboard shortcut for the Simulator is Cmd-Option-0 (zero).

> **TIP ▶** You may Ctrl-click individual project elements, the entire disc in the Outline tab, or many other places to quickly simulate specific elements in your project.

2 Check out all chapter markers in your project by clicking the Menu, Title, Next Chapter, and Previous chapter buttons on the remote to ensure proper disc operation.

3 Choose File > Save to save your project to the Lessons > My_Projects folder.

Lesson Review

1. What's a storyboard?

2. True or false: DVD Studio Pro allows you to print the graphical view.

3. What is the PAL frame dimension?

4. True or false: You must set all of your chapter markers by hand inside DVD Studio Pro.

5. True or false: you can drag assets in the Outline view to move them from folder to folder.

Answers

1. A simple flow chart that shows you how your project's buttons, menus, tracks, and other items link together, giving you a good idea of your finished DVD-Video's navigation structure.

2. True. You can even use the print dialog to "print" a PDF version of the menu to email to your client.

3. PAL video frames are 720 X 576 pixels (NTSC is 720 X 480 for DVD-Video).

4. False. You can import a plain text file (.txt) that lists your markers using timecode values and names.

5. True. The outline view works much the same way as your computer's Finder window, so you can drag assets from folder to folder, and even create new folders to group similar assets together.

Keyboard Shortcuts

Cmd-9	Track tab
Cmd-Ctrl-T	Add track
Cmd-Option-I	Show/Hide Inspector
Cmd-,	Preferences
Cmd-Shift-I	Import asset
M	Create marker
Down arrow	Move playhead to next marker
Up arrow	Move playhead to previous marker
Shift-M	Move playhead to next marker
Option-M	Move playhead to previous marker
Ctrl–right arrow	Move playhead to next marker
Ctrl–left arrow	Move playhead to previous marker
Home	Go to beginning of timeline
End	Go to end of timeline
Cmd-Option-0	Simulate (from first play)

4

Lesson Files	Lessons > 04_Swiss_start (or the My_Projects > Swiss_DVD project file you created in Lesson 3)
Media	Media > Swiss > Swiss_Assets > Menus folder
Time	This lesson takes approximately 60 minutes to complete.
Goals	Understand and create basic menus
	Learn how to create buttons
	Create professional-looking menus within DVD Studio Pro
	Create an intro menu using media from a track
	Create a button style
	Create a text style
	Use transitions
	Change font properties
	Link buttons to assets
	Use a drop zone

Creating Menus Within DVD Studio Pro

DVD menus are the gateway to a world of possibilities. The purpose of menus is to allow the DVD viewer to make choices: what to see, what to hear, and what to play, to name a few. But menus can also be as visually and aurally interesting as the content they link to.

Menus can be simple, such as a screen for choosing between two different music videos, or more complex, such as a dynamic motion menu with multiple layers of moving video and soundtracks of your choice. In fact, you can have several menus, with buttons that guide a user through a disc full of exciting video, audio, and images. And the best news is that DVD Studio Pro greatly simplifies the menu creation process. Building on iDVD's ease of use, DVD Studio Pro expands the number of ways you can customize the layout of your disc.

This lesson showcases the power of DVD Studio Pro as a DVD design tool. You'll build highly customized menus entirely within DVD Studio Pro, without the need to create assets in Adobe After Effects or Photoshop, Final Cut Pro, or other applications. Utilizing existing content in the SwissMovie track, you'll achieve great results in relatively few steps.

The Menu Creation Process

Menus provide access to material on a DVD. They include buttons linking to video tracks, slideshows, submenus, or other content on a disc. You must create at least one button for a menu, although you can create as many as 36 buttons per menu. In a way, buttons on a DVD are similar to buttons on a Web page, since they both contain links capable of activating content or other menu pages.

Menus have backgrounds, which may be composed of still images (such as a photograph or Photoshop design), a motion video clip, or a combination of both. Button designs are also incorporated into the majority of menu backgrounds. These button designs might include overlay files or different Photoshop layers. (We'll cover these methods in later lessons.)

DVD Studio Pro gives you several ways to customize your menus and create buttons, without the need to rely on Photoshop or another graphic editing application. This lesson will show you how.

Importing Assets

You'll begin this lesson by importing the menu assets for the Swiss project into the **Swiss_DVD** project file you created in Lesson 3.

1 Open the **Swiss_DVD** project file you created in Lesson 3.

 NOTE ▶ Throughout this book, we recommend using the project files you created in the previous lesson. That way, you can avoid relinking your media assets. If you did not create a **Swiss_DVD** project file in Lesson 3, use the **04_Swiss_start** file you will find on the DVD provided in this book. See "Introduction: Getting Started" for instructions on how to relink your media.

2 In the Assets tab, Ctrl-click the background and choose Import.

3 Select the Swiss_Assets > Menus folder.

4 Click Import to add the Menus folder to the Assets tab.

NOTE ▶ You can import a specific asset into the Assets tab only once, although you may use it multiple times in a project.

Working with the Assets Tab

The Assets tab organizes all of the files that are used in a project. For example, all of the video, audio, and graphics you import are displayed there. You can import files directly into the Assets tab and place them into folders. Having all

your assets organized in folders makes it simpler to work with them, particularly for large projects.

Once you have imported an asset, you can view information for it in one of the Assets tab's columns. If you have the Inspector open, you can also click a file in the Assets tab to view its information in the Inspector window.

Adding a Background Graphic

The first step in the menu creation process is to add a background graphic. In this exercise, you begin by creating a standard menu background with a single image from the SwissMovie video track. Later in the lesson, you will add other elements, such as buttons, drop zones, and a title to your menu.

1 Click the Track tab and select the timecode field above the track. Type *044021* and then press Return.

 This moves the playhead to the still image frame at 04:40:21 that you are going to use for your menu background.

Timecode field

Playhead

2 Press M to set a chapter marker.

3 In the Inspector, click the Chapter check box to deselect this marker as a chapter marker.

The purple chapter marker will turn into a green cell marker (a marker that serves merely as a placeholder) and won't be included in the chapter index menu we will create in Lesson 5.

4 In the Inspector, click Save Still to export this still frame from your movie track.

5 Name the still image *SwissMainMenu.tiff* and save it in your Menus folder. (If it's already there, click OK to replace.)

The Menus folder will be automatically selected because you just imported your menu assets.

6 Click the Import button in the Assets tab.

7 Select **SwissMainMenu.tiff**.

The SwissMainMenu still image is now imported in your Menu folder.

8 Click the Menu tab to activate the Menu Editor window.

9 Select SwissMainMenu from the pop-up menu in the top-left corner of the Menu Editor to switch to the SwissMainMenu.

10 Select SwissMainMenu.tiff in the Assets tab, and drag it into the Menu Editor.

Make sure you do not release the mouse button until the Drop palette appears.

11 From the Drop palette, choose Set Background.

The graphic has now become the background for your menu.

TIP ▶ You can adjust the amount of delay that occurs before the Drop palette appears by changing the Drop Palette Delay value in Menu Preferences (DVD Studio Pro > Preferences > Menu). Some users may like the Drop palette to respond more quickly, whereas others will find that a longer delay gives them more time to position an asset in the correct place when creating their menus.

Creating Buttons on a Still Menu

Once you have added a background to your menu, you can create the buttons that will link to the other elements of your disc. For this exercise, we will start by creating a single button on top of your still background. You will then create additional buttons, name them, and modify their text properties.

NOTE ▶ Although you can import menu graphics with buttons already created, the purpose of this exercise is to demonstrate the menu and button creation features built into DVD Studio Pro.

Drawing Buttons

For this exercise, you will learn how to work with button areas and text for a simple menu, without other graphic elements. The button area you select is the location where users can click to activate a link.

In many cases, you will have decided already where to place your buttons by creating them as part of a background image and overlay file, as described in the Tiger project in Lesson 11. But you can also begin drawing your buttons directly in the Menu Editor. You can always use overlays or add shapes later.

1 Click an area of the Menu Editor and drag to reveal a rectangular button shape.

The position you first clicked becomes the corner of a button. Dragging to an opposite corner reveals the button outline area, which is represented by dashed lines.

2 Resize the active area of the button by dragging a corner of the button outline.

When you draw buttons in the Menu Editor, you are defining the active button area. Make sure to create a bounding box that is a little bigger than the area you need for your button. This will make it easier for people viewing your disc with software players to select buttons with the mouse.

TIP ▶ You can maintain a button's aspect ratio as you resize it by holding down the Shift key as you drag an edge or corner.

3 Position the button precisely by using the arrow keys to shift it 1 pixel at a time in any direction.

Naming Buttons

After your button is created, you should name it in the Inspector. If your Inspector window is not visible, press Cmd-Option-I or click its icon in the toolbar to make it appear, and click the Style tab if it is not already showing.

1 Click your button once to select it.

2 Type *Play Video* in the Name field at the top of the Inspector window.

The Name field is where you assign an identifier, which does not actually appear in the menu, for your button. It is simply a way to identify your buttons in DVD Studio Pro or to add navigation functions. Without names, your buttons might be difficult to distinguish from each other.

3 Click the Style tab, then at the bottom of the Inspector window, type *Play Video* in the Text box.

The Text box is where you input displayed text—the name that appears in the menu and that users see when they play your disc.

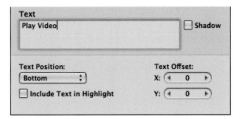

4 In the Text Position section, choose Center from the Position pop-up menu.

Adding Drop Shadows

Since your text is white, you should add a drop shadow to make it more visible against the background image.

1 Select the Play Video button in the Menu Editor to display its properties in the Button Inspector.

2 In the Text area at the bottom of the Button Inspector window, click the Shadow check box to add the drop shadow.

Choosing Fonts

With your button's text in place, you can use the formatting tools to modify the appearance of your text. The font used for the button is one of the first attributes you will want to change.

1 Select the Play Video button in the Menu Editor.

2 Select the text you want to format.

3 Activate the Font window by selecting Format > Font > Show Fonts or using the shortcut Cmd-T.

4 Choose Helvetica Neue Condensed Bold in 24 point size from the list of choices.

5 Close the Font window by clicking the Close button in the upper-left corner.

TIP ▶ You can change the default font for button text in Preferences. Open Preferences, click the Text icon to switch to the Text pane, then choose Menu Button Defaults from the Show pop-up menu. Changing settings here will change the default text that appears whenever you create a new button.

Setting Button Highlight Colors

You can add button highlights to each button you create for a menu. Button highlights, unique to DVD authoring, consist of different colors that display based on the state of your button.

Button states are defined as *normal, selected,* and *activated.* For a simple DVD, you need to set only the selected and activated highlights. When a user chooses a button with his or her remote control, the button becomes selected, and it displays the highlight color you have chosen for the selected state. The activated state shows up for a split second when the user presses the Play button on the remote control.

In this exercise, you will set the selected and activated highlight colors for the button you've created. Later in this book, you will learn more about buttons and about simple and advanced highlights, as well as how to create your own button overlays, which work with highlights.

1 Select the Play Video button in the Menu Editor to display its properties in the Button Inspector.

2 Make sure you have the Include Text in Highlight check box selected at the bottom of the Text Formatting section.

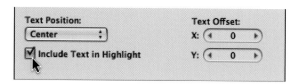

3 Click the Colors tab in the Button Inspector.

4 Select yellow from the Selected pop-up menu, and leave the Opacity slider at 15.

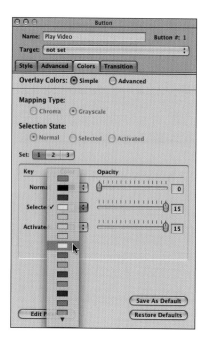

When the viewer selects the Play Video button, the button's text will be highlighted yellow because the Include Text in Highlight check box is checked.

5 Select red from the Activated pop-up menu, and set its opacity at 15.

The activated highlight will show up for only a split second when the user activates the button.

6 In the Menu Editor, navigate to the button state icons at the bottom of the window and click the Selected State icon (in the middle).

When you click the button, you should see the yellow text overlay color that you have chosen for the text.

7 Click the Activated State icon to the right of the Selected State icon.

The text color should now switch to red for the activated state.

Creating More Buttons

This project requires a total of three buttons on the main menu, so you need to create two more buttons. In this exercise, you will learn how to easily create new buttons with the same button style.

1 Click the Play Video button to select it.

2 Press Cmd-D to duplicate the button.

3 Reposition the button by dragging it directly under the first button you created.

Use the yellow snapping guides to help align your buttons.

4 Repeat steps 2 and 3 to create an additional button.

5 Click the second button.

6 In the Text and Name fields of the Button Inspector, enter the name *Chapter Index* for the second button.

7 Click the third button. In the Button Inspector, enter the name *Slideshow* in the Text and Name fields.

8 Ctrl-click the Slideshow button, and choose Set as Default Button Style from the shortcut menu.

From now on, any other buttons you create will use this default button style.

Simulating Your New Buttons

After you have created your buttons, you will want to test their appearance. You should simulate frequently while assembling a project to avoid making mistakes and to ensure proper operation of your menu elements. In this case, you just want to make sure that your buttons are displaying correctly.

1 Ctrl-click the Menu Editor background (not a button), and choose Simulate Command from the shortcut menu.

2 Use the Simulator to check that your buttons display correctly.

For this exercise, simply looking at the buttons as you use the remote control should tell you whether your fonts, colors, and images are working properly.

Making Connections from Buttons to Video

Now that you have your buttons in place, you can begin linking them to the video tracks and other disc items in your project. In this exercise, you will link the Play Video button to the video track you created earlier in the last lesson. In DVD Studio Pro, the item that is being linked to a button is called the *target*.

After you have created the connection between your button and your video track, you will want to test it in the Menu Editor to be certain that your button is linked to a video asset.

1 Ctrl-click the Play Video button in the Menu Editor.

2 Choose Target > Tracks and Stories > SwissMovie > [Track] from the shortcut menu that appears.

You may also set your links by using the Target pop-up menu at the top of the Inspector window. However, using the Ctrl-click method is quicker and more intuitive.

3 Ctrl-click the Menu Editor background, and choose Simulate Menu from the shortcut menu to activate the Simulator.

4 Click Enter to activate your Play Video button and test the link to the video track.

5 Click the Menu button in the upper-left corner to get back to the menu.

You have now successfully created your first simple menu. Your menu includes three buttons, with the first one linked to a video track.

Using the Title Safe Feature

When creating text for a DVD menu or video track, you need to be aware that some of the image area is cut off by the overscan of a television set. The *overscan area* is what falls outside of the normal viewing area. Older televisions tend to be the worst offenders—they may cut off significant amounts around the edge of your frame. Newer televisions are a bit better, although the only way to see your entire frame is with a software DVD player (such as the Apple DVD Player) or certain digital monitors. For this reason, designers consistently use two guides called *action safe* and *title safe*. Using these guides in DVD Studio Pro can help you to determine the best (and safest) placement for your text.

The title safe area is the smaller area containing important text and graphics that must be viewable on a television. If it's not already activated, you can activate it by choosing View > Title Safe Area; by clicking the Settings pop-up menu at the top of the Menu Editor and choosing Title Safe Area; or by using the keyboard shortcut Cmd-Shift-E.

The action safe area is an area closer to the edge of the screen that should contain any visual information crucial to the action or movement of the image. You can activate the action safe area guides by choosing View > Action Safe Area; by clicking the Settings pop-up menu at the top of the Menu Editor and choosing Action Safe Area; or by pressing Cmd-Option-E.

Adding Title and Text to the Menu

The next step is to add some text elements to your menu. You will type the title, tagline, and URL in your Menu Editor. The capability to add text is a nice feature of DVD Studio Pro, since you are not forced to use a separate application, such as Photoshop, to create titles for your menus or buttons. In fact, this feature makes using templates a possibility, since you can do all of your text editing and renaming within DVD Studio Pro.

1 Double-click the top of the Menu Editor window to create a text box.

2 Type *Switzerland.* into the box that appears.

3 In the Text Object Inspector, click the Shadow check box to add a drop shadow.

Now let's use the text formatting features described in the section "Creating Buttons on a Still Menu" earlier in this lesson to change the appearance of your text.

4 Activate the Font window by choosing Format > Font > Show Fonts.

5 Make sure your text is highlighted, and then use the font Helvetica Neue Condensed Bold 40 pt.

6 Once the text has changed, click next to the Switzerland text element to deselect it.

7 Double-click the background again to add a tagline for the title.

8 Type *get natural.*, and then use the Font window to format it as Helvetica Neue Condensed Bold 30 pt.

9 Align the text to the right, and click the Shadow check box to add a drop shadow.

10 Ctrl-click this text element, and choose Create Text Style from the shortcut menu.

11 Name your new style *SwissMenu*, click the Project check box, and then click Save.

12 Draw a button in the lower-right corner of your menu and name it Weblink.

This button contains the default properties we set earlier in the "Creating More Buttons" section.

13 Type *www.myswitzerland.com* in the Text field of the button.

The new font style will be automatically applied to the text. Your Swiss still menu now looks like this:

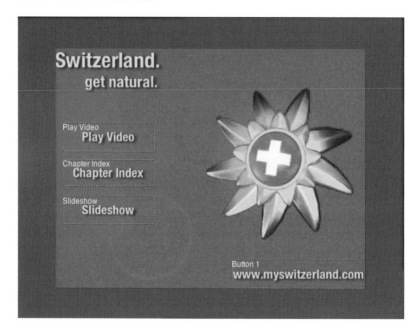

Adding Sound to the Menu

Adding sound to your still menu quickly and dramatically enhances it. For the SwissMainMenu, you will use a portion of the **SwissMovie.AC3** audio track that is called **SwissMainMenu.AC3**. This portion of the audio has been prepared in Final Cut Pro. To avoid any audio glitches when the menu loops, we recommend that you fade up the volume in the beginning and fade down the end of the menu loop.

1 From the Assets tab, select **SwissMainMenu.AC3** and drag it to the Menu Editor.

TIP ▶ Make sure that you use the same audio format (AC-3 or AIFF) at the same bit rate for all menus you create. Mixing different audio formats in the Menu domain (all menus on your DVD) is illegal, according to the DVD specification, and DVD Studio Pro will not complete the disc building process.

2 From the Drop palette, choose Set Audio.

3 Click the Motion button at the bottom-right corner of the Menu Editor to hear if the audio plays correctly.

Creating an Intro Menu

You are about to build an exciting introduction to the Swiss DVD using content from your SwissMovie asset file. The introduction menu will then transition to the main menu.

DVD Studio Pro will automatically place the matching audio for the video that you'll use for the intro menu. To ensure that your new intro menu is the first thing to play, you'll need to change the first play from the SwissMovie track to the SwissIntroMenu.

SwissMovie contains a section that would work perfectly as an introductory video segment for this DVD. Follow these steps:

1 Click the Outline tab, and select the SwissIntroMenu that you created in Lesson 3.

2 From the Assets tab, select **SwissMovie.m2v**. Drag it onto your Menu Editor, and choose Set Background when the Drop palette appears.

3 In the Menu Inspector, move the End slider as close as possible to time-code 00:09:16:06.

4 Use the up and down arrows to move the end slider to the exact frame.

5 Select the Start timecode field, and enter *090407* to define the start time-code at 00:09:04:07.

By defining the start and end points, you have reduced the duration of the SwissMovie asset to about 12 seconds. Only this section, along with the associated audio, will be rendered into the menu background when you build your disc.

6 Choose Timeout from the At End pop-up menu located in the middle of the Menu Inspector.

7 Change the Timeout value to 0 sec.

Your SwissIntroMenu will only play for about 12 seconds and then time out at 0 seconds. In the next step, you will define the timeout action.

8 Choose Menus > SwissMainMenu > [Menu] from the Action pop-up menu.

9 Click the Transition tab to reveal the Transition options for this menu.

There are over 20 built-in transitions available in DVD Studio Pro. For this situation, a fade-through color transition works really well.

10 Choose Fade Through Color in the Transition pop-up menu.

11 Click the color patch to activate the Color Picker, and choose Red.

Setting Up Navigation on Your DVD

Since you have set up a DVD that plays just the track in the previous chapter, you need to change the navigation in order to play the assets in the right order. For this project, the first thing that will play is the SwissIntroMenu. This menu plays once and then leads to SwissMainMenu.

Every DVD player remote control is equipped with a Menu button that is intended to return users to the last menu they came from. For this project, it is important to set both the Menu button and the Title button on the remote control.

1 In the Outline tab, click the Swiss_DVD disc icon to activate the disc's properties in the Inspector.

2 Click the First Play pop-up menu, and choose Menus > SwissIntroMenu > [Menu].

The next step is to set up the remote control correctly. To make changes that affect the operation of the entire disc, you must use the Inspector.

3 Make sure the disc's properties are still visible in the Inspector. In the Title pop-up menu of the Remote Control section, choose Menus > SwissMainMenu > [Menu].

This will play the SwissMainMenu in case the user presses the Title button on the remote control.

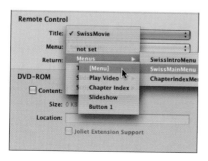

4 In the Menu pop-up menu of the Remote Control section, choose Menus > SwissMainMenu > [Menu].

This will play the SwissMainMenu when the user clicks or presses the Menu button on the remote control.

5 Choose File > Save to save your project.

Changing the Still Menu into a Motion Menu

Motion menus add excitement to a DVD interface. In DVD Studio Pro, you can play video in buttons, drop zones, and as a motion background of a menu. Instead of an ordinary static menu, you can have a menu that is pulsating with life.

Adding a Drop Zone to the Main Menu

Drop zones are simple graphics and video clips that you can use to easily customize the look of your backgrounds, especially when you want to add motion to them.

Drop zones should not be confused with buttons. Drop zones are purely graphic or video elements that do not contain interactivity. For this project, you will use a few Apple drop zones from the Palette as design elements, and allocate a 49-second portion of the SwissMovie track to one of the drop zones. You will integrate all these elements in the existing Swiss still menu that you just created.

1 In the Outline tab, select SwissMainMenu.

2 In the Palette, select the Styles tab, then the Apple tab, and then the Drop Zones tab to access the available drop zones.

3 Scroll down in the Palette window, and then select and drag the Panes Rectangle Frosted Blur Window 1 drop zone onto the Menu Editor.

As you drag, hold down the mouse button until the Drop palette appears in the Menu Editor.

4 From the Drop palette, choose Create Zone, Set Style.

5 Drag out the top-right and bottom-left corners of the drop zone so that it covers the entire Menu Editor window.

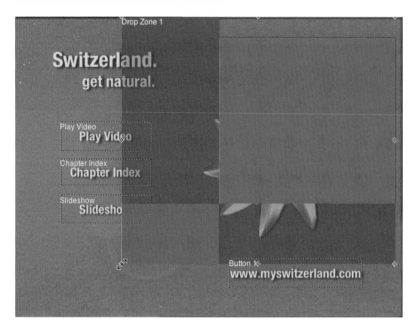

6 At the bottom-left corner of the Menu Editor, click the Send To Back icon to send the drop zone all the way to the back.

7 Click the Assets tab; choose **SwissMovie.m2v** and apply it to the drop zone.

8 In the Drop Zone Inspector, select the timecode field, enter *15121*, and press Return to get to the start frame 00:01:51:21.

Changing the Duration of Your Motion Menu

The default duration of a motion menu is set to 30 seconds. You can easily change the default settings in Preferences. For this menu, you will change the duration of the menu to match the duration of the audio, which is 49 seconds.

1 Double-click an empty space at the top of the Menu Editor to activate the Menu Inspector.

2 In the General tab, type *4907* into the Duration timecode field and press Return.

You have now extended the duration of your motion menu to 49 seconds to match the duration of the audio used for this menu.

3 Save your project in the My_Projects folder.

Lesson Review

1. How do you create a button in DVD Studio Pro?

2. Can buttons be round?

3. How do you add a drop shadow to button text?

4. What is the title safe area?

5. What is the Key command for enabing the Title Safe area?

6. True or false: you can mix both AC-3 and AIFF audio in a single project's menus.

Answers

1. Open the menu editor, then click and drag to drag out the button's outline.

2. No. Buttons in the DVD-Video must be rectangular or square.

3. Open the Button Inspector and click the Drop Shadow check-box, located in the General tab's Text area.

4. Title safe represents an area that is outside of the visible area on most picture tube TVs. Anything outside of the title safe area is not guaranteed to display in the finished DVD-Video.

5. Command-Shift-E (Command-Option-E enables the action safe area).

6. False. All audio in every one of your projects menus must be exactly the same type.

Keyboard Shortcuts

Cmd-4	Menu tab
Cmd-Y	Add standard menu
Cmd-Option-I	Show/Hide Inspector
Cmd-T	Font window
Cmd-Shift-C	Color picker
Cmd-D	Duplicate a button or other elements
Cmd-B	Make text bold
Cmd-I	Make text italic
Cmd-U	Underline text
Cmd-Shift-E	Show title safe area
Cmd-Option-E	Show action safe area
Cmd-R	Show/Hide rulers

5

Lesson Files Lessons > 05_Swiss_start
(or the My_Projects > Swiss_DVD project file you created in
Lesson 4)

Media Media > Swiss > Swiss_Assets > Menus folder

Time This lesson takes approximately 30 minutes to complete.

Goals Understand the concept of chapter index menus

Create a chapter index menu

Understand special buttons such as _PREV_, _UP_,
and _NEXT_

Select and change multiple buttons

Apply button styles

Use a chapter index menu

Creating a Chapter Index Menu

Chapter index menus provide a way to jump directly to any chapter marker in a video track. Most professional DVDs include a chapter index menu to allow the viewer to navigate through a long movie or to easily locate a specific scene. Using a track with chapter markers already in place (as you did in Lesson 3) and a chapter index menu template, you can quickly assemble a chapter index menu in DVD Studio Pro.

There are several good reasons to use menu templates. For one, templates give your disc a consistent look and feel. They also simplify the menu creation process. In this exercise, you will customize your own SwissIndex chapter index menu template and create all the connections automatically.

Rather than creating a template from scratch, in this lesson you'll customize one of the default templates included in DVD Studio Pro 4. The goal is to customize the chapter index menu in a way that works well with the previously designed SwissMainMenu.

In order to achieve this, you'll change the font, buttons, and title, and add suitable background music. Once you are satisfied with your customized chapter index menu, you'll save the template in the Palette. At that point, you will be in a position to instantly create and link this chapter index menu to your SwissMainMenu.

Toward the end of the lesson, you'll explore some of the most useful techniques for assembling menus. The lesson culminates with an exercise in creating a template for a chapter index menu, enabling you to speed up the menu creation process.

Customizing a Default Chapter Index Menu

We'll start by applying one of DVD Studio Pro's prebuilt index menus to our ChapterIndexMenu. Then we'll alter the prebuilt menu in order to customize it to our needs.

Selecting the Template

The first step is to select one of the templates provided with DVD Studio Pro.

1 Choose File > Open to open the **Swiss_DVD** project file you created in Lesson 4.

 NOTE ▶ If you did not create a **Swiss_DVD** project file in Lesson 4, use the **05_Swiss_start** file you will find on the DVD provided with this book.

2 Click the Menu tab to get to the Menu Editor.

3 Choose ChapterIndexMenu from the View pop-up menu at the top left of the Menu Editor window.

4 In the Palette, click the Templates tab, and then scroll down to the Stripes Index template.

5 Double-click the Stripes Index template to apply it to the Menu Editor window.

Customizing the Background and Buttons

In the next steps, you will customize a button so that you can use it as a style for the other buttons in your chapter index menu. You'll set various properties for the button, including the background, font, position, and overlay colors.

1 Click the Import Asset icon in the toolbar.

2 Navigate to Media > Swiss > Swiss_Assets > Slideshows and select **SwissPhoto_01.jpg** to import it.

3 From the Assets tab, select **SwissPhoto_01.jpg** and drag it onto the background of your index menu.

4 Choose Set Background from the Drop palette.

The white background will be replaced by the nice blue Swiss photo.

5 In the Palette, click the Styles tab, then the Project button, then the Text button to navigate to the SwissMenu text style you created in Lesson 4.

6 Select the SwissMenu text style, drag it to the text "PLACE TITLE HERE," and choose Apply to Text Object from the Drop palette.

The format of the text should change to the SwissMenu text style.

7 Click the text "PLACE TITLE HERE" again to select the text itself.

8 Press Cmd-T to activate the Font window. Change the font size to 40.

9 While the text is still activated, type *Switzerland. get natural.*

Switzerland. get natural.

Your title for the index menu is now set.

Creating a Button Style

Button styles are an easy way to save the properties of your buttons. Once you save a button style in the Palette, you can quickly apply the style to other buttons. This technique saves time and keeps your menu designs consistent.

1 From the Palette, select the SwissMenu text style again, drag it onto Button 1 in the upper left of the menu, and choose Apply to Button from your Drop palette.

2 In the Button Inspector, change Offset X to 0 and Offset Y to 0.

This will move the button text into a better position.

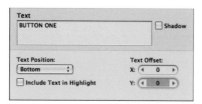

3 While the button is still selected, change the font size to 24 pt in the Font window.

If you closed the Font window, use Cmd-T again to activate it.

4 In the Button Inspector, click the Colors tab.

5 Choose white as the Selected highlight color and move the Opacity slider to 15.

6 Choose light blue as the Activated highlight color and move the Opacity slider to 15.

7 Back in your Menu Editor, Ctrl-click Button 1, and choose Create Button Style from the shortcut menu.

8 Name the style *SwissIndexButton* and click the Project check box. Then click Save.

The Project option saves this button style for this project file only. If we were to work with another project, this particular style would not show up in the Palette. However, anytime we open this project file, the SwissIndexButton style will show up in the Palette.

Applying a Button Style

Now that you've saved one button style, you can use it to set up the rest of the buttons for your chapter index menu.

1 Click the Styles tab, then the Project button, and then the Buttons button to navigate to the SwissIndexButton that you just created.

2 Shift-click the remaining five buttons to select them.

3 Double-click the SwissIndexButton to apply the style to those buttons.

4 Select all six index buttons, and drag them down a few pixels to get some distance from the title. Turn off the Title Safe Area if necessary.

Setting Up the Chapter Index Navigation Buttons

A great feature of DVD Studio Pro's chapter index menu is its capability to automatically set up the navigation to the previous chapter index menu (if one exists), the next chapter index menu (again, if it's necessary), and back to the main menu. To achieve this, you need to name the buttons in a specific way. The previous menu button needs to be named _PREV_, the button name for the main menu is _UP_, and the next menu button must be named _NEXT_. Because you have applied a pre-existing chapter index menu, the buttons are already properly named.

Note that these names are for the buttons themselves, not the text that may be in the button. As you can see from the names of the navigation buttons in our menu, their names are back, main, and next, respectively.

1 Select the _PREV_, _UP_, and _NEXT_ buttons on the bottom of your
Menu Editor by holding down the Command key and dragging the white
selection rectangle around them.

2 Click the Styles tab, then the Apple button, then the Buttons button, and
navigate to the Mosaic Square Red button.

3 Double-click the button to apply the button properties to the selected
buttons.

4 Select the back button to activate the Button Inspector.

5 Click the Colors tab in the Button Inspector, and choose white with
an opacity of 15 for Selected, and light blue with an opacity of 15 for
Activated.

NOTE ▶ You can use three different highlight sets for each menu.

6 Ctrl-click the background of your menu, and choose Simulate Menu from
the shortcut menu to test the buttons in Simulator.

All of the buttons in your menu have now been customized easily and
consistently.

Completing the Customized Chapter Index Menu Template

You're ready to complete the template. First, though, you'll add a drop zone to
put more emphasis on the title and the back, main, and next buttons.

1 In the Palette, click the Shapes tab and then the Apple button to navigate
to the Square Black 40p button.

2 Select the Square Black 40p button and drag it to the top-left corner of the menu background.

3 Choose Create Drop Zone, Set Shape from the Drop palette.

4 Drag the lower right corner of the drop zone all the way to the right to cover the title "Switzerland. get natural."

5 Press Cmd-Shift-B to send this drop zone all the way to the back.

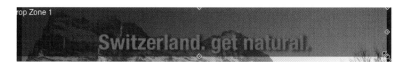

6 Click the Assets tab, select **SwissChapterIndex.AC3**, drag it to the menu background, and choose Set Audio from the Drop palette.

7 Click the Transition tab in the Menu Inspector, and choose Motion Dissolve from the pop-up menu.

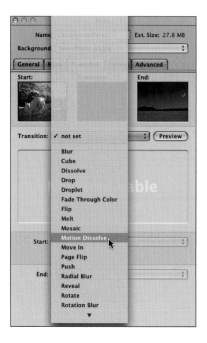

The menu is now complete, with a custom background, custom buttons, a custom drop zone and a custom soundtrack that plays while the menu is onscreen. Now let's create a template for it!

8 Ctrl-click the background, and choose Create Template from the short-cut menu.

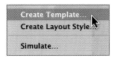

9 Name your new menu template *SwissIndex* and click the Project check box, and then click Save.

10 Press Cmd-S to save your project to the Lessons > My_Projects folder.

11 In the Palette, click the Templates tab and then the Project button to make sure that the template is there.

Since this menu is now available in the Palette, you can delete it from your project.

12 Click the Outline tab and Ctrl-click ChapterIndexMenu.

13 Choose Delete from the shortcut menu to delete this menu.

Congratulations! You have now customized the SwissChapterIndex menu, which you can use to create the chapter index of your DVD.

Automating the Chapter Index Menu Creation Process

Remember, chapter index menus provide a way to jump directly to any chapter marker in a video track. Using the SwissMovie track with chapter markers already in place and your newly created chapter index menu template, you can quickly assemble your customized Swiss chapter index menu and link it up to your main menu.

1 At the top of the Menu Editor window, select the SwissMainMenu (if it isn't already showing) from the View pop-up menu.

2 From the Outline tab, drag the SwissMovie track onto the Chapter Index button in the Menu Editor.

 As you drag, keep the mouse button held down until the Drop palette appears in the Menu Editor.

3 From the Drop palette, choose Create Chapter Index, Make Connections.

 NOTE ▶ Do not drag your original movie file from the Assets tab. Since the movie has already been added to a track, dragging directly from the Assets tab will duplicate the media in your project, and more important, the markers won't be available. Instead, drag the track from the Outline tab, which references the media and chapter markers that are already part of your project.

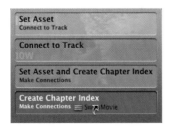

 The Choose Template or Layout Style dialog appears.

4 Click the Templates tab and then the Project button to navigate to the SwissIndex template that you just created.

5 Select SwissIndex from the list of choices.

6 Click OK.

When you click OK, all of the chapter markers from your track turn into buttons in the new chapter index menus that are created. The names of your markers are automatically added to all the buttons, which link to the corresponding markers in the track. Also, the navigation to the main, previous, and next menus is automatically set up.

Because there are ten chapter markers in your track but only six buttons in your template, two new menus are created: Menu 1 and Menu 2. Menu 1 contains buttons for the first six chapter markers, and Menu 2 has the remaining four. Best of all, every button in each of these two new menus is automatically targeted for you.

7 In the Menu Editor, click Menu 1 from the View pop-up menu to see what the first chapter index menu looks like.

8 In the Outline tab, Ctrl-click Menu 1 and choose Simulate Menu from the shortcut menu to play your chapter index menu.

Because the buttons in this chapter index menu have a lot of motion, you probably will experience a delay in the playback of the menu (especially if you have a slower machine). Once you finally build the Swiss project, however, all actions will be a lot faster.

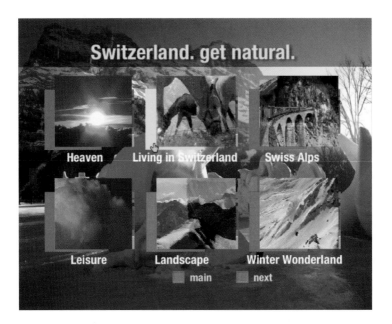

9 Click the next button to view the second chapter index menu.

Because only four buttons were needed for the second index menu (Menu 2), the other remaining template buttons were automatically deleted, allowing the user to see more of the pretty background image!

10 Save your project in the My_Projects folder.

Lesson Review

1. True or false: you can apply button styles to only one button at a time.

2. In a chapter menu, what does the _PREV_ button do?

3. True or false: DVD Studio Pro will only create chapter menus from previously saved templates.

4. How does DVD Studio Pro name new chapter menu buttons?

Answers

1. False. If you select multiple buttons, you can add the same style to all the selected buttons at one time.

2. If more than one chapter menu is created, the _PREV_ button links back to the previous chapter menu.

3. True. You must create a menu template before DVD Studio Pro will automatically create a chapter menu for you.

4. When DVD SP creates a chapter menu, it automatically gives each button the same name as the chapter marker of the Chapter it represents.

Keyboard Shortcuts

Cmd-Shift-B	Send to background
Cmd-D	Duplicate

6

Lesson Files
Lessons > 06_Swiss_start
(or the My_Projects > Swiss_DVD project file you created
in Lesson 5)

Media
Media > Swiss folder

Time
This lesson takes approximately 20 minutes to complete.

Goals
Understand the concept of a slideshow

Know what file formats can be used in a slideshow

Import slides

Add multiple audio files to the slideshow

Add transitions to a slideshow, a group of slides,
and individual slides

Change the order of slides

Change the duration of slides

Set the slideshow Fit To Audio option

Convert a slideshow to a track

Creating a Slideshow

Slideshows are a great way of displaying a sequence of still images, and a DVD is a great delivery mechanism for a slideshow, whether you're using it for a presentation, a photo album, or any of a number of other uses. DVD Studio Pro 4 lets you dramatically enhance the impact of your slideshow by adding transitions between images, or by using multiple audio tracks, including MP3 files, to add narration or music to a slideshow. In addition, you can combine slideshows with video by converting a slideshow to a track.

In this lesson, you will use a folder of already prepared images to create a slideshow for the Swiss Tourism project. The exercises explore the options available to you in DVD Studio Pro's slideshow feature. You'll start by importing images for the slides into the Assets tab. Then you'll learn how to add transitions to the slideshow and each of the slides. You'll also change the duration and the order of the slides, and add multiple audio clips to the slideshow.

Slideshows are an easy way to play still images on your DVD player. You can use them for presentations, photo albums, scrapbooks, training, corporate communications, weddings, and special events.

TIP ▶ Slideshows created in DVD Studio Pro can contain up to 99 still images. If you need to include more than 99 images, you can simply link several slideshows together. You may also choose to convert a slideshow to a track, which allows it to function like any other movie or video clip.

TIP ▶ If you want to create a slideshow with other special effects, you can build the slideshow in Final Cut Pro and bring it into DVD Studio Pro as a video track.

Once your slides are added to a slideshow, you can arrange them in the order in which you want them to display. You can also set the amount of time that each slide is shown, either by assigning an audio file to the slide (which determines its duration) or by setting the display duration value for each slide.

If you want the user to be able to advance the slides manually, you can set the Pause option. Each slide will then pause for the viewer to click the Next Track key on the remote control to advance to the next slide. This is useful for creating Microsoft PowerPoint–style presentations.

Of course, the real advantage of using DVD Studio Pro over, say, PowerPoint is that you can easily include DVD-quality video along with your static images. Also, the project you create is platform-independent (Mac or PC) and can be played back on widely available set-top and software players.

No matter how you choose to present your slides, creating a slideshow in DVD Studio Pro couldn't be easier.

File Formats for Slideshows

Creating a slideshow is simple as long as your images are prepared according to the required DVD specifications. Fortunately, DVD Studio Pro supports most of the common image formats for use in its slideshows: Photoshop (PSD), PICT, BMP, JPEG, QuickTime, MacPaint, Targa (TGA), and TIFF (TIF).

NOTE ▶ When working with PSD files in slideshows, the image layers that were visible when the file was last saved in Photoshop become the layers that are visible in DVD Studio Pro.

All images are converted to an MPEG format and, if necessary, automatically scaled to fit the frame size for the video standard you are using (NTSC or PAL). If any of the still images do not fit the aspect ratio, a background color is automatically added to fill in the gaps.

If you want to change DVD Studio Pro's resizing of an image, you can prepare your images in an image-editing application, such as Photoshop, first, and then resize them for the video format you're using (720×576 for PAL; 720×480 for NTSC). This way, you have complete control over how your image will be displayed. Also, keep in mind that the pictures and graphics have to be in the broadcast color space. Highly saturated colors look completely different on a TV monitor than on a computer screen, and, therefore, using a "broadcast" or "video safe" filter in the image editing application is highly recommended. This way, you'll be able to constrain the colors to the NTSC or PAL color space.

All DVD-compliant audio formats can also be imported into slideshows. This includes MPEG1-Layer 2, Dolby Digital (AC-3), WAVE, PCM, and AIFF (uncompressed PCM) audio. A useful feature in DVD Studio Pro is the capability to use MP3 and AAC files, which can be brought in from iTunes. DVD Studio Pro automatically takes the MP3 or AAC file and converts it to an AIFF file, which is compatible with the DVD specifications.

> **NOTE** ▶ All audio files used within a slideshow must be the same format and have identical settings for resolution and bit rate. For example, do not mix 44.1 kHz and 48 kHz audio in the same slideshow. For best results, use A.Pack to encode the audio files to AC-3 before importing them into DVD Studio Pro.

Adding a Slideshow

You will begin your exploration of slideshows by importing some images from the Slideshow folder. Then you'll connect the slideshow images to the SwissSlideshow tile in the Graphical view. (You created the SwissSlideshow tile in Lesson 3.)

1 Choose File > Open to open the **Swiss_DVD** project you created in
 Lesson 5.

 If you did not create the project, open Lessons > **06_Swiss_start** and
 relink the media if necessary.

2 Click the Assets tab and double-click anywhere inside of the Assets tab
 window.

 The Import Assets window appears. This is fastest way to import your
 assets.

3 Navigate to the Media > Swiss > Swiss_Assets > Slideshows folder and
 click Import.

 All Slideshow assets will be imported into DVD Studio Pro.

4 Drag **SwissPhoto_01.jpg** into the Slideshows folder.

 This will keep all photos organized in one folder. Notice that **Swiss-
 Photo_01.jpg** has a checkmark in the In Use column, indicating that it is
 already in use for the Chapter Index Menu.

TIP If you want to preview your images, you can select each image in the Assets tab, and the Picture Asset Inspector window will show your picture in the View Asset area. By double-clicking your picture asset, you can even preview your images in the Viewer window.

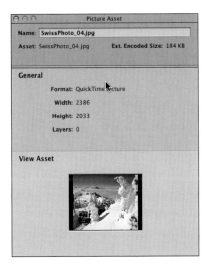

5 Click the Graphical tab to bring up Graphical view.

6 Select all the images from **SwissPhoto_01.jpg** to **SwissPhoto_14.jpg** and drag them onto the Swiss Slideshow tile in the Graphical view.

7 The Swiss Slideshow will be automatically generated.

8 Double-click the Slideshow tile in the Graphical view.

You will switch to the Slideshow tab, which contains the Slideshow Editor. At the top of the Project window, the Viewer window appears, and the Slideshow Inspector appears at the lower right of the interface.

9 Click the End Jump pop-up menu and select Menus > SwissMainMenu > [Menu]. Now, when the slideshow ends, it will jump back to the main menu.

You are now ready to make additional changes to the slideshow. The Slideshow Editor has seven columns. The three on the left show the display order (No.), a thumbnail (Image), and the name (File) for each slide. The remaining columns display various attributes of each slide, such as when in the slideshow it will appear (Time), its duration, and whether it will advance when the duration is finished or pause to allow the viewer to advance to the next slide using the remote control.

Modifying Your Slideshow

After your slide files are in place, you can assign audio files to an individual slide or to the entire slideshow. You can also adjust the duration of slides and move and delete slides. The following exercises show you how.

Adding Audio

DVD Studio Pro includes a number of flexible methods for handling slideshow audio. One of the nicest features is the way slides automatically respond to audio settings. Your options include Fit To Audio and Fit To Slides.

If you choose Fit To Audio, the duration of your slides is automatically set to have the slides play evenly over the entire length of the audio file. This is the best option to use if you want your audio and slides to finish playing at the same time. It is also an easy way to automatically set the duration of your slides, particularly for large slideshows.

Choosing Fit To Slides does not alter the duration of your slides. However, if your audio file is shorter than the duration of your slideshow, the last set of slides will continue to play without audio (unless you check the Loop Audio option). On the other hand, if your audio file is longer than the duration of your slideshow, the last slide will remain on the screen until the audio file has finished playing.

In the following exercise, you will add two audio clips.

1 Drag **SwissSlideshow_01.AC3** from the Audio tab in the Palette onto the Audio icon in your Slideshow tab.

The speaker symbol will have a black frame, indicating that an audio file has been applied to the slideshow. Also, the audio file will appear in your Slideshow Inspector with the actual running time.

No audio file Audio file applied

NOTE ▶ You can also add audio to individual slides by dragging an audio asset directly onto the space next to each slide.

2 Select any slide in the slideshow, and press the spacebar to play the slideshow.

Your slideshow will automatically begin playing in the Viewer tab, starting from the slide you have selected. This will give you a preview of your slideshow, including the audio you added to it. You can stop playback or advance to other slides by using the controls at the bottom of the window or by pressing the spacebar again. When the slideshow is finished, it will pause on the last slide.

3 From the Assets tab, select **SwissSlideshow_02.AC3**, and drag and drop it onto the Audio icon.

A second audio clip will be added to your slideshow.

4 Click the Outline tab, and select SwissSlideshow to open up the Slideshow Inspector.

In your Slideshow Inspector, you should now see both audio files listed.

You should also see that Fit To Slides is selected by default.

TIP If you choose the Fit To Audio option, DVD Studio Pro will calculate each slide's duration based on the total duration of the audio clips assigned to the slideshow. The slide duration in your slideshow will instantly change.

Changing the Duration of Slides

You can change the duration of individual or multiple sets of slides in the Slideshow Editor. The duration value indicates how long a slide is displayed. There are only a few preset choices in DVD Studio Pro: 1, 3, 5, or 10 seconds. However, you can customize your own value by double-clicking Slide Duration Value and then typing a number directly into the Slide Duration field. In this exercise, you will change the slide duration of two sides, so that the duration of the first six slides matches the duration of the audio file.

1 In the Slideshow Editor, hold down the Shift key and click
 SwissPhoto_01.jpg and **SwissPhoto_02.jpg** to select these two images.

2 Type 6 in the Duration box at the top of the Slideshow Editor to change
 the duration value for these two slides to 6 seconds.

Notice that the first six slides now exactly match the 32-second **SwissSlideshow_01.AC3** audio file.

3 Activate Pause on slide 6 by checking the box to the right of the slide in the Slideshow Editor.

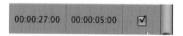

Your slideshow will only advance manually from this point. To advance in the slideshow, the user must press the Next button on the remote control.

TIP ▶ To set the Pause option on a group of slides, hold down the Shift key to select multiple slides, then click the Manual Advance check box on the Pause column of the Slideshow Editor. Any selected slides will be set to Pause.

You can only test the Pause function by using the Simulator. Let's try it now.

4 Click the Outline tab to access all of your current disc elements, and then Ctrl-click Swiss Slideshow, and choose Simulate to test the slideshow.

5 Now deselect the pause check box, as we no longer need it for this slideshow.

Moving and Deleting Slides

You can easily move and delete slides in the Slideshow Editor, just as you can with other elements that appear in lists in DVD Studio Pro.

1 In the Slideshow tab, select **SwissPhoto_02.jpg**.

2 Drag slide 2 to the top of the slide list.

You will see a black line above slide 1 and below the column headers indicating the new position of slide 2, above slide 1. Release the mouse button to complete the move.

You have now changed the order of the slideshow.

3 Select **SwissPhoto_04.jpg** in the slide list.

4 Press Delete to remove slide 4.

Once you have brought in your slides, you can easily remove slides from your slideshow. When a slide is removed, all of the other slides beneath it are automatically renumbered.

NOTE ▶ You can remove individual audio files that are added to slides in the Slideshow Editor by clicking the audio file next to the slide and pressing Delete.

5 Undo the deletion of slide 4 by pressing Cmd-Z.

6 Choose File > Save to save your project.

Slideshow Transitions

One of the best new features of DVD Studio Pro 4 is transitions. Since transitions are integrated into DVD Studio Pro, it's considerably easier and faster to build your slideshow in DVD Studio Pro, rather than using another editing application and then importing the transition. You can choose a transition effect for each slide, or apply one transition to the entire slideshow. When setting up transitions, keep in mind that transitions are considered part of the slide.

In this exercise, you will set the slideshow's default transition and choose a transition effect for several individual slides, as well as for a group of slides.

1 Double-click an empty place in the Slideshow Editor's control area to show the Slideshow Inspector.

2 In the Slideshow Inspector, click the Transition tab.

3 Choose the Motion Dissolve transition from the Transition pop-up menu.

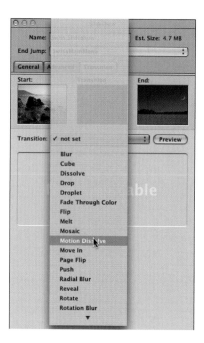

You have now set the default transition for the entire slideshow, but you can still choose a custom transition for each slide. The duration for this transition is set to 2 seconds.

Now let's set some transitions for the other slides in the show.

4 Select **SwissPhoto_02.jpg** in the Slideshow Editor.

5 Click the Transition tab, then choose the Cube transition from the
Transition pop-up menu.

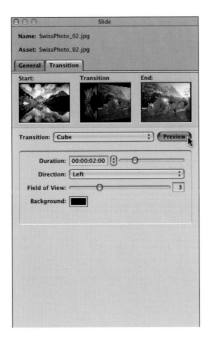

For this transition, a few more options are available for modifying the
transition. You can choose the direction in which the cube turns, as well as
the background color that is visible while the cube is turning.

6 Click the Preview button next to the selected transition.

You can now see a preview of the actual transition in the Slideshow
Inspector. This is a fast way to test the chosen transition for the actual
slide.

7 Select **SwissPhoto_01.jpg** in your slideshow, and choose Dissolve as your
transition effect.

8 Select a transition of your choice for slides 3 to 6.

9 In the Slideshow Editor, Shift-click slides 7 through 9 to select them.

10 Ctrl-click one of the slides in the selected area, and choose Transition >
Flip from the contextual menu.

You have now selected six individual transitions for the first six slides, and
a group transition for slides 7 to 9. The rest of the slideshow will play with
the default transition, Motion Dissolve.

11 Press Cmd-S to save your project.

12 Ctrl-click anywhere in your Slideshow Editor, and choose Simulate
Slideshow to simulate your entire slideshow.

Converting a Slideshow to a Track

At this point, you've explored most of the basic things you can do with
slideshows in DVD Studio Pro. If you want your slideshow to do even more,
you can convert the slideshow into a track. This gives you access to features
that are available for tracks, such as multiple audio tracks, subtitle streams,
16:9 aspect ratio slides, and buttons over video. For presentations, you can
even combine video and slides in your slideshow.

In this exercise, you will add a second audio stream that gives the user the option to choose a different piece of audio for the slideshow.

1 Click the Convert To Track button in the Slideshow Editor's control area.

Slideshow 1 reappears in the Track Editor, and its icon changes to a track icon. The duration of the slides, the slides' transitions, and all other properties you've set in the Slideshow Editor are preserved. A chapter marker is set at the beginning and end of each slide, and a cell marker is set at the beginning of each transition

2 Click the Assets tab.

3 Drag **SwissSlideshow_03.AC3** onto audio track A2.

4 Select **SwissSlideshow_03.AC3** and press Cmd-D to duplicate this audio clip.

The duplicated audio clip is too long. You can adjust it with DVD Studio Pro's trimming tool.

5 Position the pointer right at the end of the audio file **SwissSlideshow_03.AC3-2**.

The pointer turns into a trimming tool.

6 Trim the end of this second audio clip back to match the end point of the slideshow.

—————— Trimming tool

7 Ctrl-click anywhere in the slideshow, choose Simulate from Track from the shortcut menu, and make sure the slideshow works as designed. You can now switch to the second audio channel by clicking Audio 2 next to the audio symbol in the Simulator remote control.

8 Save your project to the Lessons > My_Projects folder.

Lesson Review

1. True or false: You can concatenate (add together) multiple audio streams in a single slideshow.

2. Can you mix audio formats inside a slideshow?

3. If you import a multilayer Photoshop file into a slideshow, which layers display?

4. How do you change the order of slides in a slideshow?

5. When you fit a slideshow to an audio stream, what happens?

6. What happens when you convert a slideshow to a track?

Answers

1. True.

2. No. All of the audio streams in a single slideshow must be exactly the same format.

3. Only the layers that were enabled the last time the multilayer file was saved.

4. Open the Slideshow editor, and drag slides up and down the list to reorder them.

5. DVD Studio Pro divides the total duration of the audio stream by the number of slides in the slideshow to determine the duration of each slide.

6. Each slide becomes a clip in the new track, and chapter markers are automatically created for each clip so you can navigate between them using the remote control's Next and Previous chapter buttons.

Keyboard Shortcuts

Cmd-7	Slideshow tab
Cmd-K	Add slideshow
Cmd-Option-P	Show/Hide Palette
Cmd-=	Show large thumbnails
Cmd--	Show small thumbnails
Cmd-A	Select all slides
Spacebar or L	Play slideshow in Viewer

7

Lesson Files
: Lessons > 07_Swiss_start
(or the My_Projects > Swiss_DVD project you created in
Lesson 6)

Media
: Media > Swiss folder

Time
: This lesson takes approximately 30 minutes to complete.

Goals
: Investigate the uses of subtitles

Create and edit subtitles in DVD Studio Pro

Import subtitles from a text file

Learn about using buttons over video in a subtitle stream

Learn about closed captioning

Adding Subtitles

Subtitles allow you to communicate with audiences in markets around the world. Like closed captioning for the hearing impaired, subtitles display the dialog in text, usually in the bottom portion of the screen, or provide a narration of the audio track. A feature that distinguishes closed captioning from subtitles is that closed captions also include descriptions of other sounds that are part of a scene, such as sound effects and music.

DVD subtitles have many advantages over closed captioning. One of the main advantages is that a viewer can turn subtitles on or off as they are needed, or select among 32 different subtitle streams. Each stream can represent a different language, which gives the viewer lots of control over the language to display for dialog and narration.

In addition to displaying text, a subtitle stream can contain overlays for buttons or other simple graphics. With the press of a button on the remote control, a viewer can jump to behind-the-scenes information.

In this lesson, you will learn how to easily create your own subtitles using DVD Studio Pro's built-in subtitler. You will also import one German subtitle file and use it for the SwissMovie track.

Creating Subtitles in DVD Studio Pro

DVD Studio Pro includes a powerful and convenient subtitling feature, which allows you to create subtitles directly in the Timeline window of the Track Editor. This enables you to easily sync your text with the video track and to rearrange, edit, and delete existing subtitles. For this lesson, you will create subtitles that indicate the places depicted in the **SwissMovie.m2v** track.

1 Choose File > Open and open the My_Projects > **Swiss_DVD** file that you created in Lesson 6.

 If you did not complete Lesson 6, open Lessons > **07_Swiss_start** and relink the media if necessary.

2 Click the Track tab to open the Track Editor.

3 Type *4900* directly in the timecode cursor position field, and press Enter to move the playhead to 00:00:49:00.

4 Ctrl-click in the first subtitle stream (S1), and choose Add Subtitle at Playhead from the shortcut menu.

When you choose Add Subtitle at Playhead, a subtitle is placed on the subtitle track starting at the playhead location. The subtitle is automatically selected for you and loaded into the Viewer window, so you can simply start typing the text of your subtitle immediately.

By default, all new subtitles are 5 seconds long. After your subtitles have been created, you may decide that they need to be longer or shorter to give a viewer more time to read them. Or you might need to reposition them to more accurately match the timing of a scene.

5 Type *Lucerne, Chapel Bridge.*

6 Click the new yellow subtitle in the subtitle stream to deselect the text, and then press the spacebar to play the SwissMovie including the subtitle.

This allows you to see the appearance and length of your subtitle stream. The "Lucerne" text is a little bit longer than the actual shot, but it can be easily adjusted. You'll adjust the length of the subtitle in the next exercise.

7 Type *12800* in your timecode field and press Enter to move the playhead to the next important place.

8 Ctrl-click the Subtitle stream and choose Add Subtitle at Playhead from the shortcut menu.

9 Enter *Chateau Chillon, Vaud.*

10 Click the new yellow subtitle in the subtitle stream to deselect the text, and then press the spacebar to play the SwissMovie, including the subtitle.

When you watch these two subtitles, you will see that both are playing for too long and the subtitle entries need to be adjusted. Let's deal with this next.

Adjusting the Length of Subtitles in the Track Editor

Adjusting the length or position of a subtitle in DVD Studio Pro is similar to trimming or moving a clip in Final Cut Pro, Soundtrack, or any other digital editing program. Simply drag the beginning or ending edges of the subtitle clip to resize it, or click and drag the clip itself to move the clip without altering duration. You may also choose to enter exact timecode values for your subtitles in the Subtitle Inspector, if you know exactly where you want them to begin or end.

> **TIP** ▶ You can play to a position where you want the subtitle to begin, pause the playhead on the frame you wish to start on, and Ctrl-click the subtitle and choose Move Subtitle Clip to Playhead from the shortcut menu.

As a general recommendation, text should be displayed long enough for a viewer to read through it twice before it disappears. However, you may need to leave text on the screen for longer or shorter periods of time, depending on the pace of the dialog or narration.

1 Drag the playhead to the left until it is positioned on the first subtitle clip and you can see "Lucerne, Chapel Bridge" in the viewer.

2 Zoom in to the subtitle using the Timeline Zoom control at the bottom-left corner of the Track Editor.

3 Grab the back edge of the subtitle and reduce the subtitle text by using the video in the Viewer window as a visual reference. This subtitle should stop playing at the point where the video transitions from the Chapel Bridge to the flower field.

This subtitle text should now be about 3 seconds.

4 Click the "Chateau Chillon, Vaud" subtitle text to select it.

5 In the Subtitle Inspector, enter *2* seconds for the Duration.

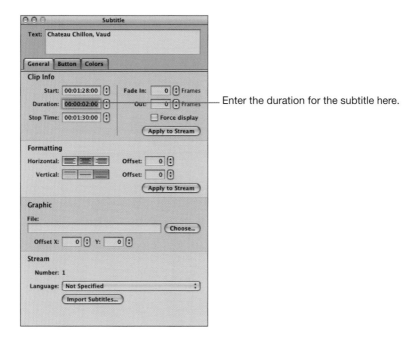

Enter the duration for the subtitle here.

Modifying the Font and Color of Subtitles

Once you have decided on where to place your subtitles and how long they should display, you should choose the appropriate font and color for your text. You do this using the same font tools you use when creating text for menus. In this example, you will change the font from Helvetica 36 to Arial Bold 30.

1 Double-click the "Lucerne, Chapel Bridge" subtitle clip in Stream 1, and use your pointer to highlight the text.

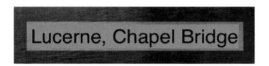

2 Press Cmd-T to open the Font window.

3 Select Arial as the font Family and Bold as the Typeface. Make the Size 30 points.

NOTE ▶ Choose fonts of 24 points or greater because they are easier to read. Also, you should avoid serif fonts whenever possible, because they are harder to read and display more jagged edges on the screen.

4 In the Formatting section of the Subtitle Inspector, click Apply to Stream.

This will apply all font and position settings to all subtitles in this stream.

NOTE ▶ To change the position of the subtitle onscreen, you can either use the Horizontal and Vertical formatting options or offset the subtitle by *x* pixels horizontally or vertically.

5 Click the Colors tab in the Subtitle Inspector.

As subtitle text is treated like an overlay graphic, you have the same options available as for an advanced overlay. You can change the color and the opacity of the actual font color, and for Outline 1 and 2. The outlines, or text borders, help improve the contrast with the video underneath the subtitle. In this exercise, you will choose orange as the font color with black outlines, which makes it easy to read the text over light and dark video content.

6 Choose Orange from the Text Color pop-up menu, and move the Opacity slider to 8.

To choose an opacity level for your subtitle, drag the Opacity slider or enter a value between 1 and 15. Usually you will set the text to 15, but for this example, we reduced the opacity of the orange color to make it less bright.

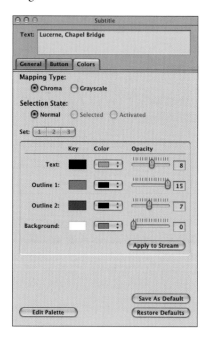

7 Choose Black for Outline 1 and Outline 2 color, but set the opacity of Outline 2 to 7 to achieve a softer outline.

You may set the outlines at full opacity or make them semitransparent. For subtitles, the Background slider is usually left at its default setting of 0, or else a color screen is added to the image.

TIP ▶ Outlines can help to make your text more visible against a dark or visually busy background. You should consider adding outlines to any subtitle text you create, since they will make reading much easier for your audience. If your subtitle does not sufficiently stand out against the background video, consider adding Outline 2 in the same color to make an outline that is twice as thick.

Importing Subtitles from a Text File

Although you can use any of the methods you've just learned about to add, trim, and move subtitles, there are easier and more precise ways to create these streams. Like Final Cut Pro markers, subtitles are best added using timecode from the source movie file.

If you have a lot of subtitles to create, or if you are receiving translated subtitle text files from a service bureau, you will find that it is easy to import subtitles from a subtitle text file. Subtitle text files are specially formatted text files that list the text of each subtitle along with its timecode in and out points. These files are easy to create one you undertand their code, and may become your preferred method of working with subtitles, even if you are doing all of the translation yourself.

You can examine the subtitle text files for this project to understand the proper formatting and placement of timecode and text information in a file. All the options you see can be easily changed in the subtitle text file.

In the following example, the font is Arial, set at 30 points, and will appear centered on the bottom of the frame. The text will be bold (TRUE), and it is not Underlined or Italic (FALSE). The subtitles are offset neither horizontally nor vertically ($XOFFSET, $YOFFSET = 0). The primary text color ($Text Contrast) is set with an opacity of 10, Outline 1 is fully opaque, Outline 2 is about 50% transparent, and there is no background contrast. The subtitles will be forced to display ($Force display = TRUE), and they won't Fade in or Fade out (value is 0). $TapeOffset = TRUE means that the asset-based timecode is used. If this

were set to FALSE, the subtitles would be referenced to the streams' zero-based timecode.

The timecode entry in the left-most column indicates when the subtitle starts playing, and the timecode entry in the middle column indicates when the subtitle ends. The entries are delimited by a tab and a comma. In the right-most column, you see the actual subtitle text.

```
● ○ ○                        Swiss_Subtitles_English.txt
$FontName              =      Arial
$FontSize              =      30
$HorzAlign             =      Center          // Left or Right
$VertAlign             =      Bottom          // Top  or Center
$Bold                  =      TRUE
$UnderLined            =      FALSE
$Italic                =      FALSE
$XOffset               =      0 // Pixel offset(can be negative)
$YOffset               =      0 // Pixel offset(can be negative)
$TextContrast      =      10
$Outline1Contrast  =      15
$Outline2Contrast  =      7
$BackgroundContrast =     0
$ForceDisplay      =      TRUE // DVD Force Display Flag
$FadeIn                =      0 // In number of Frames
$FadeOut               =      0 // In number of Frames

$TapeOffset = TRUE

00:00:25:12    ,     00:00:29:00    ,    Aelplisee (2156 m) Aroser Alp, Grisons
00:00:31:00    ,     00:00:36:00    ,    Rhinefalls
00:00:36:01    ,     00:00:40:10    ,    Zurich
00:00:40:12    ,     00:00:44:05    ,    Morcote, Southern Switzerland
00:00:49:00    ,     00:00:52:05    ,    Lucerne, Chapel Bridge
00:01:23:00    ,     00:01:26:00    ,    above Lake Geneva, Vaud
00:01:28:00    ,     00:01:30:00    ,    Chateau Chillon, Vaud
00:01:42:00    ,     00:01:45:00    ,    Appenzell
00:02:00:00    ,     00:02:03:00    ,    Matterhorn, Zermatt, Valais
00:02:09:00    ,     00:02:14:00    ,    View from the Saentis (2501 m), in Eastern
Switzerland
00:02:30:00    ,     00:02:34:00    ,    Ibex
00:02:39:00    ,     00:02:41:25    ,    Marmots
00:05:08:00    ,     00:05:11:00    ,    Matterhorn, Zermatt, Valais
00:06:13:00    ,     00:06:16:00    ,    St. Moritz, Grisons
00:07:44:00    ,     00:07:47:00    ,    St. Moritz, Grisons
00:08:11:00    ,     00:08:15:00    ,    From Wengen to Kleine Scheidegg, Bernese Oberland
```

NOTE ▶ In addition to plain text files, you can import STL (Spruce), SON (Sonic Solutions), and SCR (Daiken-Comtec Laboratories Scenarist) formats.

Now let's import some subtitle text files.

1 Ctrl-click the first subtitle stream (S1) in the Track Editor window, and choose Import Subtitle File from the shortcut menu that pops up.

2 Choose **Swiss_Subtitles_English.txt** from the Media > Swiss > Swiss_Docs folder.

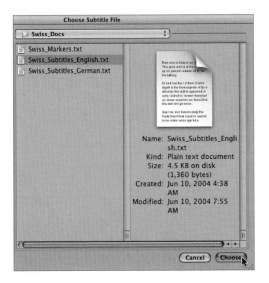

3 Click Choose to import the subtitles. An alert appears telling you that 16 subtitles were imported from the text file and automatically added to the subtitle stream. Click OK to dismiss the alert.

This will overwrite the subtitles that you were working on in the previous section.

4 Choose English from the Language pop-up menu.

5 Ctrl-click the second subtitle stream (S2) in the Track Editor, and choose Import Subtitle File from the shortcut menu.

6 Choose **Swiss_Subtitles_German.txt** from the Swiss_Docs folder.

7 Click Choose to import the subtitles, and click OK to dismiss the alert.

8 Choose German from the Language pop-up menu.

The final result should look like this:

Previewing Subtitles

Once your subtitles are created, you should preview them to make certain that they are properly aligned with your video, easily visible over the background, and displayed on the screen long enough to read.

1 Ctrl-click anywhere in your Track Editor, and choose Simulate from Track from the shortcut menu to open the Simulator.

2 Click the Next Chapter button once to move to the Zurich subtitle.

3 Click the Subtitle pop-up menu, located above the View check box, to select subtitle stream 2.

The German subtitle will now appear in your Simulator window.

4 Close the Simulator and save the project.

Creating Buttons over Video

In addition to using the subtitle streams to display text information, you can also use them to contain overlays for buttons or other simple graphics. This way, you can add the interactivity of a menu to video tracks, or animations, with a series of overlay images.

For example, you could create an overlay with a button that appears at certain points in a movie and links the viewer to information about a particular scene. You could even allow a viewer to choose whether to activate this option in a menu before watching a track. (Otherwise, the overlay graphics or buttons could be distracting.) There are many possibilities for this type of interactivity, depending on your imagination and the needs of your project.

> **NOTE** ▶ Only one subtitle stream can be displayed at a time. If you are adding overlay buttons to a subtitle stream, any other subtitles that appear at that point in time will be disabled.

You create button overlays for a subtitle stream just as you would create overlays for an ordinary menu. However, you first need to create markers in the video track to indicate where each of these buttons should appear. These markers are considered button highlight markers, and they are easy to create in DVD Studio Pro.

Button highlight markers—represented by an orange pointer—are used when you display special buttons over video tracks using the subtitle function. You can use these buttons to present viewers with choices as they watch a video track. A well-known example of this technique is the "white rabbit" feature on the DVD for the movie *The Matrix*, which lets you jump to special features if you press Enter on your remote control whenever a white rabbit overlay appears on the screen.

In this exercise, you will create a subtitle stream for activating a single button that leads to the main menu. In order to achieve this, you will need to set two button highlight markers to define when the button overlay will be playing.

1 Click the Landscape marker in your SwissMovie track.

2 Click the Button Highlight check box in the Marker Inspector.

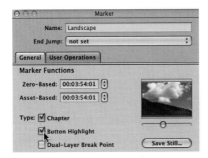

3 Type *041000* in the timecode field of your Track tab to move the playhead about 15 seconds away from your Landscape marker.

4 Press M to create another marker.

5 Click the Chapter check box to deselect it, and click the Button Highlight check box to use this marker as a Button Highlight marker.

An orange marker will appear in your timeline.

6 Double-click in the space between your two markers in the S1 subtitle stream.

A new subtitle with the correct duration will appear in the subtitle stream between your two markers.

7 Double-click the new subtitle and enter *Main Menu.*

8 Click the "Force display" check box in the General tab of the Subtitle Inspector.

9 In the Formatting area of the Subtitle Inspector, click the Align Right button to set the Horizontal alignment.

The subtitle text will move to the right of the window, and this subtitle will be forced to display.

10 Click the Background of the Viewer window, and drag your pointer to draw a button around the text "Main Menu."

Now you are going to establish the actual link from the button to the main menu.

> **NOTE** ▶ You can create a maximum of 36 buttons per video track with a 4:3 aspect ratio, and 18 buttons for a video track with a 16:9 aspect ratio.

11 Ctrl-click Button 1, and choose Target > Menus > SwissMainMenu > [Menu] from the shortcut menu.

12 Ctrl-click in the Track Editor, and choose Simulate from Track from the shortcut menu to open the Simulator.

13 Click the Next Chapter button four times to move to the Landscape chapter marker.

"Main Menu" should appear as text on the lower-right corner of your screen. If you click this button, it should lead you back to the main menu.

14 Save your project to the My_Projects folder.

Button Graphics over Video

If you want to use multiple buttons or graphics over video, you will need to use graphic overlays. These graphics can be easily imported into the subtitle stream, and you can use the same techniques as described in this exercise to create buttons and set the overlay colors. Please refer to page 427 of the DVD Studio Pro manual for more information regarding buttons over video.

About Closed Captioning

Although subtitles represent the majority of text that is created for a DVD, you may also include closed caption text, which is similar to what is broadcast by TV stations for hearing-impaired viewers. When closed captions are included, a television with the proper decoder interprets the closed caption information and displays the text on the screen. Note that only the captions themselves, plus the color and position of the text, are interpreted; the decoding device chooses the font.

The main difference between subtitles and closed captions is that closed captions include descriptions of sounds heard in a scene (telephone ringing, music playing, and so on) in addition to the usual text. Also, closed captions are included in line 21 of a video signal, which means that they are a part of the video stream and not strictly a DVD-only feature.

DVD Studio Pro allows you to include closed captioning on a DVD as an advanced feature. Please refer to page 557 of the DVD Studio Pro manual for more information regarding setting up closed captioned streams.

NOTE ▸ Closed captions on a DVD are supported only by NTSC video signals.

Lesson Review

1. How many subtitle streams can each track hold?
2. True or false: Viewers must always choose the subtitle stream they want to view from a subtitle selection menu.
3. Why should you add outlines and/or dropshadows to subtitle text?
4. Can subtitles be imported as a text file?
5. True or false: You can use images and graphics other than text in a subtitle stream.

Answers

1. 32.
2. False. If you tag the subtitle stream with a language setting, the DVD Video player will automatically display the correct subtitle stream (provided the DVD-Video player is properly set-up, of course).
3. To make the subtitles easier to view.
4. Yes, but they must be saved in a properly formatted plain text file (.txt) before they are imported.
5. True. This is how you make buttons over video, for example.

Keyboard Shortcuts

Cmd-T	Open the Font window
Cmd-A	Select all
Cmd-Option-I	Open the Subtitle Inspector
M	Add a marker at the playhead position

8

Lesson Files

Lessons > 08_Swiss_start
(or the My_Projects > Swiss_DVD project you created in
Lesson 7)

Media

Media > Swiss folder

Time

This lesson takes approximately 20 minutes to complete.

Goals

Add DVD-ROM content to your DVD

Create a menu for Web links

Understand how DVD@ccess is used

Lesson **8**

DVD-ROM Content and DVD@ccess

In addition to ordinary DVD-Video content, which includes the tracks, menus, slideshows, and other elements that form a complete project, you can include extra ROM content on a disc. By placing an extra folder alongside the VIDEO_TS folder on a DVD, you can put all types of computer data on a disc, including Flash files, PDFs, HTML, and other documents.

A DVD-Video with DVD-ROM content is called a *hybrid DVD*. These discs will play normally in a DVD player and can be put inside a computer to unlock the hidden potential of the other files.

The DVD@ccess feature can be used to activate Web links or launch an email application when a user views a menu, marker, or slideshow slide while playing the DVD from a computer with Internet access. Further, DVD@ccess can be programmed to trigger the DVD-ROM files that exist on the disc and open them on a computer, provided the computer has the applications necessary to run the files.

In this lesson, you will add DVD-ROM content to the Swiss disc and utilize the DVD@ccess feature to open a Web page.

Adding DVD-ROM Content to a DVD-Video Disc

Adding DVD-ROM content to a DVD-Video disc is simple to do in DVD Studio Pro. Use the following steps to select a folder to be placed on your disc when it is finally built. You should make certain that all of your files are in a single folder on your hard drive and that the folder is organized exactly the way you want it to appear on the finished disc.

1 Choose File > Open and open the My_Projects > **Swiss_DVD** file that you created in Lesson 7.

 If you did not create the file, open Lessons > **08_Swiss_start** and relink the media.

2 At the top of the Outline tab, click the SWISS_DVD disc icon.

 The Inspector now shows the properties of the disc. At the bottom of the General tab is a section called DVD-ROM, where you can choose to add DVD-ROM content to the DVD.

3 Click the Content check box and the Joliet Extension Support check box.

 The Joliet Extension Support is necessary to allow PC users running Windows 95 or later to access files in the DVD-ROM folder that have long filenames.

4 Click Choose.

 In the DVD-ROM Contents dialog, navigate to Media > Swiss > Swiss_ROM.

5 Select the Swiss_ROM folder.

6 Click Choose to add the selection.

Notice that the Location box in the DVD-ROM section of the Inspector lists the local file path of the folder you have chosen on your hard drive. That's all you have to do. When DVD Studio Pro formats the disc, the selected folder will be written alongside the VIDEO_TS and AUDIO_TS folders. Further, the size of the contents you have added is now listed in both binary and true bytes, and has also been added to the overall size of the disc.

7 Look to the top right of the Inspector and see that the Est. Size number has increased. Also, your Disc Meter in the toolbar has increased to reflect the size of the added ROM material.

> **TIP** It is important to remember that any DVD-ROM content you add to a disc should be factored into the total file size of your project. You should view the file size of the data you have added to a project before adding it to a DVD project. For this reason, you may wish to wait until the last moment to add the DVD-ROM content, so that you can add the finished project size (estimated size, located in the toolbar and at the top of the Disc Inspector window) to the size of the extra files.

Creating a Web Link with DVD@ccess

DVD@ccess is a feature in DVD Studio Pro that allows a menu, marker, or slideshow slide to automatically trigger a computer to open a Web browser and load a URL specified by the DVD menu.

Setting Up the Web Link Menu

In order to smoothly integrate Web links into a DVD project, you should create a special informational menu page. Since DVDs can be played in set-top players as well as computers, you will usually want to create a special menu that informs viewers that they need to be viewing the DVD on a computer with an Internet connection in order to access the links. You will also use this special menu to launch the Web link. In the case of our project, we'll point the user toward www.myswitzerland.com.

Let's try this now.

1 In the Outline tab, select SwissMainMenu to activate it in the Menu Editor.

2 Click the Assets tab, then select Menus > SwissMainMenu.tiff, and drag it onto the Weblink button.

3 Choose Create Submenu from the Drop palette.

A submenu will automatically be created and linked to this button in your main menu.

4 Double-click the Menu 3 button to jump to the submenu you have just created.

5 At the top of the Menu Inspector window, name the menu by typing *WeblinkMenu* into the Name field.

6 Double-click the menu background to activate your Text tool.

7 Type *Launching www.myswitzerland.com.*

8 Double-click again in the middle part of the menu and type

This feature will only

work on a computer

connected to the Internet.

9 Shift-click both text elements to select them.

10 Click the Styles tab, then the Project button, and then the Text button in your Palette to navigate to the SwissMenu style.

11 Double-click the SwissMenu style to apply it to both text elements.

12 Click the menu background to deselect the text elements.

13 Select the "Launching www.myswitzerland.com" text, and move it to the top left of the Menu Editor inside the title safe zone.

14 Select the "This feature…" text and move it to the left of the Swiss logo.

15 Click the Position Left button in the Formatting section of your Text Object Inspector.

16 Press Cmd-T and choose 24 pt font size.

17 Move the text to align it on the left with the title text.

Your menu should now look like this:

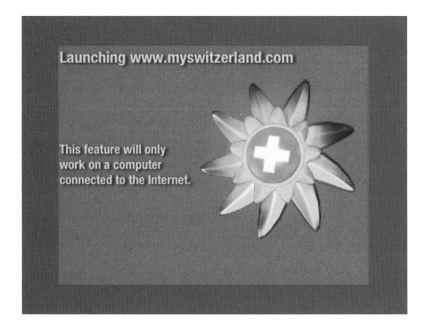

Establishing the DVD@ccess Link and Menu Actions

In the next few steps, you will establish the DVD@ccess link and set up a time-out action for the Web link menu.

1 Click the menu background to activate the Menu Inspector.

2 Click the Advanced tab.

3 Click the DVD@ccess check box in the Playback Options section of the Menu Inspector.

4 In the Name field, type *Switzerland Tourism* as the name for the link.

This text is used for your reference while creating the DVD and is not added to the final disc. Use a name that will help you to identify the link in your project.

5 Enter *http://www.myswitzerland.com* into the URL field.

TIP ▶ The URL needs be written in the format http://*www.yourwebsite.com* for Internet links, or in the format mailto:*yourname@yourprovider.com* for email links.

Now that your DVD@ccess link has been created, you should create a timeout action. The timeout action will return the viewer to the previous menu. This way, you don't need to create a Back button, and viewers are required to read the page.

6 Click the General tab of the Inspector.

7 Choose Timeout from the At End pop-up menu in the bottom portion of the General tab.

This is where you can set the amount of time before the menu jumps to the asset you'll choose from the Action pop-up menu.

8 Enter an appropriate value, such as 10, into the Sec (seconds) field.

9 In the Action pop-up menu, choose Menus > SwissMainMenu > [Menu] to return the viewer to the main menu.

10 Choose File > Save to save your project.

Testing the DVD@ccess Link

It is quite important to test your DVD@ccess link before you distribute your completed DVD. Follow these steps to use the Simulator to launch your DVD@cccess links:

1 Press Cmd-, (Cmd-comma) to open DVD Studio Pro Preferences.

2 Click the Simulator icon and make sure that the Enable DVD@ccess Web Links check box is selected in the Simulator pane.

3 Click OK.

4 In the Outline tab, Ctrl-click the WeblinkMenu icon and choose Simulate Menu from the contextual menu.

If you are connected to the Internet, your default Internet browser will be launched and www.myswitzerland.com will be displayed. Your Weblink-Menu will time out after 10 seconds, and your SwissMainMenu will be displayed again.

> **TIP** ▶ DVD@ccess works fine on Macintosh computer systems, but there are a few known issues on the Windows platform. You can choose Help > Late-Breaking News to check out some of those issues.

Testing the Link Using DVD Player

After you test the Web link using Simulator, you should further ensure that it works by using the DVD Player application to test the built DVD. First, of course, you'll need to finish your DVD, as described in Lesson 9.

It's important to make sure that you've selected the Enable DVD@ccess option in the DVD Player Preferences. Follow these steps once you have completed the formatting and building steps for the Swiss Tourism project as explained in the next lesson.

1 Be sure you have used the Build and Format or Burn command in order to include the DVD@ccess installers in the ROM portion of your DVD.

See Lesson 9 for details.

> **TIP** ▶ If you want to burn your project using Roxio's Toast, you should consult the DVD Studio Pro 4 manual. The manual elaborates on how to include the DVD@ccess installers using a third-party application.

2 In the Applications folder of your hard drive, double-click the DVD Player icon to launch it.

3 Press Cmd-, (Cmd-comma) to open DVD Player Preferences.

4 Make sure the "Enable DVD@ccess web links" check box is selected, and click OK.

5 Open the VIDEO_TS folder, play the DVD, and test the Web link from your built folder.

Activating DVD-ROM Content with DVD@ccess

You can trigger DVD-ROM content by adding a DVD@ccess link that references a local file on the DVD instead of a Web site. To do this, you enter a pathname in the DVD@ccess area of the Inspector. The pathname must have the following format:

file:///*DVDName*/*FolderName*/*Filename*

▶ The *DVDName* is the name of the disc that was entered into the Disc Inspector, such as SWISS_DVD.

▶ The *FolderName* is the folder the file is in.

▶ The *Filename* is the name of the file itself.

Using this structure, you can link to any content you have included on the DVD-ROM portion of a disc.

NOTE ▶ The file path information is case sensitive, so it must be typed exactly as it appears for files and folders on a disc.

Although Simulator and the Apple DVD Player can be used to test DVD-@ccess Web and email links, they cannot be used to test the opening of files located on the DVD. A disc must be burned in order to test links to DVD-ROM files.

Lesson Review

1. What's the name of a DVD-Video disc that has DVD-ROM content on it?

2. What does DVD@ccess do?

3. What is the file path to link to the Internet?

4. What is the file path to link to an email address?

5. What is the file path to link to a file on the DVD-Video disc's ROM section?

Answers

1. A Hybrid DVD.

2. It launches web links from your DVD-Video, on computers that have DVD@ccess installed.

3. http://www.yourDomain.com

4. mailto:yourName@yourDomain.com

5. file:///discName/folderName/yourfile.extension

9

Lesson Files	Lessons > 09_Swiss_start (or the My_Projects > Swiss_DVD project file you created in Lesson 8)
Media	None
Time	This lesson takes approximately 30 minutes to complete.
Goals	Understand the building and formatting process
	Build a DVD project
	Burn a disc
	Test projects in Apple DVD Player
	Understand DVD media choices
	Understand the replication process
	Prepare a project for replication
	Learn about copy protection
	Design graphics for DVD labels and inserts

Finishing Your DVD

After your project is complete, it's time to systematically test it to make sure that all of the menus, tracks, slideshows, and other items function properly. After it has been tested, the next step is to build and format your project for output.

If you aren't familiar with the terms *build* or *format*, don't worry. *Build* is just a fancy word for exporting your project from DVD Studio Pro into files that adhere to the DVD specification. In most cases, *format* is just another way to say *burn to disc*. But the term *format* also takes into consideration that we may be placing the finished VIDEO_TS folder on a DLT (digital linear tape) or exporting it as a disc image to a hard disk drive. *Format* is a blanket term for any final process of writing the files to a particular medium.

DVD Studio Pro offers more options for finishing your project than ever before. There are two primary finishing methods: The first is building and formatting your project directly to a DVD-R (DVD-recordable) disc, using a DVD burner, or to digital linear tape using a DLT drive. The second is building to a folder on your hard drive that you can test with the Apple DVD Player, just as you did at the beginning of this project (in Lesson 3).

In this lesson, you will learn the best and most thorough methods for testing and finishing a DVD. You'll also learn how to prepare your project for distribution.

Testing Your Project

Once you are finished assembling your project, you should test the entire disc's functionality with the Simulator. The Simulator works like a DVD player, using the same controls to navigate a disc as a DVD player's remote control. However, testing with the Simulator is not a replacement for testing your project in a real DVD player. It is simply the first phase of testing your DVD to ensure that all of the links and other elements you have added to your project function as you intend. Once you have tested the DVD with the Simulator, it is always a good idea to build the DVD to a hard drive and test it with Apple's DVD Player.

Unlike a DVD player, which plays a properly formatted VIDEO_TS folder that was created in the building process, the Simulator uses assets that may not be formatted for a DVD. As a result, your playback may skip or stutter a little. The amount of difficulty that you experience when playing back a project with the Simulator depends on the performance of your computer and the type of assets you are using. In most cases, it will be fine for gauging the performance of your project. Just know that your final disc will probably operate much more smoothly after it has been built.

> **NOTE** ▸ In the Simulator pane of Preferences (DVD Studio Pro > Preferences), you can set up the Simulator to operate like a real DVD player, with options for region codes, languages, and player aspect ratios.

You can simulate an entire project (instead of individual disc items, as you have done in previous lessons) by accessing the Simulator from the File menu, or by clicking the Simulate icon on the toolbar.

1 Choose File > Open to open the **Swiss_DVD** project created in Lesson 8. If you did not create the project, open Lessons > **09_Swiss_start** and relink the media if necessary.

2 In the Project window, click the Log tab (next to the Outline tab).

By clicking the Log tab, you tell DVD Studio Pro to generate a log file. The log file contains status information that may be useful for fixing problems when you simulate a project, build a disc, or encode content.

3 Click the Simulate icon on the toolbar.

The Simulator interface consists of a preview window on the right and a bank of remote control buttons on the left. These buttons are just like the buttons you would find on a standard DVD player remote control or in Apple's DVD Player. Using these buttons, you can test your project, just like you tested it in Lesson 3, or as you would any commercially produced disc.

Here's a close-up of the Simulator's remote control buttons.

On the bottom portion of the Simulator window you can view the current time for the asset you are playing. You can also use the pop-up menus to access alternate video, audio, and subtitles, if any.

Things to Look Out For When Testing Your Project

It is important to be thorough when testing a project. Make sure all of your buttons and links work correctly. Once you proceed to the next step and build the project, even if you don't format (or burn) it to disc, you will not be able to fix any problems without opening up the project file again and building again from scratch. In the Simulator window, use the controls on the left side of the screen to test the playback of your disc. Explore the disc as you would any DVD that you rent or buy.

1 Click the Simulator icon in your toolbar.

2 First, and most important, make certain that your startup action has been set for the DVD.

 You should see the SwissIntroMenu playing to the SwissMainMenu fading through red. If this is not playing first, you may need to go back and set the First Play action in the Disc Inspector.

3 Click the Play Video button to activate the SwissMovie track.

Make sure that the buttons on the remote control operate correctly.

4 Click the Menu button from the remote control in the upper-left corner of the Simulator window to get back to the SwissMainMenu.

5 Check all of the links from your menu buttons, including the chapter index menu, which links to the various markers.

6 Click the Title button from the remote controls.

The Title button should take you to the top menu of the disc.

7 Observe the output of the log file.

| Assets | Outline | Log |

View: Simulate

6/17/04 5:21:50 AM
SPRM 14 (Player Config) register changed: 512
SPRM 0 (Menu Language) register changed: 513
SPRM 16 (Audio Language) register changed: 513
SPRM 18 (Subtitle) register changed: 513
SPRM 20 (Region Code) register changed: 0
Beginning from first play target
Menu timeout expired
SPRM 8 (Highlight Button) register changed: 1024
Jumping to Menu: SwissMainMenu – Play Movie
User activated: Play Movie
Jumping to Track: SwissMovie – Heaven
SPRM 6 (Title PGC) register changed: 1
SPRM 4 (Title Number) register changed: 1
SPRM 5 (VTS Title) register changed: 1
SPRM 7 (Part of Title) register changed: 1
SPRM 3 (Angle Number) register changed: 1
SPRM 1 (Audio Stream) register changed: 0
SPRM 2 (Subpicture Stream) register changed: 0
User action: Menu
SPRM 8 (Highlight Button) register changed: 1024
Jumping to Menu: SwissMainMenu – Play Movie

Every process the DVD player invoked, or the user chose, right down to which buttons are navigated, is listed.

Building and Formatting a DVD

After testing, the next step in creating a finished DVD is performing a build. You can either build and format your project in two separate steps, or combine both steps in one process by using Build and Format or the Burn command. In this section, we'll first take a look at building and formatting as separate steps. Then we'll go back and take a look at the "all-in-one" method.

Building a project means, in effect, that a VIDEO_TS (Video Title Set) folder is created. The VIDEO_TS folder contains your finished DVD project. At the end of the building process your files will be multiplexed, which means that all audio, video, menus, and other disc items are woven together to create DVD-compliant files.

Every DVD player, regardless of type (software or hardware), looks for the VIDEO_TS folder on the first level of the DVD to play a disc. Without this folder, your disc will not play. However, you do not have to put the VIDEO_TS folder onto a disc. You may choose to create the folder, which can be opened and tested with Apple's DVD Player application, on your hard drive instead. Outputting a finished project to your hard drive also makes it available for duplication at a later time.

> **NOTE ▶** When you build a disc, an AUDIO_TS folder is created along with the VIDEO_TS folder. Although the AUDIO_TS folder is empty (and relevant only to specialized DVD-Audio titles), you should include it with your VIDEO_TS folder on any discs you create. Since the DVD specification includes the use of an AUDIO_TS folder, most DVD players automatically look for it. If that folder is not found on a disc, you might experience playback issues (although most discs and players operate fine without it). For this reason, it is good practice to include the AUDIO_TS and VIDEO_TS folders together on a disc.

Setting Your Build Preferences

Before you actually build your disc, you should make certain that your prefer-
ences are set correctly. Follow these steps.

1 Choose DVD Studio Pro > Preferences and select the Destinations pane.

 The important thing to check is that the location, or destination, where
 you want to place a completed build is correct. To check or change the
 destination for your built VIDEO_TS folder, you must choose
 Build/Format from the Show pop-up menu.

2 From the Show pop-up menu, choose Build/Format.

 The default destination for your build is set to a folder called DVD Studio
 Pro Files, which was created by DVD Studio Pro inside your Users folder
 when you installed the software. Your Users folder, located on your boot
 drive, is not a great place for your build. A better option is a dedicated
 media drive. (External FireWire hard drives are great for this.) You should
 create a dedicated folder on the drive as the location for your build. Further,
 it's best not to use the same location (drive and folder) for both the build
 and your DVD assets.

3 Click the Choose button.

4 Select an appropriate location in which to save your builds, and then click
Choose.

5 Click OK to close the Destinations pane.

Creating a Build of Your DVD

Now that the preferences are set correctly, you can go ahead and build the
Swiss_DVD project. While building a project, you should watch the Log tab,
which is useful for checking your work while the VIDEO_TS folder is being
created.

1 Click the Build button in the toolbar, or use the keyboard shortcut
Option-Command-C.

NOTE ▶ By choosing Build here, you are making the choice to build and
format your project in two separate steps. Later in this lesson, you'll learn
about building and formatting in one step using the Build and Format
command.

2 In the Choose Build Folder dialog that appears, select a location for your
finished build folder, or accept the default location (which you just set in
the Destinations pane) and click Choose.

The build process is now initialized, and DVD Studio Pro has begun com-
piling the menus and multiplexing (or *muxing*) your tracks. You can view
the progress of your build with the status bar that appears. The build
process will take a while, depending on the speed of your computer. This
will give you a chance to explore the Log tab as it outputs its information.

3 Check the Log tab for any error messages. If you have any, it's easy to see
from the Log where you went wrong.

As your VIDEO_TS folder is built, you can see in the Log tab which part
of the process is currently taking place. In most cases, the Log simply lists
each part of the process as it is completed. But in some cases, it may list
errors, such as a missing asset or the first-play action not being set.

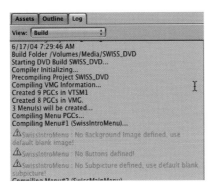

You can disregard the DVD Studio Pro alerts, because you have inten-
tionally set up the SwissIntroMenu without buttons or any other
elements.

When the build is complete, an Alert dialog appears when the files have
been successfully compiled. If there were any problems in your project
such as mismatching audio files in your menu domain, your build would
not have been completed and you would have received the appropriate
error message.

4 Close the Alert dialog and check the location where you saved your build.

The Build command has taken your project and compiled it into a fin-
ished VIDEO_TS folder, which you can burn onto a DVD disc or view
with a software DVD player on your computer's hard drive.

Contents of the VIDEO_TS Folder

Every VIDEO_TS folder that is created contains a unique set of files, which make up a DVD title set. The following are a few of these files:

▶ DVD Studio Pro Layout file—This file is unique in DVD Studio Pro and contains all formatting information about the DVD project.

▶ VIDEO_TS.IFO—An IFO file contains the information about a disc, including its capacity, and the way navigational elements should work, such as menus, buttons, and links.

▶ VIDEO_TS.BUP—The BUP files are backups of IFO files. Backups are important if a disc is damaged or a player cannot otherwise read the original IFO file.

▶ VIDEO_TS.VOB—A VOB file is the video object file containing all the actual video, audio, and subtitle information for the menus, tracks, and slideshows you've created. Each VOB file may contain up to 1 GB of information. Larger projects may be broken up into several VOB files.

Formatting Your Project

Formatting your project can occur either as a separate step after the building or as part of the build. In the last exercise, you chose the Build command, rather than Build and Format, so now you need to format your project as a separate step, after compiling is completed. (In the next section, we'll take a look at the one-step Build and Format process.)

The Format command takes the finished VIDEO_TS folder, which was assembled with the Build command, and writes it to a DVD-recordable drive, to a DLT (digital linear tape) drive, or as a disc image to a hard drive. There are specific settings for each one of these output options.

> **NOTE ▶** In this process, a folder containing DVD-ROM content and DVD@ccess installers can be included. This option is also available if you build and format in a single step, as described later in this lesson, or burn a DVD.

One advantage of building and formatting in two separate steps is that you can choose any VIDEO_TS folder you want to burn. If, at a later time, you decide you would like to use an older VIDEO_TS folder you created, you can use the Format option in DVD Studio Pro to place it on a disc.

A second and perhaps more important advantage of building and formatting in separate steps is that you can test the build for errors with Apple's DVD Player before physically burning those errors into a DVD. This is frequently referred to as "burning a coaster," because placing drinks on them to avoid leaving a ring on a table is about the only thing an unplayable DVD is good for.

> **NOTE ▶** You may also use a separate DVD-burning application, such as Roxio's Toast Titanium, to place the VIDEO_TS folder on a disc.

Building and Formatting in a Single Step

If you are satisfied with your project and want to simply finish and place it on a disc, you can build and format in a single step. To do this, choose File > Advanced Burn > Build and Format or choose Build and Format from the toolbar.

The Build and Format command combines these separate tasks: assembling a VIDEO_TS folder and then writing it to the drive of your choice (DVD, DLT, or hard disk).

1 Choose the Build and Format command from the toolbar.

The Build and Format window will appear.

2 Make sure you have chosen the appropriate settings for your project.

In the Source section, it is important to choose the correct build of your project. As you will include DVD-ROM content, the DVD-ROM check box has be checked and the correct Location needs to selected. In the Destination section of your Build and Format window, you can choose the Output device. As a default, the DVD Recorder (in this case the SONY DVD-RW drive) is selected. You can also output your project onto a hard drive or to a DLT drive. If you have the Lossless Linking check box selected, it adds protection against buffer underrun conditions. This is achieved by allowing the DVD Recorder to pause during the writing process, and then pick up where it left off once additional data becomes available.

TIP ▶ DVD-ROM content can be added to a DVD project, although you need to carefully consider the amount of content and space required to fit it on a disc. In addition to affecting the way you encode your video and audio assets (for example, using a lower bit rate for your movie to fit extra content on a disc), a project with DVD-ROM files might influence your choice of a DVD-5 or DVD-9 disc to hold all the material.

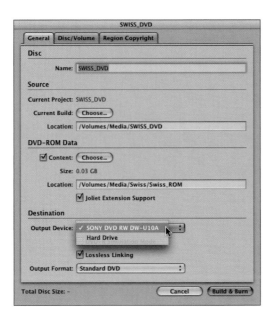

3 Insert a blank DVD-R disc into your recordable drive.

4 Click Build & Burn. An alert will come up.

5 Choose Reuse VIDEO_TS.

Choosing Reuse will reuse as much of the current VIDEO_TS contents as possible. As you did not change anything since you built the project, all the contents will be reused.

Using the Apple DVD Player

Once the build is complete, the next step in finishing your DVD is to use the Apple DVD Player to play back the VIDEO_TS folder's contents and test the project.

1 Locate the Apple DVD Player application in your hard drive's Applications folder, and double-click its icon to launch the application.

> **NOTE** ▶ You may have already placed the Apple DVD Player icon in your Dock in Lesson 3.

2 Choose File > Open DVD Media.

3 Select the VIDEO_TS folder you created for this project and click Choose.

4 Click the Play button on the Apple DVD Player's remote control to begin playing the project.

Test all of the links as you did when you used the Simulator at the beginning of this lesson, and as you did with the sample build in Lesson 3.

5 Quit DVD Player.

6 Go back to DVD Studio Pro 4 and select File > Save to save your project.

Burning a Disc Using the Burn Command

The Burn command simplifies the output of a project by automatically build-
ing a VIDEO_TS folder and burning it in one step to a DVD-recordable disc in
an Apple SuperDrive or external DVD recorder. You used Burn in Lesson 1 as
a quick way to create a disc. It's also a convenient function for making multiple
copies of a project.

In this lesson, we have already built, formatted, and burned the Swiss Tourism
project using the Build and Format command, but you should know that you
can also use the Burn command to build, format, and burn a disc in on step.
Burning a disc is the only way to accurately test a finished project. Whenever
possible, you should burn a disc and then test it in a set-top DVD player; these
often function differently than software players. Since you may experience
variations in performance among different brands and models of DVD play-
ers, it's a good idea to test your disc in as many types of players as possible.

> **NOTE** ▶ If you are creating a DVD-9 project (a disc with dual layers on a
> single side), you can test it with the Apple DVD Player. Another option is
> to use one of the newly introduced dual-layer DVD recorders, allowing
> you to burn your entire DVD-9 project on a single DVD disc.

For this lesson, you do not need to go through the process of burning a second
disc, particularly if you are using DVD-R media, which is more expensive than
CD-R media, but is the most common choice to burn recordable DVDs. If you
don't wish to burn the disc, skip the exercise below.

Follow these steps to burn a DVD using the Burn command.

1 Insert a blank DVD-R disc into your recordable drive.

2 Click the Burn icon in your toolbar or choose File > Burn to initiate the
process.

3 Watch the Log tab as DVD Studio Pro builds, formats, and burns your project onto a disc.

Since your next project will be in NTSC, you will need to reset your encoding preferences.

4 To do this, choose DVD Studio Pro > Preferences to get to the Preferences menu.

5 Click the Project pane and select the NTSC radio button to switch your video standard from PAL to NTSC.

6 Click OK to save the changes.

Choosing Recordable DVD Media

There are many flavors of DVD media. If you purchase a new Apple computer today, you will get a multiformat DVD recorder. DVD Studio Pro 4 now supports the RW format. If your built-in DVD recorder is a multiformat drive, you can even write DVD+R and DVD+RW media. The only drawback to using recordable media, such as DVD-R, is that it will not work in every player. (It does, however, work fine with most new players.) Replicated discs, produced at a DVD-manufacturing plant, are the only discs guaranteed to work in all DVD players and computers equipped with DVD-ROM drives.

Of course, the type of media you choose is dependent on the formats supported by your recordable drive. Here is a list of the available formats of DVD media.

▶ DVD-R is still the preferred format for burning DVD discs, since it is still the most compatible format. Also, the variety and availability of DVD-R Media—including inkjet printable discs—mean that it is the least expensive option.

NOTE ▶ DVD Studio Pro supports the DVD-R Authoring media, using the Pioneer S201 for preparing projects for DVD replication.

▶ DVD-RW is the rewritable flavor of the DVD-R discs. All Apple SuperDrives support this format.

▶ DVD+R is a newer writable format initially introduced by Philips and HP. It is now supported by all newer multiformat DVD recorders and by DVD Studio Pro 4.

▶ DVD+RW is the rewritable version of the DVD+R media.

TIP ▶ Rewritable DVD-RW and DVD+RW media are great for testing discs, because you can rewrite numerous times.

▶ DVD+R DL (double-layer) is a new format introduced in 2004. This is highly recommended for anyone who wants to burn or replicate DVD-9 discs, as it allows you to test DVD-9 discs before going to DVD replication.

NOTE ▶ DVD-RAM media, which is only compatible with a very small number of players, is mostly used for storage and backup.

Dual-layer DVD+R media

Burning Speed

Currently, DVD-R and DVD+R both write at a maximum 8x speed, allowing you to burn a full disc in less than 8 minutes. Current drives write DVD-RW/DVD+RW discs at 4x speed, and the new dual-layer recorders also support 8.5 GB DL (dual layer) DVD+R at 2.4x speed. You can expect that future releases of DVD burners will have even faster burning speeds. In addition to the hardware used, the burning speed of a disc is influenced by the type of media you use.

Distribution of Your Completed DVD

Once you've completed a DVD project, you must decide how to deliver your final disc. The most common option is to duplicate a disc with a recordable DVD drive or a DVD duplication tower. However, for professional projects that require several hundred to thousands of discs, replication is the best option. Replication also ensures that your discs are compatible with all players.

Duplication vs. Replication

In the world of DVD production, *duplication* is the process of creating copies of a disc using recordable media and drives. For example, burning discs using Apple's SuperDrive, an external DVD recorder, or a DVD duplication tower is considered *duplication*. Discs duplicated in this way are relatively easy to produce. This method is best suited for quantities of up to 300 discs. Duplicated discs are not 100 percent compatible with all DVD players, but using better quality media will improve the playback compatibility.

Replication, on the other hand, uses a glass master process to produce a large quantity of discs on media that is usable in any player. This process must be done at a special facility possessing the equipment to create a professional DVD from a disc, FireWire hard drive, or DLT—Digital Linear Tape (10/20 GB or 20/40 GB)—that you provide.

Replication is impractical for small runs of discs, because the price per disc is too high unless large quantities are required. It is usually cost-effective when you need 500 discs or more. Replication is, however, the highest-quality and most reliable method for producing DVDs.

In addition, DVD replication is the only method of adding copy protection to your DVDs. Until recently, it was the only way to produce dual-layer discs (DVD-9) holding up to 8.5 GB of information.

Choosing a Disc Type

Before you decide either to duplicate your disc or to send your project off to a manufacturing plant for replication, you should carefully consider the different options available for your disc. Some of the options—especially the selection of the type of disc to use—should be a part of the planning that takes place as you are beginning a new project.

There are several types of discs to choose from when you are distributing a DVD. Although the size of your project (the amount of data) is the most important consideration for choosing a disc type, other factors are important, too.

DVD-5 A DVD-5 disc is the most common type of disc used for both duplication and replication. This disc format is the most practical for short films or other projects that do not require a lot of space. DVD-5 discs can hold 4.7 GB of data, which is roughly equivalent to about 2 hours of video and audio content (encoded at lower bit rates), on one side of a disc.

Dual-Layer DVD-9 The next step up from a DVD-5 is a DVD-9 disc, with a maximum capacity of 8.54 GB. DVD-9 discs utilize a single side with two thin layers stacked on top of each other. The laser in a DVD player can read through the first layer to the one beneath, which nearly doubles the capacity of a single-sided, single-layer DVD-5.

For any projects over 2 hours (or for projects with lots of extra content), this is the recommended type of disc. In fact, DVD-9 discs are used for the majority of Hollywood releases. What's more, since only one side of the disc is used, labels can be placed on the unused side. In addition, the use of dual layers makes these discs notoriously hard to copy, since amateur video pirates cannot write the same amount of content to a DVD-5.

DVD-10 and DVD-18 The next larger disc is a DVD-10, which is essentially a dual-sided disc with a DVD-5 on each side. This means a DVD-10 needs to be manually flipped over in order to play the other side. For this reason, and the lack of an adequate solution for labeling (since both sides are occupied), these discs are rarely used.

For extremely large projects that need to squeeze as much data as possible onto a single disc, there are DVD-18 discs. These are dual-sided, dual-layer discs that are basically two back-to-back DVD-9s. They are more expensive and difficult to create, and they are rarely used, because two separate DVD-9 discs are usually cheaper and easier to produce. Also, DVD-18 discs, like DVD-10 discs, do not have space for disc labels.

Mini-DVDs Mini DVDs can be created using small, 3-inch/8 cm discs, which are similar to the miniature CD singles you sometimes find at a record store. These discs can hold up to 1.47 GB of data. Although these discs are impractical for most projects, they can be a good way to deliver a DVD "business card" or other short, promotional pieces.

NOTE ▶ The small 3-inch discs will not play in slot-loading DVD drives. In order to play these discs, you must use a DVD player with a tray.

Media Issues for Replication

If you are planning to use replication as your distribution method, you should also consider the following:

▶ If you are using DVD-R general media, it is critical to use DVD-R rather than DVD+R/+RW or DVD-RW media. Because of a different recording process, DVD+R media seems to cause problems for DVD replication. The problems occur when the discs are read for glass mastering. Also, if you decide to use DVD-R media, make certain you use the highest quality discs available. Sending an extra disc as a backup whenever possible is a good idea as well.

▶ DVD-R Authoring media is supported by DVD Studio Pro 4. DVD Studio Pro 4 added support for DVD-R Cutting Master Format, which allows you to write extra information, including copy protection information, to special DVD-R Authoring media. You need a device such as Pioneer S201 and special DVD-R Authoring media.

▶ If you are using DLT tapes for replication, the preferred type of media is Type III, 10/20 GB and 20/40 GB tapes, because most of the DVD replication plants are equipped to read these tapes. Just remember to always write uncompressed information to a DLT.

> **NOTE** ▶ You can receive check disc packages from a replication plant, which consist of a small quantity of discs to test your project before going forward with the replication of the entire order.

Setting a Layer Break Point

For DVD-9 projects, you need to set a layer break point. The layer break point determines where to switch between layers in a disc.

If you are authoring a DVD-9 project, DVD Studio Pro will automatically set a break point. If you are not happy with the automatic layer break point, you have the option to set it manually. Typically, you should place a layer break at a point in a movie where there is no picture or sound, such as a point where audio and video fade to black. This makes the freeze that occurs while the disc switches layers less noticeable to a viewer, although you are still likely to notice the layer

break. Layer breaks must also occur on the I-frame of a closed GOP MPEG stream.

> **TIP** ▶ The easiest way to ensure a perfect layer break point is to create a chapter marker in Final Cut Pro, which you can convert into a layer break point marker in DVD Studio Pro.

1 In the timeline of the Track Editor window, click a chapter marker that is a suitable break point.

You will turn this chapter marker into a layer break marker.

2 In the Inspector, click the Dual-Layer Break Point check box.

3 You can choose to deselect the Chapter check box if you wish to make this marker a break point exclusively.

You have now set the break point for the disc.

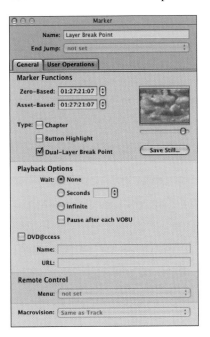

Adding Copy Protection

Copy protection is an important option for DVDs that are commercially pro-
duced and sold. However, copy protection systems are not always effective and
are relatively easy to circumvent. Typically, copy protection is only important
for discs sold in stores, and not for corporate projects distributed internally at
a company. In fact, you might decide that the cost and risk factor are negligible
for a commercially distributed project as well, particularly if you are producing
only small quantities and do not wish to pay the licensing fees.

If you decide your project would benefit from some form of copy protection,
you currently have two choices: CSS (Content Scrambling System) or Macro-
vision. Basically, CSS is a form of protection that prevents a disc from being
copied digitally (from a DVD to a hard drive or another disc). Macrovision
prevents the copying of video using analog connections from a player to a
recording device.

Before you decide to use either one of these protection schemes, be sure the
replication plant you have chosen offers them, because only certain plants
license these services. Additionally, any copy protection information you add
to a project, such as CSS, can be transmitted to a replicator only on DLT tapes
or DVD-R Authoring media (as opposed to DVD-R General media). This is
because the DVD-R General media is unable to unlock a portion of the disc
where copy protection information needs to be written. A final issue to con-
sider is that the addition of copy protection to a disc may delay the replication
process.

If you choose to add CSS to your project, you can "flag" or mark it in DVD
Studio Pro, although you will need to add a "CSS-key" from the replication
plant to activate this form of copy protection. Macrovision also requires you to
sign a contract in order to license its copy protection technology. The price is
usually determined by the quantity of discs produced.

Here are the steps to set up copy protection for your disc:

1 In the Outline tab, click the Disc icon to activate the Inspector.

2 Click the Region/Copyright tab to get to the copyright information.

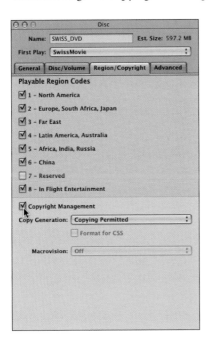

3 Click the Copyright Management check box to activate the copyright options.

4 From the Copy Generation pop-up menu, choose No Copy Permitted.

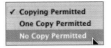

5 Click the Format for CSS check box, or set Macrovision to one of the Type settings (contact your replicator).

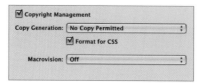

Designing Disc Labels and DVD Case Inserts

The last step for producing a professional DVD is designing the packaging for the disc. This includes the label to be printed on a disc and the case in which it is placed. You can also create special inserts for a DVD, such as a booklet providing information about the disc and its contents.

Most manufacturers offer packages for printing and labeling, so make sure to check with them before sending out your project. Many companies will also provide the necessary templates to make the layout and design of your labels easier. It's prudent to ask for a sample of a labeled disc before you send your project out. It's a good idea to evaluate printing quality, which can vary from one manufacturer to the next.

In addition, once you have sent your project to the manufacturer for replication, you should demand a proof print of your finished DVD inserts and labels, before they proceed to print hundreds or thousands of copies that do not meet your specifications.

All graphics you create for disc labels and inserts should be 300 dpi to allow for enough detail in the printing process, particularly when graphics are being resized. You should also be aware of how the number and types of colors are used in the printing. For example, a white background is often considered a fifth color, while other colors look different against a silver background. These are examples of printing issues to be resolved up front with the replicator and verified with a proof print.

The standard DVD packaging method is to use Amaray cases. These cases are like a shell that opens to reveal a place for the disc to snap into, and two clips

on the inside cover for holding inserts. Other standard packaging options are jewel cases, paper sleeves, or cardboard mailers, but a full range of packaging options are available. Of course, you can also use similar packaging options in case you duplicate your DVDs. For best results in playback, it is recommended to use inkjet printable DVDs rather than DVDs with disc labels.

Lesson Review

1. Before outputting a project what should you always do?
2. What is the name of the folder where DVD Studio Pro records all the DVD-Video formatted files?
3. Why is it a good idea to format a copy of your project to a folder on your hard drive before you burn a DVD disc?
4. Which command allows you to build, format, and burn a disc all in one step?
5. What's a DVD-9?
6. How do you set a dual layer disc break point?

Answers

1. Simulate the project inside DVD Studio Pro, and check every button on every menu to ensure your navigation structure does not contain any errors.
2. The VIDEO_TS folder.
3. Because you can open the project in the Apple DVD Player and test it in an actual DVD-Video player before burning a disc. If it works in the Apple DVD Player, it will work on a set top DVD-Video player.
4. The Build and Format command.
5. A disc with two data layers on one side that holds 8.54 GB of data.
6. Find a marker in one of your tracks where you want to make the break point, select it, and select the Dual-Layer Break Point check box.

Keyboard Shortcuts

Cmd-Option-0	Simulate (from First Play)
Cmd-P	Burn
Cmd-Option-C	Build
Cmd-F	Format
Cmd-Option-F	Build and Format

Tiger Project: Creating a Complex DVD

Adrian Ramseier is the founder and principal of All4DVD, an award-winning DVD authoring and production house that also specializes in training and curriculum development. Located in Irvine, California, All4DVD's team of noted instructors have extensive experience in video editing and DVD authoring. They have created DVDs for clients including Sony Pictures, BMW Motorcycle, Road Stunt Awards, and Reuters. Adrian is the author of *Apple Pro Training Series: DVD Studio Pro 2*. He can be reached at www.all4DVD.com.

10

Lesson Files	None
Media	Media > Tiger folder
Time	This lesson takes approximately 60 minutes to complete.
Goals	Learn the definition and use of bit budgeting
	Learn about various encoding parameters
	Import files into Compressor
	Encode files with Compressor
	Set up a batch encode
	Create a droplet
	Understand the difference between PCM and AC-3 audio

Lesson 10
Introduction to Encoding

Now that you have gone through the various steps of authoring and building a simple DVD, it's time to kick it up a notch. In the next four lessons, you will build a DVD that contains a movie and a slideshow, just like the Swiss Tourism DVD. Your new project—which is a promotional tool for a documentary on tigers—will introduce some of the more advanced features of DVD authoring. You'll learn how to build stories using markers, how to set up navigation using scripting, and how to use movies to transition in and out of menus. The **Tiger_DVD** project will also show you how to use multicolor overlays and multi-layer graphic documents or video as background assets.

For a complex project like Tiger that has many assets, it is better to acquire and encode your assets before you begin to author. This lesson will show you how to encode DVD-Video using Compressor. Bundled with both DVD Studio Pro and Final Cut Pro, Compressor offers many more options than DVD Studio Pro's built-in encoder, without sacrificing ease of use. With Compressor, you can quickly encode one file or batches of QuickTime files into MPEG-2 for your DVD project, using presets or adjusting the compression settings to achieve optimal results.

At the very start of the encoding process, you need to do a little math. In order to accommodate all of the assets you intend to fit on one disc, we need to make sure that their aggregate size will not exceed the disc's capacity. You will create this "budget" of digital assets first.

Bit Budgeting

Bit budgeting is a system of calculating the final size of a disc based on the elements that are included in the project. It is important to be aware of your project's final size, since you can fit only a certain amount of information on a disc. This is especially relevant for encoding purposes, due to the large amount of space that video occupies on a DVD. In fact, the majority of your disc is taken up by large MPEG-2 video files, which (despite their extreme compression ratio) can fill up a disc very quickly.

It is often helpful to use bit budgeting equations or special calculators to estimate the size of a DVD project. These formulas can assist you in choosing a bit rate for your video, so that it fits easily on a disc. For example, if you have video that is 2 hours long, a very high bit rate, such as 8 Mbps (megabits per second), might make the resulting MPEG-2 file too large for a 4.7 GB DVD-5 disc, after other assets (audio, subtitles, slideshows, and so on) are factored into the equation.

Compressor empowers you to control the file size of your final project. There is a little bit of math involved, but don't worry, you will learn a few tricks that make it very easy to calculate the estimated disc size. But take bit budgeting very seriously. Even experienced authors are sometimes forced to re-encode asset files if they don't properly budget their projects, especially when encoding feature-length materials. In encoding time alone, the process will cost you a lot of time. These mistakes are common ones, and they're easily avoided if you take the time to bit budget your project before you begin to encode your assets.

A Bit About Bits

Bit budgeting gets its name from the smallest unit of measurement in the digital world: a bit. A bit has a value of either 1 or 0, and these two digits make up the only two numbers in the binary system we refer to as *digital*. Bits are small, so small they're usually measured in units of a thousand (kilo), a million (mega), a billion (giga), or a trillion (tera). Chances are, you've heard of these prefixes before, followed by the word *byte*, as in kilobyte, megabyte, gigabyte, and terabyte. A byte is really just a packet of 8 bits, and both bits and bytes are units of measurement, like grams (kilograms). Bits are usually used to measure speed (56 kilobit per second modem), whereas bytes are usually used to measure size (120 gigabyte hard drive). When abbreviated, measurements of bits use lowercase letters, and measurements of bytes use uppercase letters, as in kbps (kilobits per second) versus MB (megabytes).

Bit rate, then, is a measurement of how many bits per second are moving through a phone line, Ethernet cable, or, for our purposes, a DVD player. The more bits there are per second of video, the more bits there are to carry color and luminance information, and the better the image quality.

The goal of bit budgeting is to encode your video and audio assets at the highest possible quality, while keeping the combined file sizes of your assets under the total disc capacity. Figuring out the maximum bit rate with which you can encode your files without making them too large to fit on the DVD is where the "budgeting" part of bit budgeting comes in.

Disc Capacity

The capacity of a disc can be misleading. For example, a DVD-R disc may say it can hold 4.7 GB of data, but the technically accurate amount, which is based on binary number systems, is a little less. Although you might think that 1 MB of information is equivalent to 1,000 kilobytes, it is actually equivalent to 1,024 kilobytes. This means that a 4.7 GB disc actually holds 4.37 GB of information, which is a significant discrepancy when you are working with large projects. A

DVD-9 disc, which would seem to hold 8.54 GB of information, actually holds only 7.95 GB.

What If It Doesn't Fit?

If the assets will not fit on the DVD (as calculated based on a bit rate), you have a number of options:

▶ Encode your audio to Dolby Digital AC-3 files. This is almost a must for programs longer than 90 minutes. If you encode a 2-hour movie, the available bit rate for the video is a mere 3.4 Mbps. Using Dolby Digital files, you can still encode your video at 4.7 Mbps. How do you save this much room? Because PCM files, although high in quality, are the least efficient file format in the DVD-Video specification. PCM audio files take up 1.5 Mbps of the total bandwidth for playback. However, encoding audio files using Dolby Digital at 192 kbps frees up an additional 1.3 Mbps for your video bit rate.

▶ Use stories rather than duplicating media. Since stories allow you to perform seamless branching, you can combine several versions of the same program on a disc by reusing media. However, viewers will likely notice a brief pause while the jump occurs.

▶ Leave assets off the disc. This works only if you are not required to use all elements in your project.

▶ Author a DVD-9, which will give you a total disc size of 7.95 GB. This will require replication, discussed in Lesson 9.

▶ Split your project to fit on a second DVD-5 disc.

▶ Use MPEG-1 compression. This is recommended only if you are not that concerned about the video quality. MPEG-1 will allow you to put almost 8 hours of video on a DVD-5. It is also a valid format for DVD-Video, and you can encode your video using Compressor or any other MPEG-1 encoding tool.

Using the Disc Size Indicator

The DVD Studio Pro toolbar includes an indicator to measure how much space your assets are taking up on a disc.

The problem with using this indicator to monitor progress is that by the time the assets are in your project, they're already encoded. Unless you want to waste time re-encoding video (and you don't), calculate the combined file sizes of all your audio and video assets, including motion menu backgrounds, audio for slideshows, and all alternate audio and video streams, before adding them to your project.

Bit Budgeting Methods

An easy bit budgeting method is to calculate a bit rate for your video using the formula $560 \div x$, where x is the length of your video assets. This formula assumes that you are using compressed audio, such as AC-3. If you are using PCM audio, you need to subtract another 1.3 Mbps from the result of this equation.

For example, if you have 120 minutes of video, you get an approximate bit rate of 4.67 Mbps ($560 \div 120 = 4.67$). If you are using AIFF uncompressed audio that the QuickTime encoder supplies, your available bit rate for your video will be 3.37 Mbps.

> **TIP** ▶ Do not forget that this bit rate is the combined bit rate for audio and video, so you will have to split it between the audio and video streams.

If you are using multiple audio and video streams, you can also use a bit budget calculator, which is usually a simple spreadsheet that helps you calculate the bit rate for your video and audio assets.

Using Storyboards to Bit Budget

Storyboards are useful for bit budgeting, since the storyboard helps you figure out what assets you need. Once you know what assets you need, and their length in minutes, all you have to do is apply the formula to each audio and video asset, and then add them together to see if they will fit on the DVD. If they do not fit, plug a lower bit rate into the formula, recalculate, and try again. Once you've determined that all of the assets will fit into your project, you can begin the encoding process with Compressor.

Using Compressor to Encode a File

Compressor can work with files in a variety of ways. When you encoded the Swiss Tourism assets with DVD Studio Pro, you were in effect using Compressor, because DVD Studio Pro's encoding engine uses the same encoder architecture as Compressor's. However, DVD Studio Pro lacks some of Compressor's best features, such as batch encoding and adding professional filters.

By far the most popular and convenient method for using Compressor is to export directly from Final Cut Pro into Compressor. This is especially useful when you have finished editing a project and do not want to compress the file with QuickTime before encoding it with Compressor. You can simply load the sequence you have been editing directly into Compressor without adding steps or compressing it a second time. If you do not want to use extra hard drive space or reduce the quality of your original video, you should export directly into Compressor from Final Cut Pro.

For this lesson, you will be encoding a small video file into MPEG-2 for use on the **Tiger_DVD** project. Although this file is smaller than a full-length movie, it demonstrates the capabilities of Compressor equally well.

Compression Terminology

This section briefs you on some important compression-related terminology.

Variable Bit Rate vs. Constant Bit Rate

Variable bit rate (VBR) video uses less space on a disc while producing excellent quality, since high bit rates are only allocated to portions of your video that need it the most. For example, a complex scene with lots of motion will get a higher bit rate to handle the extra information, whereas a static scene will use a lower bit rate. In this way, you can save a great deal of space on a disc, which is ordinarily taken up with *constant bit rate (CBR)* settings on less sophisticated systems.

VBR settings that take two passes—one to analyze a file and the other to encode it—are even better because they save you more space on the disc by using the VBR more accurately due to the initial analysis of the file. The disadvantage of two-pass VBR is that it takes longer to encode.

Average and Maximum Bit Rates

The *average bit rate* and *maximum bit rate* settings should match the needs of your project. In general, you want to use the highest quality encoding option your project will allow. For most projects, a setting of 5 or 6 Mbps is best for your average bit rate, which should maintain excellent quality while keeping file sizes manageable. A setting between 7 and 7.5 Mbps is typical for the maximum bit rate.

The maximum bit rate you should use for any video is 8 Mbps, since some DVD players (such as DVD software players on laptop machines) may have difficulty reading data rates that are too fast.

In addition, if you use a high bit rate for your video, you may encounter more problems when building a disc. At times the bit rate will spike, or hit a high point slightly above the maximum value. This causes the disc to be unreadable, and for this reason you should use more conservative bit rate values for your projects.

Finally, there are bit rate limits imposed by the number of camera angles and audio streams used in your project. If you use five angles or fewer, you could encode with 8 Mbps, although it is not recommended. The maximum bit rate for six to eight angles is 7.5 Mbps, and 7 Mbps for nine angles.

GOP—Group of Pictures

Each MPEG stream contains three types of frames that define the video. A *group of pictures (GOP)* setting defines the pattern of the three frame types used: intra (I) frames, bi-directional (B) frames, and predicted (P) frames. I-frames are also known as *reference frames*, *key frames*, or *compression frames*, and they contain the complete image of the current frame. Markers on a DVD track can be placed only on an I-frame. P-frames are encoded from a "predicted" picture based on the closest preceding I- or P-frame. B-frames are encoded based on interpolation from I- and P-frames.

Lesson 17 explains GOPs in detail. As a general rule, though, you should use a GOP structure with an IBBP pattern, with Closed GOP selected and a GOP size of 15 frames. This is the format that is preferred for most projects, particularly those with multiple angles, which require a closed GOP structure for smoothly switching between track layers. However, if you have to go down to a very low bit rate (such as 3 Mbps), the open GOP structure can help improve the video quality.

For a full review on bit budgeting, including precise calculators and other useful information, please see Appendix B.

Importing a File into Compressor from Final Cut Pro

Use the following steps to see how easy it is to move a video file from Final Cut Pro to Compressor. This is the preferred method of working when your project originates in Final Cut Pro.

> **TIP** ▶ If you don't have Final Cut Pro or Final Cut Express installed on your computer, you can also import any QuickTime files directly into Compressor. In this case, launch Compressor (Startup disk > Applications > Compressor), choose File > Import, and select the Tiger > Tiger_Assets > Tracks > **Tiger_Intro.mov** clip. Click Open. Proceed to the next section, "Encoding a Movie."

1 Launch the Final Cut Pro application by clicking its application icon in the
 Dock or in the Applications folder on your hard drive.

2 Choose File > Import > Files. Navigate to the Tiger_Assets > Tracks folder
 and select **Tiger_Intro.mov**. Click Choose.

3 Select the **Tiger_Intro.mov** clip in the Browser, and drag it to the Timeline.

4 In the Browser, double-click Sequence 1 and name it *Tiger_Intro*.

5 Choose File > Save Project As to save your project as *Tiger_Movie* in the My_Projects folder on your hard drive.

6 Select the Tiger_Intro sequence in the Browser, and choose File > Export > Using Compressor.

Once you've exported your movie, the Compressor application automatically launches and the Batch window appears. The Batch window is a list of files and their associated encoding settings. You have only one file to encode at the moment—that file is listed in the Batch window's Source Media column, by the project and sequence name.

This indicates that the file has been successfully exported from Final Cut Pro to Compressor, and it is now ready to be assigned compression settings.

7 Click in the Batch Name field of the Batch window, name your batch *Tiger_Encodes1*, and press Enter.

Encoding a Movie

Once your movie has been imported into Compressor, you can begin the encoding process. To fit on a DVD, QuickTime media must be converted and compressed using an MPEG-2 encoder such as Compressor.

In typical Apple fashion, Compressor simplifies the encoding process by offering a number of preset compression settings. Compressor's presets run through the entire spectrum of encoding options, from faster but lower-quality constant bit rate encoding, to slower but vastly superior one-pass and two-pass variable bit rate encoding with motion estimation. These presets allow you to quickly pick encoding settings and get on with authoring your DVD, even if you haven't the slightest idea what any of the terms in the previous sentence mean.

In this exercise, you will apply a basic preset. Later in this lesson, you will learn how to modify default settings and create your own presets, and you'll even learn how to create droplets, which will simplify the compression process even more. Ready? Let's encode.

1 In Compressor's Batch window, select Media Filename Style, and click to open the Setting pop-up menu.

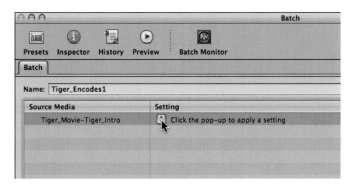

TIP ▶ If you did not import from Final Cut Pro, your file will be called **Tiger_Intro.mov**.

2 Choose DVD: Best Quality 90 minutes – 4:3 > All from the list of presets.

Compressor automatically assigns three presets to the file: an AIFF preset, a Dolby Digital AC-3 preset, and an MPEG-2 preset (For more information on AIFF and Dolby Digital files, see the "About Dolby Digital (AC-3) Audio" section). There have been three presets assigned to the file, and two of them are audio presets. Of course, you need only one final audio stream, and it's up to you to choose between the uncompressed AIFF or the file-size compressed Dolby Digital file. But keep this in mind: In many situations, the file size and data-rate savings of a Dolby Digital file more than make up for the very slight decrease in audio quality that results from compressing the sound. By encoding both an AIFF and a Dolby Digital file in the same batch, you can quickly open and audition both streams after encoding has finished, and then choose the one that most suits your project's needs.

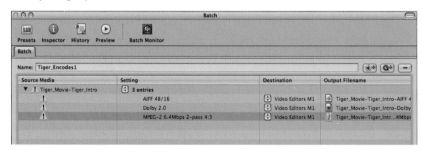

The higher the bit rate, the better the quality your encoded video will have, and if you look at the MPEG-2 preset, you can see that this video stream will be encoded at 6.4 Mbps (it's ok if your preset is 6.2). However, along with this higher quality setting comes a larger file size. Usually, to fit 60 minutes or more onto a single disc, the video must be compressed at a lower bit rate in order to take up less space on the disc. Since the disc you are building has less than 60 minutes of video, you can safely use a bit rate of 6.4 Mbps, or even higher to encode the video stream.

3 Click to open the Destination pop-up menu for the AIFF 48/16 File.

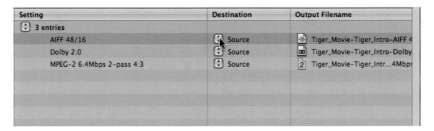

Source is the default option, which places the encoded files in the same directory as your original media. This is not recommended, especially when exporting directly out of FCP, since it places the encoded files on the root level of your hard drive. From the pop-up menu you can choose Desktop, your Movies folder, and other destination options.

4 From the Destination pop-up menu, choose Other. A menu appears.

5 Select a destination for your encodes files. Click the New Folder button. In the New Folder dialog, name the folder *Encodes*.

6 Click Create, then click Open in the pop-up menu to link the Encodes folder to its destination. Now you've established that the destination of the encoded AIFF file is the Encodes you folder.

7 In the Presets window, click the Destinations tab. (If you can't see the Presets window, choose Window > Presets, or press Cmd-2.)

8 Click the plus (+) button and choose Local from the pop-up menu to cre-
ate a new destination.

9 Select the Media > Encodes folder you just created, and click Open in the
pop-up menu that appears.

10 In the Destinations tab, select the new Untitled Local-1 destination.

The Inspector updates to show you information about this destination.

11 In the Inspector, name the preset *Encodes* and press Return.

12 Choose Compressor > Preferences to open the Preferences window.

13 From the Default Destination menu, chase the *Encodes* folder.

This sets the Encodes folder as your default destination so every newly encoded file is always sent to a place where you can easily find it (of course, you can override the default destination at any time by simply selecting a new destinations preset).

14 Click Apply to close the Preferences window.

15 In the Batch window, assign the Dolby Digital file and the MPEG-2 file to the Encodes Destination preset.

You are now ready to encode this **Tiger_Intro** movie to MPEG-2. In the next excercise, you will explore what kinds of settings you have chosen for this particular clip.

About Dolby Digital (AC-3) Audio

Properly encoded audio is important for any DVD project, particularly larger projects where the size of your audio files may take up a lot of disc space, not to mention the bandwidth that they must share with video streams. Before creating a DVD, you should decide what type of audio your project requires. The two primary choices are PCM and Dolby Digital (AC-3) audio.

PCM (Pulse Code Modulated) audio is an uncompressed format that takes up a lot more disc space than compressed audio such as AC-3. Its primary file types are AIFF, WAV, and Sound Designer formats. The QuickTime MPEG Encoder (used by QuickTime Pro, Final Cut Pro, and DVD Studio Pro) automatically creates a PCM file when compressing a video file with an audio track attached.

Dolby Digital audio, which is also called AC-3, is a compressed 48 kHz file that maintains excellent quality while significantly reducing the amount of space (and bit rate) on a disc. You might think of the com-

parison between PCM and AC-3 as similar to audio on a compact disc and an MP3 file. One is significantly larger than the other, although the difference in quality can be negligible. Another advantage of AC-3 is that it can contain up to 5.1 channels of audio in a single file. This makes it possible to deliver true surround sound mixes that come close to re-creating the movie theater experience.

In addition to using different formats for uncompressed audio and surround sound, DVD Studio Pro can utilize multiple audio streams within a track. In fact, with DVD Studio Pro, you can make use of the maximum of eight audio streams allowed by the DVD specification.

Exploring Encoding Settings

Although the presets included with Compressor offer a full range of encoding options, it's important to see how these presets were made, in case you wish to tweak the settings of a preset and create your own.

1 Choose Window > Presets to open the Presets window, or if it's already on your screen, simply click it to bring it to the front.

TIP The four main windows of Compressor can be brought up in the following ways:

 ▸ Selecting the window from the Window menu

 ▸ Pressing Cmd-1 through Cmd-4

2 In the Presets window, click the Settings tab.

Take a look at one of the Apple Presets to see how encode settings work.

3 Click the disclosure triangle next to the Apple settings group, next to the disclosure triangle the DVD: Best Quality 90 minutes – 4:3.

4 Double-click the MPEG-2 6.4 Mbps 2-Pass 4:3 setting.

The setting opens in the Inspector, where you can now see a summary of its properties. For example, the Summary pane lists the various attributes of your video and audio, including the original frame rate, frame size, and aspect ratio, as well as the compression settings that will be applied.

5 Click the Encoder button.

The Encoder pane opens with the Video Format tab selected. A quick glance at this tab shows that the Aspect ratio is 4:3, and the Field dominance is set to Automatic. The Automatic setting usually does a good job of determining the order of your video fields.

6 Click the Quality tab to view the bit rate settings.

In this example, we have chosen the highest quality settings, which create the best possible image quality, but doing so will require the greatest amount of time to encode.

7 Click both the GOP and Extras tabs to see what they contain.

Okay, let's finally encode this file.

8 In the Batch window, click Submit.

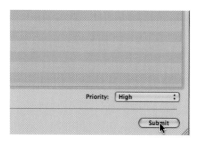

The Batch Monitor launches, which is a separate application from Compressor.

9 Click the disclosure triangles to the left of your batch listings to see the progress of the encoded files.

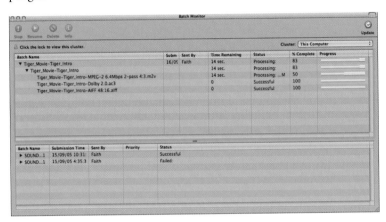

Creating a Preset

In addition to the many presets already available in Compressor, you can create your own presets for encoding video and audio files.

1 Launch Compressor, if it isn't already open.

2 Open the Presets window by choosing Window > Presets.

3 Choose an encoder setting from the plus (+) menu to create a preset.

The new preset, named Untitled MPEG-2, appears in the Custom settings group.

5 Double-click your new preset in the presets list.

The Inspector opens and/or updates to display the new presets properties.

6 In the Inspector, name your new preset *MPEG-2 180min High Quality Encode.*

Using the formula 560 ÷ *x*, or 560 ÷ 180, the max bit rate for 3 hours of video would be 3.1 Mbps.

7 In the Inspector, click the Encoder button. Click the Quality tab, enter *3.1* in the Average Bit Rate Mbps field, and choose "Two pass VBR Best" for the Mode. Leave the Maximum Bit Rate at 7.5.

8 Enter *3.1Mbps,2-Pass VBR, 4:3* in the Description field.

9 Click Save.

Your custom MPEG-2 preset has been saved, and you can now apply it to video files in Compressor's Batch window.

Creating a New Preset Group

You can create folders to hold groups of new presets. This allows you to assign multiple presets to a single source media file in the Batch list. You will assign audio and video encoding presets that will create both MPEG-2 video and PCM audio files needed for DVD Studio Pro.

1 In the Presets window, click the Create New Preset Group button.

This creates a new Untitled folder in the Custom settings group.

2 Select the MPEG-2 180min High Quality Encode preset, and move it into
the Untitled folder.

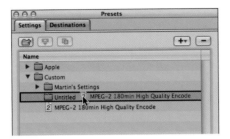

3 Click the disclosure triangle next to the Apple settings group and open any
DVD preset folder.

4 Select the AIFF 48/16 preset.

5 Click the Duplicate Selected Setting button.

A copy of the AIFF 48/16 setting is created and moved to the bottom of the Custom settings group.

6 Double-click the AIFF 48/16–Copy preset. Use the Inspector's Name field to remove the "–Copy" text at the end, and press Return. Move it into the Untitled settings group.

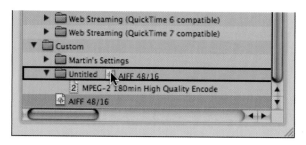

7 Select the Untitled settings group.

The Inspector updates to display the untitled settings group's properties.

8 Click the Inspector's Name field, and name the settings group *MPEG-2, 180min High Quality Encode.*

9 Press Return to confirm changes.

You have now created a new preset group for 180-minute encoding.

Creating a Compressor Droplet

The only thing that makes the encoding process simpler than using a preset is applying a Compressor droplet. A *droplet* is an alias, or shortcut, for launching an application that you can store as an icon on your Desktop or even in your Dock. What makes droplets different is that they not only activate an application, but also perform actions in that application in the background, automatically.

Compressor droplets are useful for quickly and easily encoding several files with the same settings. Dragging a QuickTime file or even a group of files onto a Compressor droplet icon launches Compressor and encodes the files according to the preset it represents. For example, you might decide to create a high-quality MPEG-2 droplet (such as MPEG-2 60min High Quality Encode) for converting a folder of short video clips into MPEG-2 files that can be imported into DVD Studio Pro.

Follow these steps to create a Compressor droplet:

1 In Compressor, open the Presets window by choosing Window > Presets.

2 Select a preset or group of presets you want to save as a droplet from the presets list.

3 In the Settings tab, click the Save Selection as Droplet button.

4 From the Where pop-up menu in the Save dialog, choose Desktop as the destination for your droplet.

5 From the "Choose Destination for Droplet results" pop-up menu, choose your Encodes folder.

6 Click Save to create your new droplet.

You will now see a droplet sitting on your Desktop. To use the droplet, simply drop a file onto the droplet icon.

MPEG-2, 180min High
Quality Encode

7 Select the **Tiger_Transition1.mov** and **Tiger_Transition2.mov** files from the Tiger > Tiger_Assets > Tracks folder, and drag them onto the droplet on the Desktop.

The Droplet window appears with both files listed.

8 Click Submit, and your files will be automatically encoded into your Encodes folder.

Lesson Review

1. What's the difference between variable bit rate (VBR) and constant bit rate (CBR) encoding?

2. What is the benefit of VBR versus CBR encoding?

3. True or false: You can encode MPEG-2 files using Compressor, directly from a Final Cut Pro Timeline.

4. What's a droplet?

5. True or false: you can create your own custom Compressor presets.

Answers

1. In VBR files, the data rate can vary over time. In a CBR encode, the data rate stays constant at all times and never varies.

2. VBR encoding provides better picture quality at a lower average data rate because scenes of higher visual complexity (action scenes, fast fades, or pans) can use a higher data rate than scenes with low visual complexity (a tripod mounted shot of a person speaking). In a CBR encode, the data rate never varies. Consequently scenes with high visual complexity suffer in quality, while scenes with low visual complexity have a higher data rate than needed to maintain a good image.

3. True. You can, and you should, because encoding files directly from the Final Cut Pro timeline saves you from rendering out a finished movie, and then encoding.

4. A droplet is a Compressor preset packaged into an icon you can keep on your desktop (or any other folder). To encode a file, just drop it on the droplet.

5. True. While the default presets are great for fast encodes, to configure exactly the type of encode settings you need, you have to create your own preset.

11

Lesson Files Lessons > 11_Tiger_finished

Media Media > Tiger folder

Time This lesson takes approximately 60 minutes to complete.

Goals Understand button states

Learn about the creation of menus and overlays

Create a simple overlay

Add a motion background and make it loop

Understand chroma mapping for advanced overlays

Create an advanced overlay

Creating Menus with Overlays

Menu creation is the heart of DVD authoring. In this lesson, you will learn how to create simple and intermediate menus using overlay graphics and highlights, which are an essential part of the menu creation process. When users select buttons by pressing arrow buttons on their remote controls, they need a way to know which button is currently selected or activated. An overlay provides visual feedback to indicate whether buttons are in their normal, selected, or activated states.

In addition to working with overlays, you will also learn more about creating motion menus and using Adobe Photoshop with DVD Studio Pro.

We'll start with a preview of the Tiger project.

The Tiger DVD Project

The Tiger project is a promotional tool for a documentary called *Tigers: Tracking a Legend.* In Lesson 10, you encoded the video and audio assets for the Tiger project. Now let's take a closer look at the navigational structure for this project, which will be our focus in this lesson and the next two lessons.

The Tiger project contains a "making of" documentary, as well as a slideshow. In addition to these elements, there are two transitional movies that are designed to play seamlessly into and out of the main menu. The main menu employs sophisticated features such as advanced overlays, which allow your buttons to be any shape and have multiple highlight colors. Using markers to create stories, and a couple of simple scripts, you will learn how to add exciting visual and navigational enhancements to your DVDs while taking negligible disc space away from the all-important video and audio assets.

As you can see in the following storyboard, the first-play action in the DVD is called TigerIntro, which is the first of two transitional movies used in this project. When TigerIntro is finished, it links to the main menu, which is a

motion menu with an MPEG-2 file as the background asset. TigerIntro is a transitional movie because the video asset that is the basis for TigerIntro and the asset that is the background for the main menu are two parts of the same movie. When the DVD is inserted, TigerIntro will play seamlessly into the main menu, as if the two elements were one movie—because, of course, they are.

The main menu has two buttons—Play Title and Slideshow—which will lead viewers to the "making of" documentary and the slideshow, respectively. However, instead of the Play Title button linking to the TigerMovie track directly, it links to a second transitional movie called TigerTransition1. Just as you can have a transition into a menu, you can have a transition out of one. TigerTransition1 is the bridge between the main menu and the Tiger-Movie track. When the Play Title button is activated, the TigerTransition1 movie will play.

Note that transitional movies don't necessarily have to use a frame adjacent to the menu's last frame as a starting point, although the transition will be smoother if it does. Since the TigerTransition1 movie is triggered by the viewer's selecting a button with the remote, and the viewer could make that choice at any time during the motion menu's duration, matching frames isn't an option anyway. Although the transitional movie out of the main menu is not a continuation of the menu background movie, the content is similar enough to create a suitably smooth transition.

Let's play a sample build of the Tiger DVD in Apple DVD Player.

Playing the Tiger DVD with DVD Player

1 Insert this book's DVD-Video into your DVD-ROM drive or a DVD player.

This will automatically launch the DVD Player application, which will start playing the disc.

2 Click the Tiger DVD button to begin playing the project.

The first thing that plays is the TigerIntro movie. Watch how it transitions into the main menu. That's the purpose of a transitional movie—it helps one element flow into another.

NOTE ▶ If you're watching on a computer, you may notice a slight pause between the end of the TigerIntro and the main menu, which is due to limitations of the software DVD Player and may or may not be present on the final DVD.

In the main menu the Play Title button is in its selected state, indicated by yellow highlighting of the text and an orange tiger pawprint graphic to the right of the text.

3 Select the Slideshow button by clicking the down arrow button on the remote control, by pressing the down arrow on your keyboard, or by using your mouse to position the pointer over the Slideshow button.

Note that the yellow highlight and the orange pawprint have moved to the Slideshow button.

4 Click the Slideshow button.

Did you notice the yellow highlight moving from the text to the pawprint? Clearly something new is going on that indicates selected and activated button states. You will learn how to do this in the following exercises.

The slideshow will play. When it is finished, the screen will return to the main menu.

5 Select the Play Title button by clicking the remote control arrow buttons, using the arrow keys on the keyboard, or dragging the mouse.

6 Activate the button by pressing Return on the keyboard, clicking the Enter button on the remote control, or clicking the button with the mouse.

7 Watch the movie to familiarize yourself with the content. If you wish, click the Chapter Skip Forward button on the remote or press the right arrow key on your keyboard to jump to other chapters.

When the movie is done, it will jump back to the main menu.

8 Watch the menu loop twice.

After the second menu loop, the menu will time out, and a script will randomly play one of four pieces of video that you will define as stories in Lesson 12. In that lesson, you will also learn how to write a menu loop script and a random play script. This will help you to make your DVD more interesting and interactive.

9 Quit the player application when you're finished.

NOTE ▶ Chapter markers in movies still function when accessed by the remote control, even if there is no chapter index menu. Creating a chapter index menu at a later time is simple, so creating chapter markers for your movies is usually a good idea even if you're not sure whether you will be creating a chapter index menu.

Now that you have seen the blueprint and final build for the Tiger DVD, let's get down to the topic of this lesson: menu design with overlays.

Creating Menus with a Simple Overlay

The interactive experience you create for a user should be attractive, easy to understand, and as seamless as possible. Creating your own menu designs is an important part of the process. In order to incorporate your own designs into a DVD project, you need to understand overlays, which define how buttons look when they are selected or activated. Overlays are the fastest method for navigating and displaying menus on a DVD player and are used in nearly all professional DVD titles.

Every button has three states you can define: normal, selected, and activated. Each state can be assigned a different highlight color in DVD Studio Pro. (Highlights are discussed in a later section of this lesson.) The normal state is how a button looks before the user has selected it. Once a viewer uses the remote control to choose a button, it is considered selected. When the user presses Enter on the remote control, the button is activated.

An *overlay* produces the simple outline or graphic that is used to highlight a button in order to indicate its state. The result is that when you assign a highlight color to a button state in DVD Studio Pro, only the area defined by the overlay will be highlighted when the button is selected or activated.

Just as a stencil constrains a brush stroke of color to a defined shape or character, the overlay constrains the color of the highlight to specifically defined words or shapes. Therefore, an overlay is actually an additional still image, usually created in Photoshop, that contains a map of where these words or shapes appear, corresponding to the look and composition of the menu. You

can create simple overlay files, which contain one color map, or more complex overlays with up to four colors, as described later in this lesson.

> **MORE INFO** ▶ Lesson 14 builds on many of the concepts introduced in this lesson. For an in-depth treatment of how menu overlays are created, see Lesson 14.

Tips for Designing Menu Graphics

The following are some suggestions for creating graphics that will look best on a television set or video monitor. Since video is restricted in its use of colors (graphics applications such as Photoshop have a much broader palette) and image resolution, you need to consider some basic design principles for motion design work before creating your menus and overlays:

▶ Avoid text that is smaller than 18 to 24 points, depending on the font.

▶ Use sans serif fonts whenever possible (fonts without the "curls" at the ends of letters).

▶ Design your overlays without any soft or feathered edges.

▶ Make all of the lines in your graphics at least 3 pixels thick. Since most video still uses fields instead of progressive frames, thin lines will appear to flicker or buzz on an interlaced display.

▶ Be wary of any colors that are shifted toward the red end of the spectrum, since they tend to flicker, especially in thin graphics.

▶ Avoid heavily saturated colors (particularly bright red), which tend to bleed and look bad on a television screen.

▶ Because TV colors are not as rich, vibrant, or precise as computer colors, be wary of subtle shades of red and blue, which tend not to reproduce accurately.

▶ To avoid problems with bright colors interfering with the audio on older TV sets, keep your primary color levels (red, green, and blue) to a value of 235 or lower.

Perhaps the most important and peculiar issue when creating graphics for a menu is how the images are sized. Since graphic applications use square pixels, which are the standard for computer displays, you need to account for the nonsquare pixels that are used by video. For this reason, you always begin by creating a document in Photoshop with an image size of 720 × 534, which DVD Studio Pro will later resize down to 720 × 480. If you are creating menus with a 16:9 aspect ratio, they should start at 864 × 480 (for NTSC) before DSP resizes them to 720 × 480.

Aspect Ratio	Photoshop Image	Resize to
4:3	720 × 534	720 × 480
16:9	864 × 480	720 × 480

If you do not resize your images in this way, they will appear stretched on your DVD. Circles will become ovals, and squares will become rectangles. Fortunately, Photoshop 7 and CS include presets for proper DVD proportions, which should make it easier to remember the correct size when creating a new document.

For more information about this important topic, see the discussion of pixel aspect ratio in Lesson 14.

> **NOTE ▶** Always remember to select the proper aspect ratio (4:3 or 16:9) as the first step when you create a new menu. Do this before adding graphics. Otherwise, your overlays will not be aligned properly, and you will need to delete them and add them back to the menu.

Importing the Tiger Assets Folder

Since you will be using the files in the Tiger_Assets folder for the remaining lessons in this project, you should simply import the entire folder into the Assets tab. All of the files you will need for this project will be available for use in the Assets tab.

1 Launch DVD Studio Pro. Create a new project by choosing File > New.

2 Press F3 to make sure you are in the Advanced configuration.

3 On the Disc Inspector's General tab, click the NTSC radio button in the
Disc Inspector to switch the Video Standard setting to NTSC.

NOTE ▶ Directly above the NTSC radio button there is an SD radio but-
ton. SD stands for "StandardDefinition Video," or the 720 × 480 NTSC
video you are editing now.

4 Click the Import button at the top of the Assets tab.

5 Navigate to your Media folder on your hard drive, then the Tiger folder,
and select the folder Tiger_Assets.

6 Click Import to bring the entire folder into DVD Studio Pro.

The main folder with all of its subfolders should now be named and organized for you in the Assets tab.

7 Choose File > Save and save your project as *Tiger_DVD*. Put it on your media hard drive, in the My_Projects folder.

Adding a Motion Background and Overlay

For this exercise, you will be creating a motion menu with an overlay for the main menu of the Tiger project.

As you know, DVD Studio Pro enables you to create motion menus, which are much more exciting than still menus, by assigning an MPEG-2 movie as the menu background instead of a still image or Photoshop document. Many DVD titles include some form of motion menu to add interest to the interactive experience. The background can be motion video, but so can the buttons, which can display video from the asset they are linked to.

The majority of motion menus consist of a video clip that is approximately 15 to 40 seconds long. A motion menu is usually set to loop, although you can make it jump to a track or other menu element when it times out, after playing for a set amount of time.

Typically, motion menus are created in applications such as Final Cut Pro or Motion. Using their powerful compositing features, you can design complex

animations, motion graphics, and buttons for use as menu backgrounds. Button areas, including text, can be composited directly onto a motion background in an application such as Final Cut Pro or Motion and then used as a basis for an overlay file created in Photoshop.

You can use both simple and advanced overlays with motion backgrounds. In the following exercise, you will learn how to work with simple overlays. Later in the chapter, you will use the same menu with an advanced overlay.

1 In the Assets tab, click the **TigerMainMenu.mov (Video)** file from the Tiger_Assets > Menus folder and drag it onto the Menu Editor.

Do not release the mouse button until the Drop palette appears and you have made your selection in the next step.

2 Choose Set Background from the list of choices in the Drop palette.

Your main menu now has a motion video background in place. The **TigerMainMenu.mov (Audio)** was automatically imported as well.

Take a look at the words "Play Title" and "Slideshow" on the menu. These background button graphics represent the normal state for buttons in your menu. The normal state is how a button looks before a user has selected it. Since this state does not require an overlay to help define it, you can just incorporate the normal state of a button by making it a part of your background, as we have done for you in this menu. Creating a

button graphic on a still image or compositing it onto a video is all you need to do for a normal-state button.

3 In the Assets tab, double-click the **TigerMainMenu_ol.tif** file to preview the overlay graphic file.

This image is now being displayed in the Viewer tab. As you can see, this simple overlay graphic is a black-and-white image, with the black pixels indicating the overlay area and the white pixels indicating transparency. Notice that the overlay graphic representing the text is a little bit larger than the text that is rendered into the motion background.

4 Click the Menu tab to get back to the menu.

5 Again drag **TigerMainMenu_ol.tif** from the Assets tab, but this time onto the Menu Editor.

6 Choose Set Overlay from the list of choices in the Drop palette.

The simple overlay graphic is assigned to the menu.

NOTE ▶ You can also assign background and overlay layers in the Inspector, which you will do for the more complex overlays you'll create later in this lesson.

OK, nothing happened…yet. When you create button areas in the next exercise, the intersection of the button area and the overlay will produce the shape of the highlight colors that indicate the button states.

Creating Buttons for the Overlay

Now that your menu background and overlay are in place, you need to define the active button areas for your menu. You can do this using the same techniques you used to create buttons in previous lessons.

1 In the Menu Editor window, click the Show Button Selected State button.

> **NOTE ▶** Make sure your Menu Editor window is wide enough to display the button state icons. If it is too narrow, these button state icons in the bottom right of the window will disappear.

Keeping the selected state showing for your button overlays will help you to accurately draw and position your button selection areas in the next steps. You will notice the overlay graphic as you click each button while creating it in the Menu Editor. Since the overlay will help define the active area for your buttons, the overlay must precisely match the positions of any buttons or graphics you have added to the background.

2 Click and drag on the menu background to create a new button selection area.

3 Resize the active area of the button by dragging a corner of the button outline to cover the overlay image exactly. Then choose View > Display State > Composite.

When drawing buttons in the Menu Editor, you are defining the active button area.

NOTE ▸ Depending on the color assigned to the selected state, your button may appear different from the one pictured here.

4 Click the first button area and duplicate it by holding down the Option key while dragging it.

5 Position the new button area precisely over the next button graphic on the menu background, as you did for the first button.

TIP ▸ You can use align and distribute tools to help you precisely position your buttons. Select each button while holding down the Shift key, Ctrl-click one of the buttons, and choose a command from the Align Objects or Distribute Objects selections of the contextual menu.

6 Click Button 1 and name it *Play Title* in the Name field of the Inspector.

TIP ▸ If the Inspector is not open, you can always get there by clicking the Inspector icon in the toolbar or pressing Cmd-Option-I.

7 Click Button 2 and name it *Slideshow*.

Choosing Highlights for Selected and Activated States

After your button areas have been drawn and named, it is time to set the selected and activated highlights for each button. The highlights you will select use the overlay graphic as the basis for the area where the colors show up.

1 Click your menu's background in the Menu Editor to open the Menu Inspector.

This will deselect any buttons and put the menu's parameters into the Inspector. The title bar now displays "Menu."

2 Rename your menu by typing *TigerMainMenu* in the Name field.

3 Click the Colors tab.

4 Make sure that the Overlay Colors option is set to Simple. If it's not, click the Simple radio button.

Selecting this button will provide the highlight color choices only for simple overlays. Later in this lesson, you will learn how to use advanced overlays.

5 Make sure that the Opacity slider for your normal button state is set to 0.

Since your normal state buttons are part of the background image, you should set the Opacity to 0 (completely transparent), so that the menu graphics are always visible and your overlays are not.

6 Choose a yellow color for your selected button state and set the Opacity to 5.

On the scale for Opacity settings, 15 is the maximum value and is considered 100 percent, or completely opaque. A setting of 5 will give you an Opacity value of approximately 33 percent, which should make your underlying button graphics easily visible, even with the overlay on top of them.

Remember, if the Opacity values are set too high, the overlay colors might appear too bright on a television set.

7 Select an orange color for your activated button state, and set the Opacity slider to 5.

Although the activated state is not as crucial as the selected state (since the activated state just flashes briefly on the screen before the disc jumps to the item), it does help to provide additional feedback and a more consistent user experience.

NOTE ▶ You can change the colors chosen for this project to suit your own design preferences.

8 Save your project.

9 Click Simulate in the toolbar to see the selected and activated states of your buttons.

10 Close the Simulator.

Looping the Motion Menu

When a motion menu loops, it plays through and then jumps back, by default, to the first frame. For this reason, a simple choice when designing a motion menu in Final Cut Pro (or any other application) is to fade up your audio at the beginning and fade it down at the end. Because the ending and beginning volume is zero, the resulting loop will not contain any noticeable changes in audio that would bother a viewer.

As far as the video of your motion menu is concerned, you may also fade in and fade out the video to create a smoother point for transitioning back to the beginning. Another common technique is to find a suitable frame to end on, which you also set as the first frame of the video asset, to create a seamless or "invisible" loop. Once you have your motion background designed for a nearly perfect loop, you should set the looping option in the Menu Inspector.

> **NOTE ▶** Loops will not be "perfect" on a DVD, since there will be a pause as the player jumps from the last frame back to the beginning of the clip.

1　In the Menu Inspector window, click the General tab.

2　Make sure that Loop is selected from the At End pop-up menu.

The At End pop-up menu allows you to decide what the motion menu does when it reaches the end of a clip. You can choose to freeze on a still frame (the last frame of your video clip), continue looping, or time out

after a defined number of seconds. When you decide to time out, you can then choose where the menu should jump to, such as another menu or track in your project.

Creating Menus with Advanced Overlays

In addition to using simple overlays, you can use what DVD Studio Pro refers to as *advanced overlays* to create more colorful button overlays. Although an advanced overlay is limited to the use of four simultaneous colors, you can still create many interesting designs.

> **MORE INFO ▶** Lesson 14 builds on many of the concepts introduced in this section. For an in-depth treatment of advanced overlays, see Lesson 14.

Understanding Key Colors

Advanced overlays contain advanced color mapping—that is, key colors—which gives you a lot more flexibility in your designs. For instance, you can assign more than one highlight color to the selected and activated states, or even modify the appearance of the overlay to include a graphic or other elements.

There are two methods of creating these key colors for advanced overlays: *chroma mapping* and *grayscale* (or *luma*) *mapping*. Essentially, both methods produce the same result, since each uses four key colors or shades to define the overlay colors. The chroma mapping method uses black, red, blue, and white; grayscale (luma) uses black, dark gray (at 66 percent), light gray (at 33 percent), and white. You would use one of these sets of colors in Photoshop to create your button elements.

When you import the overlay into DVD Studio Pro, you choose the colors with which you replace each of these four key colors. For example, a red button element you created in Photoshop could be designated as your yellow highlight in DVD Studio Pro.

As an introduction to the concept of key colors, you will use a graphic file with an advanced overlay in the next series of exercises.

Adding an Advanced Overlay

In the following exercise, you will use an advanced overlay to use in place of the simple overlay you created for the main menu of the Tiger DVD. By seeing both of these overlays in the menu, you will understand the benefits of each one and how you can use them.

1 Double-click **TigerMainMenu_aol.tif** from the Assets tab to preview this graphic file.

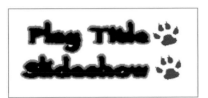

This advanced overlay graphic has four colors: black, red, blue, and white. Each of the colors in the overlay constrains a highlight color to the pixel areas that are defined by that particular color, as you will see after completing the following steps. The color white is almost always assigned an Opacity of 0 so that only the black text, red outline, and blue graphic will receive highlights. The pawprint graphic, which is a new element not indicated by anything in the background layer, will probably receive an Opacity of 15 so that it will stand out. The two remaining colors will have their Opacity values set somewhere in between to reveal the text beneath them, and they can be any color you wish.

2 Click the Graphical tab, and double-click the TigerMainMenu tile.

3 On the Menu Inspector's General tab, click the Overlay pop-up menu and
 choose Tiger_Assets > Menus > **TigerMainMenu_aol.tif**.

4 Expand the button selection area for each button farther to the right, to
 encapsulate the new design elements on the advanced overlay graphic.

Since our button areas were already created for the simple overlay in an ear-
lier exercise, you can use the existing button areas by changing their sizes.
You can enter precise button dimensions in the Coordinates & Size area of
the Advanced tab in the Inspector if you want to have exact button sizes.

Choosing the Highlight Colors for an Advanced Overlay

Once the advanced overlay graphic is in place over your background, you can make decisions regarding the use of different highlight colors.

1 In your Menu Editor, click the Play Title button to load the button's parameters into the Inspector.

2 In the Inspector, select the Colors tab.

3 Click the Advanced radio button in the Overlay Colors area.

4 Select Chroma as the Mapping Type.

Notice that the four colors listed under Key are black, red, blue, and white, just like in the overlay.

5 Click the Normal radio button in the Selection State area.

6 Make sure that all of the Opacity sliders are set to 0.

The Opacity sliders are set to 0 by default. Since the normal state for the Menu button is to be part of our background image, the overlay should not be visible.

7 Click the Selected radio button in the Selection State area.

All of the adjustments you make will be applied to the buttons using the overlay when the viewer selects them. You can test the effects of the changes you make by selecting the buttons and clicking the Show Button Selected State button at the bottom of the Menu Editor window, just as you did for the simple overlay.

8 Using the Color pop-up menus, choose yellow for the black key, and set an Opacity of 5.

If you followed the previous simple overlay exercise to the letter, you may notice that this step was already done. This is because the simple and advanced overlays both use black as the main selection area for this project.

9 Choose yellow for the red key with an Opacity of 2.

10 Choose orange for the blue key with an Opacity of 15.

As you saw earlier in the lesson when you worked with simple overlays, the scale for Opacity settings has a maximum value of 15, which is considered 100 percent, or completely opaque. A setting of 5 will give you an Opacity value of approximately 33 percent, which should make your underlying button graphics easily visible, even with the overlay on top of them. You should set the Opacity slider to 0 for the color white, since that is the color used as the background. Note that if the Opacity values are set too high, the overlay colors may appear too bright on a television set.

NOTE ▶ For most projects, the key color white will always be removed (made transparent) by setting the Opacity slider to 0.

Next, you'll invert the color set in the selected state to give it a nice touch when the button state changes from selected to activated.

11 Click the Activated radio button in the Selection State area.

12 Choose orange for the black key with an Opacity of 5.

13 Choose orange for the red key with an Opacity of 2.

14 Choose yellow for the blue key with an Opacity of 15.

All of the adjustments you make will be applied to all of the buttons using the overlay when they are activated by a user. You can test the effects of the changes you make by selecting a button and clicking the Show Button State Activated button at the bottom of the Menu Editor window.

15 In the Menu Editor, Ctrl-click the menu's background and choose Simulate Menu to test the menu's button states for the correct selected and activated highlights.

> **TIP** ▶ Testing highlights is a lot simpler before linking button areas to project elements, because you can test each button's activated state without jumping away from the menu.

16 Close the Simulator window.

17 Choose File > Save to save your project.

Lesson Review

1. What does an overlay do?
2. How many button states can you define in DVD Studio Pro?
3. What is the pixel width of the thinnest horizontal lines you should use when designing for video?
4. True or false: Overlay graphics outside of a button's hotspot will not display.
5. Can menu's loop seamlessly (without a pause or glitch)?
6. What are the two types of color mapping you can use with DVD Studio Pro?

Answers

1. It produces the simple outline or graphic that is used to highlight a button in order to indicate it's state.
2. Three: Normal, Selected, and Activated.
3. Three pixels. Lines that are horizontally thinner than that will appear to flicker on interlaced TVs.
4. True. If you want to see the overlay graphics, they must be inside the button's rectangular hotspot.
5. No. When a menu loops, the player jumps from the last frame back to the first frame, and there will be a pause of up to one second.
6. Chroma mapping (100% Black, Red, Blue, and white), and grayscale/luma mapping (100% black, 66% black, 33% black, and 0% black/100% white).

Keyboard Shortcuts

Cmd-1	Assets tab
Cmd-4	Menu tab
Cmd-5	Outline tab
Cmd-9	Track tab
Cmd-Option-I	Inspector tab

12

Lesson Files Lessons > 12_Tiger_start
(or the My_Projects > Tiger_DVD project file you created
in Lesson 11)

Media Media > Tiger folder

Time This lesson takes approximately 45 minutes to complete.

Goals Create chapter markers in Final Cut Pro and DVD Studio Pro

Export chapter markers in a QuickTime movie

Create, import, and work with markers in DVD Studio Pro

Learn how to use other types of markers

Understand the concept of a story

Create stories

Working with Markers and Stories

One of the most useful features of DVD authoring is being able to add chapter markers to a video track. Chapter markers allow a viewer to easily and quickly navigate through long movies. You can also use these markers to create stories. Stories are like playlists in iTunes, which allow you to play all or just some of your chapters, in any order. However you decide to use chapter markers, there are a number of ways to create them. Final Cut Pro is one of the most convenient and powerful methods, although you can just as easily import markers from Final Cut Express, iMovie, Compressor, a text file—or just set them in DVD Studio Pro as you did in Lessons 2 and 3. In this lesson, you will learn several different methods for creating and manipulating chapter markers.

Working with Chapter Markers

Chapter markers provide a convenient method for moving around in a video track on a DVD. Once chapter markers have been set, users may jump from one point to the next, either using the chapter keys on their remote controls, or through specific experiences that are defined by menus and stories. For instance, you can create a single video track with chapter markers and then allow users to access different portions of the track using a menu with buttons linked to those chapter markers.

> **NOTE** ▶ The maximum number of chapter markers in a single track is 99.

The process of creating chapter markers centers on the use of timecode, which allows you to precisely place markers in the video. You may use the timeline near the top of the Track Editor window in DVD Studio Pro to create markers. Or you can add markers in Final Cut Pro, Final Cut Express, or even iMovie, which will import directly into DVD Studio Pro along with the audio and video. You can also preview your video with Final Cut Pro, QuickTime, or even an analog video editor or tape deck (using tapes with timecode window burn, of course), and log the positions of chapter markers using Apple's TextEdit by noting the timecode in the window burn as it plays. You can then import these text files directly into your DVD Studio Pro Track Editor, provided they are formatted properly.

A major dilemma in chapter marker creation is the issue of having to place them at I-frames only. If you are working with video that is already encoded into MPEG-2 in DVD Studio Pro, you can only place chapter markers on an I-frame, which occurs at the beginning of a GOP (group of pictures), typically every 15 frames. If the frame you wish to place a chapter marker on happens to fall between I-frames, you will have to settle for the nearest one, which can make for some awkward jumps in the DVD if you need a chapter to start precisely—before a fade-up, for example, and not in the middle of one. To circumvent this issue, you can always add your markers in Final Cut Pro, Final

Cut Express, iMovie, or Compressor *before* you encode your video. Using this method, you can *force* an I-frame onto whichever frame you choose.

> **NOTE** ▸ The main difference between using Final Cut Pro and DVD Studio Pro to add markers is that DVD Studio Pro can only add markers to I-frames. In Final Cut Pro and Final Cut Express, however, you can add a marker to any frame, and it is automatically stamped as an I-frame during export from Final Cut Pro or when encoded using Compressor. The GOP (group of pictures) just before this special I-frame is reduced to compensate for its presence.

Creating Markers in Final Cut Pro

Since most video that is added to a project in DVD Studio Pro originates from an editing application such as Final Cut Pro, it is often easiest to add your chapter markers in your NLE (nonlinear editor) before exporting the video. In this lesson, you will learn how to add markers in Final Cut Pro that can be used to set chapter markers for your DVD. Working in this way simplifies the marker creation process, since your markers are automatically imported into DVD Studio Pro with the clip. Also, the tools you are accustomed to using in Final Cut Pro are often quicker and easier to use for precisely placing markers in a video track.

> **NOTE** ▸ If you don't have Final Cut Pro, refer to Lesson 3 to set markers in DVD Studio Pro.

Types of Markers in Final Cut Pro

In Final Cut Pro, you can add three types of markers to a clip or sequence: chapter markers, compression markers, and scoring markers. You create these markers by creating a simple marker and then adding a specific tag to the marker in the Edit Marker window. These markers can then be exported with the video and audio of the clip sequence, and read by another application such as DVD Studio Pro or Soundtrack.

Chapter markers in FCP are identical to those in DVD Studio Pro, except for one major difference. Chapter markers can only occur on I-frames, so adding chapter markers in Final Cut Pro is advantageous because when you click Add Chapter Marker, Final Cut Pro forces an I-frame onto the video when it is compressed to MPEG-2. This allows you to place a chapter marker on the exact frame you want, instead of the nearest I-frame (+ or − 15 frames) as when adding markers in DVD Studio Pro. As stated before, this special I-frame is preceded by a GOP that is smaller than the regular 15 frames for NTSC or 12 for PAL.

You can also add a compression marker without adding a chapter marker. Forcing an I-frame has other applications besides adding chapter markers. I-frames are the least compressed frames of a GOP, and placing them on important edit points (particularly those that occur on transitions or contain a lot of motion) ensures that they maintain the highest quality when encoded to MPEG-2.

Scoring markers, like chapter markers, can be embedded in video and read by another application, such as Soundtrack, which is included with Final Cut Pro and also sold separately. Scoring markers can mark important moments in a movie where music needs to be particularly loud or soft, or of a certain tempo or feeling. In Soundtrack, these markers create snapping points and thumb-nails, which aid in the placement of Apple Loops in Soundtrack. However, scoring markers are not used by DVD Studio Pro.

Creating Chapter Markers in FCP for DVD Studio Pro

In this exercise, you are going to create four chapter/compression markers in Final Cut Pro that are going to be used for two stories. We will use these stories later on in this project for a random play script.

1 Launch Final Cut Pro by clicking its icon in the Dock.

 If you haven't added it to your Dock, locate the Final Cut Pro icon in the Applications folder on your hard drive and drag it to your Dock.

2 Choose File > Import > Files.

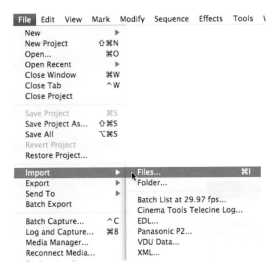

3 Select Media > TigerBasic > TigerBasic_Assets > Tiger_Video > **TigerMovie1**, and click Choose to bring it into Final Cut Pro.

The video **TigerMovie1** now appears in the Browser window.

4 Drag the video file from the Browser window onto the Timeline window.

You can also drag the file onto the Canvas window and choose Overwrite from the menu that appears.

For this project, you will set four chapter/compression markers at precise spots, which you will use to build a story later on.

NOTE ▶ Stories use chapter markers to mark a specific section of a video track (such as a chapter's beginning and end). Because you are going to create a story in a later exercise, you should choose a start and end point for each chapter or section you intend to use in the story, or it will not play properly. A chapter in a story starts at one chapter marker and plays until the next chapter marker (the end marker) is reached.

5 Navigate to 01:00:27;04 by typing this timecode into the timecode field in the upper-left corner of the Timeline window and pressing Return.

Entering a timecode will move the playhead to an exact location.

NOTE ▶ There are several methods for moving the playhead in Final Cut Pro. You can drag it across the Timeline window by using the mouse; use the J, K, and L keys to move forward and backward through the video; or press the left and right arrow keys to precisely position the playhead one frame at a time. If you know the exact timecode where you want to place the marker, however, entering the timecode value is the fastest.

6 Once you have located a point for your marker, press the M key twice.

The first M automatically places a marker at this particular timecode, and the second M brings up the Edit Marker window, where you can choose more options for the marker you are placing. You can also view or change the timecode of the exact frame that the marker is placed on, add

comments about it, and place a few different types of markers, depending on your needs (as discussed in the next few steps).

7 Type *Dance Start* into the Name field of the Edit Marker window to name the marker.

> **NOTE** ▶ You might decide to keep the markers named in the order you create them (Marker 1, Marker 2, and so on), although this doesn't tell you anything about the contents of the video at that point. A more precise name—even if it is simply Introduction, Dance Start, Dance End, and so on—is often a better way to name your markers because you can easily refer to these names when you build your stories. Also, if you were to place a new marker between existing markers (for example, a new marker between Marker 1 and Marker 2), it would appear to be out of order, since markers are numbered in the order they were created, not by their relative positions in the Timeline.

8 Click the Add Chapter Marker button in the Edit Marker window.

This button automatically adds a text tag in the Comment field, which, once exported, will inform any other QuickTime-aware application that both a compression marker and a chapter marker should be set for this frame.

> **NOTE** ▶ You can automatically create a chapter index in DVD Studio Pro by using a track with chapter markers added in Final Cut Pro.

9 Click OK when you are finished editing your marker.

10 Repeat steps 5 through 9 to create the following additional chapter markers in your **TigerMovie1** video clip:

01:00:34;23 Dance End

01:00:39;06 Jeep Start

01:01:10;08 Jeep End

11 Practice navigating between your markers by holding down the Shift key and pressing the up arrow key to move to the next marker or the down arrow to move to the previous marker.

TIP ▶ You can also Ctrl-click in the ruler section of the Timeline and choose to jump to a specific chapter marker in the shortcut menu.

12 Choose File > Export > QuickTime Movie when you are ready to export your video.

You can also choose to export this movie using Compressor. For this exercise, you are simply learning how to add and export a video with markers. You can import the video you create here into DVD Studio Pro as a QuickTime file and encode it from within that application. You may even encode it in the background while you author a project (depending on your settings in the Encoding pane of Preferences), in case you need to save time and quickly finish a project.

13 Choose DVD Studio Pro Markers from the Markers pop-up at the bottom of the Export dialog.

This will ensure that the tags placed on your markers in the Timeline will be embedded in the resulting QuickTime file.

14 Make sure that the Make Movie Self-Contained check box is *not* checked.

NOTE ▶ The Make Movie Self-Contained option is important to understand. When its box is checked, the resulting QuickTime file will have all video frames and audio samples packed into a new, large file, which is perfect for loading onto a FireWire drive and handing over to a collaborator or a client. These QuickTime files are called *self-contained*, simply because they contain all the content needed for playback within themselves. When the box is not checked, the QuickTime file is called a *reference movie*. These movies are much smaller and contain links to the proper video files, but they're relatively useless when moved to another computer, because the links they contain will be broken.

The simple rule for deciding whether to make a movie self-contained is this: If it's staying on this machine, the box is unchecked. If it's leaving the machine, the box is checked.

15 Click Save to export your Final Cut Pro movie to your Desktop and name it TigerMovie2.mov.

A status window will appear, estimating the time until export is complete.

Working with Markers in DVD Studio Pro

Once you have an exported QuickTime movie with embedded markers, you can easily import it into DVD Studio Pro just as you would any other video asset. Once the movie is imported into a DVD Studio Pro project, you can add more chapter markers and even edit the existing markers in an imported file. However, there is one other difference between adding markers in DVD Studio Pro and Final Cut Pro. As noted in the previous section, DVD Studio Pro can only place markers on existing I-frames in encoded video, which occur at the beginning of a GOP (group of pictures). Since most NTSC GOPs are 15 frames long, this means that you can only place a marker every 15 frames (depending on how the video was encoded). Also, the markers you add in DVD Studio Pro are a part of your project file only, and not embedded into the imported file, like the markers you added in Final Cut Pro. If you decided to export an MPEG from DVD Studio Pro, these new markers will not be embedded into it.

However, with the addition of a new timeline and the Track Editor, creating markers in DVD Studio Pro 4 is much easier than it was in previous versions of the software.

For this exercise, you will be importing a video clip and setting chapter markers in DVD Studio Pro using a list of timecodes in a text file. These chapter markers will then be used in the creation of stories.

1 Launch DVD Studio Pro and open the My_Projects > **Tiger_DVD** file you created in Lesson 11. If you didn't create the file, open Lessons > **12_Tiger_start** and relink the media, if necessary.

2 Press F11 to get to your Desktop, and select **TigerMovie2.mov** and hold down the mouse button.

3 Press F11 again and drag **TigerMovie2.mov** onto the Track1 tile in the Graphical tab.

TIP ▶ If you have disabled or reassigned the keys for Exposé, you can import this file using any of the import methods we described earlier in the book, and then drag it from the Assets tab onto the Track1 tile in Graphical tab.

You can now see **TigerMovie2.mov** in your Track tab with all the markers you have just set in Final Cut Pro.

4 In the Graphical tab, select TigerMovie2 and press Delete to remove TigerMovie2 from your project.

To complete the next exercise, we will use **TigerMovie.m2v** with the same chapter markers you set for **TigerMovie2.mov** in the last exercise.

5 From the Assets tab, find the Tiger Assets > Tracks >TigerMovie.m2v
 asset, then drag and drop it into an empty spot on the Graphical tab.

A new track tile will form in the Graphical tab.

6 Below, in the Track Editor, Ctrl-click in the marker area above the timeline
 and choose Import Marker List from the shortcut menu.

 NOTE ▸ You can also choose File > Import > Marker List to import a
 marker list for a selected track.

7 Select the text file called **Tiger_Markers.txt**, located in the Media > Tiger >
 Tiger_Docs folder, and click Choose.

 DVD Studio Pro provides a message that states how many markers were
 imported. Your new markers should appear automatically in the timeline.

<ant—>
</ant—>

NOTE ▶ If the markers that are added from a text file do not fall on an I-frame, they will be moved to the next available I-frame. You can set which GOP will be chosen (Previous GOP, Next GOP, Nearest GOP) by changing your settings in the Track pane of Preferences.

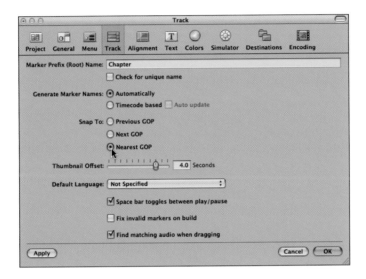

Using Stories as Playlists

A story is simply a way to rearrange the playback of track segments defined by the chapter markers. You may want to create a version of a track that skips some objectionable content, or you may want to use a short piece of the track as a preview. You can create up to 98 stories for each track.

With stories, you can create several different versions of a movie or video program without reusing material or creating additional video tracks that take up valuable space on a disc. A story offers a simple way to rearrange the playback of the track cells defined by the chapter markers in a playlist. A story has access to the entire track, but it does not have to include it all. You can choose which chapter markers to include and in what order—you can even play a marker's video more than once. Additionally, you can exclude specific subtitle and

audio streams from a story. By excluding selected streams, you can force the DVD player to play the alternate audio and subtitle streams.

In this exercise, you will build four stories that will play four sections of a short piece of the track as a preview. You will also create stories to make the main menu more interactive. These stories will be part of a random play script that randomly plays one of the stories after the menu has looped twice.

> **NOTE ▸** The actual playback of a story is not strictly seamless, since a jump must occur at each new marker (similar to skipping chapters using the Next and Previous buttons on your remote control).

So whether you want to allow viewers to see the "director's cut" of your movie without the happy ending the studio made you tack on, or show the movie with the scenes that were left on the cutting room floor put back in, or even provide a random play timeout action for a motion menu, stories will do the job without creating so much as a kilobyte of new media.

> **NOTE ▸** You can include up to 99 tracks, slideshows, and stories in a single project. But please note, this is the total number of tracks, stories and slideshows *combined*.

Chapter markers in stories may be thought of as aliases that point to the original material—in this case, points in a video track. These markers can be placed in any order you want. Buttons may link to these stories and activate a series of chapter markers.

Working with the Story Editor

In this exercise, you will learn how to create four stories from the markers you have already created by placing the markers in the Story Editor window. Initially, you are going to link these stories to another menu. In the next lesson, these stories will be used as a timeout action in a random play script.

1 In the Graphical tab, click the TigerMovie track tile.

2 In the toolbar, click the Add Story button.

TIP ▶ You can also Ctrl-click the track in the Graphical or Outline tab and choose Add > Story from the shortcut menu.

Add Story

3 Double-click the new story (Story 1) tile to open the Story tab.

The left side of the Story Editor window contains all of the markers from the track you have selected (the source list). On the right side of the window is the list where you can arrange these markers to create a story (the entry list).

4 Drag the marker called Dance Start from the source list on the left to the entry list on the right.

By dragging markers from your track marker list on the left to the story marker list on the right, you are creating entries for your story.

5 Click the Play button in your viewer window to watch the story.

The story will play for 7 seconds until it hits the Dance End marker, then stops.

The Dance End marker indicates the end of this story. Don't drag it to your entry list; otherwise, it will play the Tiger End marker as well and stop at the next marker, which is Jeep Start. In order to have stories play

just the part of the track we want them to play, we create these "End" chapter markers to stop the playback at a specific point.

TIP ▶ To change the order of markers in the entry list, simply drag the markers to new positions in the list, just as you would slides in a slideshow.

6 In the Graphical tab, double-click the name field of the Story 1 tile.

7 Type *Dance Story* to rename the story.

8 Click the TigerMovie track tile.

9 In the Inspector, set this track's End Jump to Menus > TigerMainMenu > [Menu].

The End Jump for the stories is set to Same as Track as a default. Therefore, all stories will jump back to the same place as the main track (in this case, TigerMainMenu) once they are finished.

10 Repeat steps 1 through 7, using the TigerMovie track, to create three new stories for Jeep, Water, and Tiger Mother.

 To delete a marker in the entry list, select it and press the Delete key.

11 In the Story tab, choose Dance Story from the View pop-up menu to get back to the Dance Story.

12 Ctrl-click the empty space to the right of the Story tab, and choose Simulate Story from the shortcut menu to simulate the story.

No.	Story Markers	Running Time
1	Dance Start Entry	00:00:07:19

Change Chapter ▶

Play
Stop

Simulate

Dance Story should now play for 7 seconds and then jump back to the TigerMainMenu. You may also want to simulate the Jeep, Water, and Tiger Mother stories.

You have now created four stories that are going to be used in a random play script to make the Tiger menu more interactive.

No.		Duration	No.	Story Markers	Running Time
1	Start	00:00:27:04	1	Water Start Entry	00:00:42:00
2	Dance Start	00:00:07:19			
3	Dance End	00:00:04:13			
4	Jeep Start	00:00:31:01			
5	Jeep End	00:03:04:15			
6	Water Start	00:00:42:00			
7	Water End	00:04:01:00			
8	Tiger Mother Start	00:01:03:00			
9	Tiger Mother End	00:01:00:11			

Creating a Story with Multiple Markers

Stories are not only easy to create, but they are also flexible. You can add markers from the source list to the entry list multiple times to replay part of a track. (Each new appearance of the marker is given another number at the end of its name.) You can also put markers into any order you want, even after adding them to the story.

1 In the toolbar, click Add Story.

2 In the Inspector, rename this story *Tiger Playlist*.

3 Move the markers Dance Start, Water Start, and Dance Start from the source list on the left to the entry list on the right.

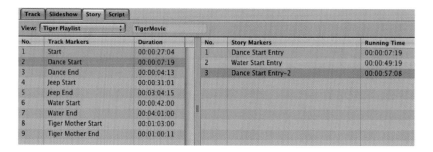

4 Choose File > Save to save your **Tiger_DVD** project.

When the Tiger Playlist story is activated, all of its markers will play in the order in which they appear in the list you created, until the last marker has finished playing. As you can see, you can even play the same markers twice.

Lesson Review

1. What is the maximum number of chapter markers you can add to a single track?

2. Can you set markers frame accurately (on an exact frame) inside DVD Studio Pro itself?

3. What is the process for setting chapter markers inside Final Cut Pro?

4. How many stories can you include in a project?

5. True or false: To create a story you must first select the track the story will be assigned to and then add the story to the project.

6. Can a story play chapters from two different tracks?

Answers

1. 99. Or 98 new chapter markers in addition to the default chapter marker that gets placed at the first frame of each track (this marker cannot be moved or altered).

2. No. To set markers frame accurately, you must set them in Final Cut Pro (or Compressor) before encoding the MPEG-2 stream.

3. Park the playhead on the frame you want to tag with a marker, then press the M key twice to set a marker and then open the Edit Marker window. Next, click the "add Chapter Marker" button to turn the marker into a Chapter Marker.

4. That depends upon how many tracks and slideshows the project has. You can have a maximum of 99 tracks, slideshows, and stories in a single project.

5. True. DVD Studio Pro needs to know which track the story belongs to, so you must select the track first in either the Graphical or Outline view.

6. No. Stories can play only chapters from the track they are assigned to.

Keyboard Shortcuts

Cmd-8	Opens the Story Editor tab
Cmd-9	Opens the Track Editor tab
Cmd-Shift-T	Adds a story
Ctrl–left arrow	Moves the playhead to the previous marker
Ctrl–right arrow	Moves the playhead to the next marker
Option-M	Moves the playhead to the previous marker
Shift-M	Moves the playhead to the next marker
Option–left arrow	Moves the playhead to the previous GOP
Option–right arrow	Moves the playhead to the next GOP
M	Creates a new marker in the Track Editor timeline

13

Lesson Files Lessons > 13_Tiger_start
(or the My_Projects > Tiger_DVD project you created
in Lesson 12)

Media Media > Tiger folder

Time This lesson takes approximately 60 minutes to complete.

Goals Set up a simple project with an advanced menu design

Learn how to create advanced motion menus with transitions

Learn how to make a DVD look professional

Use the Connections tab to link all the elements in your
project

Create a random play script

Create a menu loop script

Lesson 13

Connections and Basic Scripting

Now that you have prepared your menus, stories, and video and audio assets for the Tiger project, it is time to assemble the elements into a finished DVD.

In this lesson, you will give the Tiger project a motion menu with video transitions that bridge the gaps between menus, tracks, and slideshows. You will then create advanced menus that link with these transitions.

You will also learn how to create navigation that occurs without any input from the viewer. You can do this using a menu loop and a random play script, without the need to insert any new content or take up more space on the DVD.

For the Tiger DVD, you will program the menu to loop two times, and if there is no input from the viewer through the remote control, a random play script will then jump to one of the four stories before coming back to the main menu. This makes the DVD a lot more interesting, especially for viewers who insert the DVD into their players and let the main menu loop for several minutes while they're making popcorn.

Assembling the Tiger Project

Since the elements required for the Tiger project have already been created, you can simply use the steps in the following exercises to put them together into a finished DVD. Examining the way these pieces are used should give you ideas for your own menu designs and disc layouts.

Adding Transition Tracks

As a part of the menu design process, transition movies can bridge the space between the start of a disc and a menu, or between a menu and a track. Automated transition movies are easily one of the most exciting additions to DVD Studio Pro 4. You can even build your own alpha transitions in DVD Studio Pro 4, which we cover in depth in Lesson 16.

However, if you want to include sound or you want to build very specific transitions, you can easily create these transitional movies in an application such as Final Cut Pro. Since any sequence in Final Cut Pro can be the background for a menu, you can export the first part of the sequence as an MPEG-2 transition movie, and then export the remaining part of the sequence as the background for a motion menu. In this way, you can create smooth transitions into and out of menus. You can set up these transition movies just as you would any other track in DVD Studio Pro. In a later section of this lesson, you will set the links that activate these tracks from the main menu, as well as set a first-play action for the disc itself.

In the following exercise, you will create a track that contains the Intro Transition movie, which will be used as the first-play action that takes you seamlessly into the main menu. You will also create a track that will contain a transition movie. The transition movie will activate whenever the viewer makes a choice to jump from the main menu to other DVD content.

1 Open the My_Projects > **Tiger_DVD** file you created in Lesson 12, or the Lessons > **13_Tiger_start** file.

2 Click the Graphical tab to make the Graphical view active.

3 From the Assets tab, drag the **Tiger_Intro.mov** video into an empty space in the Graphical view.

A track named Tiger_Intro is created in the Graphical view. In a moment, we will reassign this track as the first play, so that it becomes the first thing a user sees when inserting the disc into the player.

4 From the Assets tab, drag the **Tiger_Transition1.mov** video into an empty space in the Graphical view.

A track named Tiger_Transition1 appears in the Graphical view. This track will contain a transition from the TigerMainMenu to the TigerMovie track.

5 From the Assets tab, drag the Slideshows folder into an empty space in the Graphical view.

A slideshow named Slideshow 1 is created.

6 Click the Slideshow 1 tile to bring its parameters into the Inspector.

7 From the Assets tab, drag **TigerSlideshow.aif** onto the Audio area of the Inspector.

8 In the Inspector, click the Transition tab and choose Dissolve as your Transition for the entire slideshow.

It is almost a must to use this great transition feature for slideshows.

Establishing Connections

In previous lessons, you have established links between buttons, tracks, stories, and other disc items using several intuitive techniques. You will now learn how to connect all your items by using the Connections tab. The Connections tab will be most useful in this lesson, because there are only a few links established between disc items so far.

Using the Connections tab is perhaps the quickest way to check and establish links between the different items in a project. The way you set the connections determines how the viewer experiences your DVD title. You will make these connections so that the viewer jumps from a starting point, or source, to a destination, or target.

The following steps illustrate how to make connections in the Connections tab, where you will complete the Tiger project by establishing the first play for the Tiger_Intro movie, making the logical connections between all tracks, and linking the remaining buttons to their corresponding track and slideshow. As a last step, you'll complete the DVD by making sure that all of the links between menus, tracks, and slideshows are in place. Once all of your disc items are in place for the project, you can link them to your buttons in the main menu. You will also need to set the appropriate targets for your transitions.

1 Press F3 to switch to the Advanced window configuration.

2 Click the Graphical tab, and then click the background of the Graphical view to activate the Disc level in the Connections tab.

3 Click the Connections tab.

4 Make sure that Basic is selected in the View pop-up menu in the top-left corner of the Connections tab.

 The Connections tab offers you different views of the connections in your project. You can determine the level of detail you want to see by setting View to Basic, Standard, or Advanced. For our purposes, Basic will be sufficient.

In the Basic view, you will find all major jumps, such as the first-play action; jumps from buttons to menus and tracks; and end jumps from tracks to menus. By using Basic view to connect all project elements, you can make sure that your disc is not missing any major links.

5 Click the pop-up menu next to Basic, and make sure that All is selected.

The All setting shows us all available Basic connections, whether they have targets or not. If we switched to Connected, the list below would just show which links were connected, and Unconnected would just display those links that do not currently have targets. We'll keep this set to All to view all available links.

The Connections tab has two panes. The left pane is divided into two columns. The left column, Source, lists the source links: menus, menu buttons, tracks, slideshows, and other items. The Target column lists what the buttons or items are linked to. If there is nothing in the Target column, the source is not linked to anything.

In the pane on the right side is a third column, Targets, which lists the possible disc items—menus, tracks, slideshows, and stories—that are available to be set as targets.

Let's start with changing the first-play action to the Tiger_Intro movie.

6 Drag the Tiger_Intro track from the Targets column onto the first entry in the Target column, which is currently filled with TigerMainMenu.

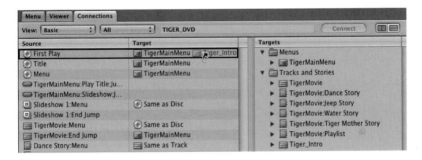

Tiger_Intro replaces TigerMainMenu as the first-play item on the disc.

Finding the Unconnected Elements

Working with the Connections tab set to display only unconnected items is a good way to quickly check your disc for links that have not been established yet. In effect, it provides a "to-do" list. When only unconnected items are viewed, items will disappear from the list as soon as they are connected to something. When the Source and Target columns are both empty, you have correctly connected everything in your DVD.

1 Click the pop-up menu to the right of the View pop-up menu and choose Unconnected.

Now the Connections tab displays only the items that you still need to connect before finishing your project. Let's go ahead and connect these items now.

2 Drag the Tiger_Transition1 track from the Targets column onto the TigerMainMenu: Play Title target in the second column.

For the Tiger DVD, Tiger_Transition1 will bridge the space between TigerMainMenu and the TigerMovie track.

As soon as you connect the Play Title button from your TigerMainMenu, this item disappears from the list of unconnected source items.

3 Drag the TigerMovie track from the Targets column onto the Tiger_
Transition1: End Jump target in the second column.

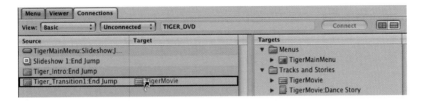

4 Drag Menus > TigerMainMenu from the Targets column onto the
Tiger_Intro: End Jump target in the second (Target) column.

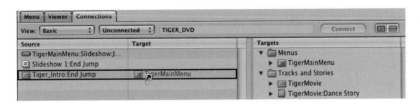

5 Click the disclosure triangle next to the Slideshows folder in the Targets
column to get access to the Slideshow 1 target.

6 Drag Slideshow 1 from the Targets column onto the TigerMainMenu:
Slideshow target in the second (Target) column.

7 Select Slideshow 1 End Jump in the Source list and double-click TigerMainMenu in the Targets list.

Double-clicking an item in the Targets list is an alternate way to add the item to the currently selected source.

Now let's set the Connections tab to show All connections. This will enable us to be sure that we've set up all the links.

8 Click the pop-up menu to the right of the View pop-up menu, and choose All.

You have now successfully set up the navigation of your **Tiger_DVD** project. This view gives you a chance to examine all the connections on your DVD.

9 Click the pop-up menu next to View, and choose Standard from the list of choices.

To get access to additional sources of your DVD project, you can use the Standard view. If you choose the Advanced view, your source list will display every single detail. For the **Tiger_DVD** project, it is not necessary to use the Standard or Advanced view.

TIP ▶ Since they are so detailed, the Standard and Advanced views work better if you choose only a single item, such as a menu or track, in your Outline or Graphical tab rather than the Disc or global view.

You should now simulate your disc to make sure that all links work properly.

MORE INFO ▶ For more detailed information on the Connections tab, please refer to page 485 in the DVD Studio Pro 4 manual.

10 On the toolbar, click the Simulate icon to preview the disc.

Now, the Tiger_Intro movie starts playing and leads to the menu. If you choose Play Title from TigerMainMenu, a video transition will lead you to the TigerMovie.

11 Close the Simulator window.

Creating a Menu Loop Script

Scripts are a powerful, advanced feature included as a part of the DVD-Video specification. Although many users may never need to use these scripting features, it is nice to know that they are available, particularly when you come accross a sophisticated project that requires unique solutions or workarounds.

Scripting in DVD Studio Pro allows you to accomplish complex tasks that could not otherwise be performed. For example, you can create a script that tells a track to loop a certain number of times, or create a script that randomly selects a story to play when a user activates a button in a menu or even when the user fails to make any selection. You can combine several functions into a single script that you attach to a disc item in DVD Studio Pro.

In this lesson, you will get exposed to some basic scripting. You will create a script that loops a predetermined number of times. You will also add random play commands that choose a particular story to play from the TigerMovie track.

NOTE ▶ For in-depth practice with scripting, see Lesson 20 in the Advanced section of this book.

1 On the toolbar, click the Add Script button.

2 In the Outline tab, double-click the new script (Script 1), which opens up the Script Editor.

3 In the Inspector, rename the script *Menu Loop Script*.

You've created a new script. Now let's put something in it.

Setting Up the Counter

The first thing that needs to be set up is a counter for the number of times the menu is going to loop before it jumps randomly to one of the four stories you have created in a previous lesson.

1 In the Inspector, click the disclosure triangle to the left of GPRM 0.

GPRM stands for General Purpose Register Memory. This is a fancy term for variables. You have eight of them to use when you author your disc, and they can be assigned any number of useful values. In this case, we are going to create a counter variable to keep count of how many times our main menu has looped.

2 In the newly expanded area or GPRM 0, double-click the word "GPRM 0" and type in "Counter."

Naming this GPRM value is simply a way to help you identify it later on. You can name your GPRM variables anything you want (hopefully related to what that GPRM is doing for you), or you can leave them with their default names.

3 In the Script Editor, click the first command line, Nop.

It will become highlighted when selected.

The Nop, or No Operation, command is the simplest of all commands in scripting. It means do nothing, and in this case it is simply a placeholder for the first line of the script until you assign a useful command, as you will do now.

3 From the Command pop-up menu at the top of the Inspector window, choose Set GPRM.

This command simply allows you to set the value of a GPRM. We are going to add the number 1 to the current value of our Counter variable (GPRM 0).

4 From the Operation pop-up menu, choose "add."

5 From the Source Type pop-up menu, choose Immediate.

6 Type the number *1* into the Source Value field and press Return.

This command will add an immediate value of 1 to our Counter variable. Notice that Counter is automatically set as the target of this command.

Setting Up the Compare Condition

In the next few steps, you will set up a compare command that will loop the menu again if the menu has played fewer than two times. This will be achieved by a Jump command, which lets the menu jump to itself and play again. But if the menu has already looped twice, it will jump to a random play script, which will play one of the four stories randomly.

1 Click the Add button (+) at the top of the Script Editor.

Another command line is added to the script.

2 Select the new command line you added in the Script Editor, Nop.

3 In the Inspector, choose Jump from the Command pop-up menu.

4 From the Jump To pop-up menu in the Inspector, choose Menus > TigerMainMenu > [Menu].

So far, this command is jumping us out of this script and back to the main menu. Now we will add a condition to this command, so that the jump back to the main menu happens only when a certain condition is met.

5 Click the Compare Command check box.

6 From the Execute If pop-up menu, choose Counter.

7 From the "is" pop-up menu (which contains operation types), choose less than (<).

8 From the "to" pop-up menu (which is the element type to compare), choose Immediate.

Immediate means that instead of comparing with a number stored in a variable somewhere, we will use a value that we input immediately into the command.

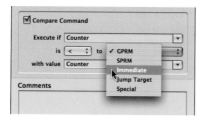

9 Type the number *2* in the "with value" field and press Return.

Now the jump command executes only if there is a number 0 or 1 in Counter (the GPRM 0 that we renamed). If not, the script will move on to the next command. This is important to understand: If the compare command in a line of a script is false, the action of that line will be ignored, and the script will begin to execute its next line. Let's create that next line now.

Resetting the Counter

In the preceding exercise, you learned how to set up the counter. Now, you will add another command that resets the counter to 0 whenever it reaches a value of 2.

1 Click the Add button (+) at the top of the Script Editor.

Another command line is added to the script.

2 Select the new command line in the Script Editor (Nop).

3 In the Inspector, choose Set GPRM from the Command pop-up menu.

4 From the Operation pop-up menu, choose "mov."

5 From the Source Type pop-up menu, choose Immediate.

6 Type the number *0* into the Source Value field and press Return.

7 From the Target pop-up menu, choose Counter.

We have now entered a command that resets our counter to 0.

Adding Random Play Commands

Now that you have set up your script to loop a menu two times, you'll want to add a random play action to the script, which will randomly choose a story to play from the TigerMovie track. The first step is to set up a random number variable that will generate a random number from the number of stories you have.

1 In the Outline tab of the main window, click the Menu Loop Script.

At this point, you should rename another GPRM variable to be used in the following steps. Although you don't need to rename GPRMs, it is a good way to keep track of variables that you use in your scripts.

2 In the Inspector, rename GPRM 1 "Random Number".

3 Click the Add button (+) at the top of the Script Editor.

Another command line is added to the script.

4 Make sure the new command line is selected in the Script Editor.

5 In the Inspector, choose Set GPRM from the Command pop-up menu.

6 From the Operation pop-up menu, choose "ran."

7 From the Source Type pop-up menu, choose Immediate.

8 Type the number 4 into the Source Value field and press Return.

This command will generate a random number between 1 and 4. The random number that is generated by the Source Value is placed into Random Number (the GPRM 1 variable that you renamed) and will be used to determine the next track that will play.

9 From the Target pop-up menu, choose Random Number.

Setting Up Random Play Jumps

Now you create the commands that play the random stories from the Tiger-Movie track. More specifically, you will create four jumps to one of the four stories using the Compare command.

1 Click the Add button (+) at the top of the Script Editor.

Another command line is added to the script.

2 Make sure the new command line is selected in the Script Editor.

3 In the Inspector, choose Jump from the Command pop-up menu.

4 From the Jump To pop-up menu, choose Tracks and Stories >
TigerMovie::Dance Story > [Story].

5 Click the Compare Command check box.

6 From the "Execute if" pop-up menu, choose Random Number.

7 From the "is" pop-up menu (which contains operation types), choose
equal (=).

8 From the "to" pop-up menu (which is the element type to compare),
choose Immediate.

9 Type the number *1* in the "with value" field and press Return.

This jump command executes and plays the Dance Story, if there is a number 1 in the Random Number variable (the GPRM 1 that you renamed). Otherwise, the script moves onto the next command line.

10 In the Script Editor, select command line 5, "Jump TigerMovie: Dance Story if (Random Number = 1)."

11 Press Cmd-C to copy this command line.

12 Press Cmd-V to insert a copy of this command line.

13 In the Inspector, change the Jump To command to TigerMovie::Jeep [Story] and the "with value" for the Random Number compare command to *2*.

14 Press Cmd-C once and Cmd-V twice to insert two more copies of command line number 6.

15 In the Script Editor, click command line number 7.

16 In the Inspector, change the Jump To command to TigerMovie::Water [Story] and the "with value" for the Random Number compare command to *3*.

17 In the Script Editor, click command line number 8.

18 In the Inspector, change the Jump To command to TigerMovie::Tiger Mother [Story] and the "with value" for the Random Number compare command to *4*.

When you are done, the finished script should look like this:

Connecting the Script to the Menu

After you create your script, it is time to connect it to your TigerMainMenu. The easiest way to achieve this is to set the script as a timeout action for the menu.

For this project, you will make the TigerMainMenu do a timeout jump to the Menu Loop Script you created. This causes the script to play the two loops you want for the menu before the script randomly plays one of the four stories that are linked back to the TigerMainMenu.

1 In the Graphical tab, click TigerMainMenu tile.

2 In the Inspector, select the General tab.

3 Set the At End value to Timeout.

4 Type a duration of *0* seconds for the timeout.

A timeout value of 0 simply means that there should not be a pause before the menu jumps to the next disc item.

5 From the Action pop-up menu, choose Scripts > Menu Loop Script.

6 Choose File > Save to save your **Tiger_DVD** project.

7 On the toolbar, click the Simulator icon to simulate the disc.

Without clicking any buttons or remote control buttons, allow the main menu to loop, time out, then loop again. You should now see the script executing one of the four stories randomly. You should then return back to the main menu, and the process starts again.

8 Close the Simulator window.

9 Click the Log tab to view the actions of your script in detail.

Congratulations! You have just set up a sophisticated DVD project, including a script that makes the menu more interactive.

As you have learned in previous lessons, you should now thoroughly test your DVD. Then you can build or burn your project if you wish. Please see Lesson 9 for further information on finishing your project.

Lesson Review

1. What does the Connections tab do?

2. True or false: you can filter the connections tab to show you only the unconnected items in your project.

3. What does GPRM stand for?

4. What do GPRMs do?

5. When creating a random play script, what operation do you choose from the Set GPRM command's Operation menu?

6. Can you target a script from a menu time-out action?

Answers

1. It allows you to quickly check and establish links between the different items in a project.

2. True. You can also filter the connections tab to display only the connected items, or to display all items (both connected and unconnected).

3. General Purpose Register Memory.

4. GPRMs are variables you can use to hold values as a script executes.

5. Choose the operation called "ran."

6. Yes. In fact, you can target a script from any target menu inside DVD Studio Pro.

Black Box Project: Advanced Authoring Techniques

Vancouver-based Martin Sitter is a veteran audio producer, multimedia artist, and author specializing in track-based video and audio applications. After producing electronic music albums (house/tech house) for record labels including Peng Records UK and Phatt Phunk Records LA, Martin went on to embrace interactive video. He has authored and produced numerous commercial DVDs, and is a lead instructor for Apple Certified trainings and the director of macProVideo.com. Martin is the author of *DVD Studio Pro 3 for Macintosh: Visual QuickPro Guide* and *Apple Pro Training Series: Logic 6*, and is a contributing author of *Apple Pro Training Series: Advanced Editing and Finishing Techniques in Final Cut Pro 4.*

14

Lesson Files	Lessons > 14_Advanced_Menu_Design-Start
Media	Media > Blackbox folder
Time	This lesson takes approximately 60 minutes to complete.
Goals	Learn how to create standard menu assets
	Discover how menu overlays are created
	Explore the way DVD Studio Pro automatically updates when source assets are altered
	Learn more about adding audio to menus
	Concatenate multiple audio files together in a single menu
	Add motion backgrounds to a standard menu
	Create a menu intro transition and set a loop point to delay the display of button state overlays
	Explore layered menus

Advanced Menu Design

DVD-Video is all about the menus. Without menus, you have just a linear progression of video, and that's not much more exciting than a standard VHS tape. Menus provide interactivity, and it's the menus that make a DVD-Video both engaging to watch and memorable. While it is important to ensure that your video is encoded properly and looks good, menu design consumes the bulk of the effort that goes into making any professional DVD-Video.

And speaking of professional, this chapter is aimed at designers who already have graphics chops but need a little extra information about the menu creation process. If you're a DVD author who uses Adobe Photoshop as an integral part of the design process, this lesson is for you.

The following pages build on menu creation concepts covered in previous lessons, particularly Lesson 11, "Creating Menus with Overlays." You'll start the lesson by dissecting a properly configured Photoshop document to see how a menu source asset is created. You'll also see just how easy it is to create a motion menu in DVD Studio Pro, and you'll add audio files to give your menus some aural ambiance. Finally, you'll explore the world of layered menus, which make it possible to turn on graphics outside a button's hotspot.

The Two Types of Menus

In DVD Studio Pro, there are two types of menus: standard menus and layered menus. Up to this point in the course, all the menus you've created have been standard menus.

Standard menus—a.k.a. overlay or highlight menus—are the preferred menu format for DVD-Video. Check your favorite Hollywood DVD, and chances are it uses this type of menu. Standard menus use a background image that includes the button graphics, and an overlay image that is a template for "stamping" button states onto the menu.

The advantages of standard menus are that they respond quickly to user input when the DVD-Video material is played on a computer, and they can have audio playing along, as well as moving video backgrounds. However, standard menu button states are limited to three colors, and you cannot enable graphics outside of the button's hotspot.

Layered menus use a specific layer of a Photoshop document for the menu background and for each button state. When a button is selected or activated, DVD Studio Pro enables the entire layer for that button state. The advantage of a layered menu is that you can "turn on" graphics outside of the button hotspot, and you can also use full 16-bit color in the design of your button states. However, layered menus cannot have audio or use video backgrounds, and they respond slowly to user input when played on a computer.

> **NOTE** ▶ This lesson assumes that you own Photoshop and know your way around it. Specifically, you'll need to understand the layering structure of Photoshop documents.

Each type of menu has its advantages and disadvantages. In this lesson you will make one of each to explore the differences between these two types of DVD Studio Pro menus.

Creating a New Menu in Photoshop

DVD-Video uses a frame dimension of 720 × 480 pixels (720 × 576 PAL). But that's only half the story, because when this 720 × 480-pixel video frame is displayed on a television, it is always horizontally squeezed, which means it displays thinner on a TV than it does on a computer. The reason? Computers and televisions display pixels differently. To understand why, you need to understand pixel aspect ratio.

Understanding Pixel Aspect Ratio

Computers display pixels as perfect squares, while televisions display pixels as rectangles that are slightly taller than they are wide. Defined as a ratio, a pixel on a computer is 1 unit wide by 1 unit tall (1:1), while a pixel on an NTSC television is 0.9 units wide by 1 unit tall (0.9:1). In other words, pixels displayed on an NTSC TV look approximately 10 percent thinner than they do on a computer screen.

We've all heard the saying "TV adds 10 pounds," but this dramatic thinning of the image is just not the right way to take those pounds off! Instead, you need to compensate for this difference when you create your computer-generated graphics.

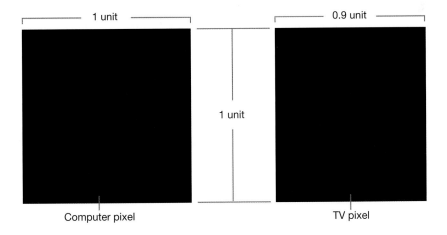

NOTE ▶ PAL TVs stretch pixels horizontally, instead of squeezing them. A PAL television displays pixels at an aspect ratio of 1.066:1.

MORE INFO ▶ CRT televisions do not actually display pixels. Instead, an electron gun fires charged particles at the front of the picture tube, causing colored phosphors to glow red, green, and blue. The combination of colors in these glowing phosphors creates the actual picture, not pixels. While it's common to refer to CRT televisions as displaying "rectangular pixels" (as we do in this book), this is a bit misleading because no pixels are actually used in the display of a TV image. Once the video is printed to tape, transmitted down the copper cable wire, or played off of a DVD-Video disc, all those little digital pixels get converted to analog waves.

Creating a New Photoshop Document

So, computers display square pixels, while NTSC televisions display horizontally squeezed, or rectangular, pixels. How do we get around this fundamental difference between computers and televisions?

You know NTSC TVs horizontally squeeze the image by approximately 10 percent. To avoid this problem you *could* design your menus to be 10 percent thinner and then stretch them out before bringing them into DVD Studio Pro. For example, you could design your menus at 640 × 480 (a 4:3 aspect ratio), and then stretch them out to 720 × 480 before importing them. At playback, your menus would be squeezed 10 percent to display at the computer equivalent of 640 × 480 pixels—exactly the size and aspect ratio you designed them at!

However, there is a problem with designing menus at 640 × 480: When you resize the menu to 720 × 480, Photoshop (or DVD Studio Pro) has to interpolate the image to make it physically bigger, which means it has to *add* extra pixels to fill out the frame. When graphics programs interpolate images, they are better at throwing data away than they are at adding new data. For this

reason, you will achieve better image quality by starting with a larger image and resizing to make it smaller.

> **NOTE** ▶ Regardless of their original dimensions, DVD Studio Pro will automatically resize all menu source assets to 720 × 480 pixels for NTSC or 720 × 576 pixels for PAL. If you are graduating to DVD Studio Pro 4 from version 1 or 1.5, you'll be happy to know that you no longer need to resize menu assets before importing them into the program.

When designing in Photoshop, start your new documents at 720 × 534 pixels for NTSC, and at 768 × 576 for PAL. The following exercise demonstrates why this works so well.

> **MORE INFO** ▶ It's a common mistake to design Photoshop NTSC menus at 720 × 540 pixels. These dimensions are the proper square pixel dimensions for Standard Definition video (also called SD, or D1 video), or video that uses a frame dimension of 720 × 486 pixels. To understand why, multiply 540 by 0.9 (the horizontal part of the NTSC pixel aspect ratio). The result is 486. However, if you multiply 534 by 0.9, the result is 480 (rounded to the next lowest whole number). Because DVD-Video uses a frame dimension of 720 × 480 pixels, starting your Photoshop graphics at 720 × 534 will help preserve the correct aspect ratio in the final DVD.

1 Open Photoshop.

2 Choose File > New (Cmd-N).

The New dialog appears.

3 Enter 720 pixels for the Width setting and 534 pixels for the Height setting.

For PAL, use a width of 768, and a height of 576.

MORE INFO ▶ The resolution setting in Photoshop's New dialog is used to increase pixel density for graphics that are going to be printed on paper. If you come from a print background, you are probably used to designing Photoshop documents at a pixel resolution of 300 pixels/inch, or higher. DVD Studio Pro will still accept and display these images correctly, though it will convert them to 72 pixels/inch before multiplexing your project. Because DVD Studio Pro automatically converts, you don't gain an increase in image quality by designing at higher pixel resolutions.

4 If you are using Photoshop CS or later, at the bottom of the New dialog, ensure that the Pixel Aspect Ratio menu is set to Square.

NOTE ▶ Photoshop CS introduced several new video functions, including the ability to automatically compensate for rectangular pixels. However, if you're following the steps in this exercise, you are already compensating for rectangular pixels by designing your menus approximately 10 percent taller than the video frame dimensions, so there's no need to have Photoshop display using rectangular pixels. In general, when creating graphics on a computer, it's always best to design the way the computer displays the pixels—that is, square.

5 Click OK.

A new Photoshop document appears.

6 Draw a perfect circle in the Photoshop document and fill it with black.

TIP ▶ To draw a perfect circle in Photoshop, hold down the Shift key as you drag the Elliptical Marquee tool. If you can't see the Elliptical Marquee tool in Photoshop's Toolbox, it's because the tool is hidden under the Rectangular Marquee tool. To expose the Elliptical Marquee tool, click and hold the Rectangular Marquee tool in Photoshop's Toolbox, and select it from the pop-up menu.

Elliptical Marquee tool

7 Choose File > Save and save the file using the name **Circle_720X534.psd**.

8 Launch DVD Studio Pro 4.

9 Choose File > New.

10 Import the **Circle_720X534.psd** asset into DVD Studio Pro.

11 Create a menu out of the **Circle_720X534.psd** asset.

12 Open the new menu in the Menu Editor.

There are a few things to notice here. First, the rulers along the top and bottom of the Menu Editor clearly show that this menu is 720 × 480 pixels, not 720 × 534, as designed. Second, the circle looks like a perfect circle. DVD Studio Pro has automatically resized the document to 720 × 480, and it is also automatically compensating for rectangular pixels.

13 From the Menu Editor's Settings menu, choose Square Pixels.

Settings menu

The Menu Editor now displays the file at *exactly* 720 × 480 square computer pixels. In other words, DVD Studio Pro has automatically resized the Photoshop document from 720 × 534 to 720 × 480. This causes the circle to look vertically squashed by approximately 10 percent. It now looks like an Easter egg lying on its side.

However, as you learned in the last section, when displayed as rectangular pixels on an NTSC television, this same circle is squeezed horizontally by about 10 percent. In short, the circle is squeezed 10 percent vertically to become an oval, and then it is squeezed 10 percent horizontally, which turns it into a circle once again!

The moral of the story is:

Always design your NTSC menus at 720 × 534 (768 × 576 for PAL)! If you take care to begin your menus at the correct frame size, in the finished DVD-Video your circles will look like circles, your squares will look like squares, and all aspect ratios will look correct.

NOTE ▶ Apple DVD Player displays NTSC DVD-Videos at 640 × 480 square pixels. This has the effect of horizontally squeezing the 720 × 480 square pixel frame by about 10 percent, causing it to display the exact same way it would on a TV.

14 From the Menu Editor's Settings menu, choose Rectangular Pixels.

It's easier to design DVD-Video while looking at the assets as they'll appear on a TV, so make sure you reset the menu to display using rectangular pixels.

15 Close the project.

Now that you understand the difference between square and rectangular pixels, let's look at how menus are designed in Photoshop.

A Closer Look at Standard Menus

Often a standard menu is designed as a multilayer Photoshop document that contains all of the layers needed to create the background graphics, plus an additional single layer containing the overlay graphics. The background graphics

include all imagery that sits behind the menu buttons, as well as the button shapes in their normal state (the graphics that display when the user is not interacting with the button).

The overlay layer uses four distinct grayscale or chroma colors to define shapes that are "laid over" the background graphics when a viewer selects or activates menu buttons.

Let's examine a standard menu in Photoshop.

Menu background Menu overlay

1 From this book's companion files, open the DVD Studio Pro Project named **14_Advanced_Menu_Design-Start**.

This is just a brand new DVD Studio Pro project with a default empty menu and track tile, but the Assets tab has been preloaded with all the media you'll need for the next several lessons.

2 In the Assets container's Menus folder, Ctrl-click the **standardMenu.psd** file, and choose Open in Editor.

The **standardMenu.psd** asset opens in Photoshop.

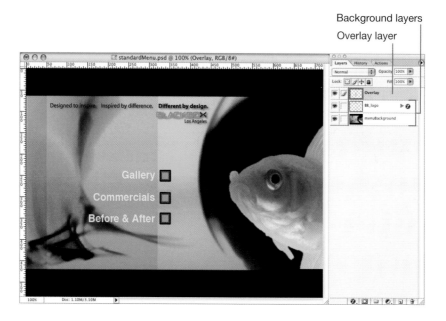

3 In Photoshop's Layers palette, click the visibility icons to turn document layers on and off, and take a look at the graphics on each layer.

Visibility icon

As you can see, the BB_logo and menuBackground layers are both part of the menu background; the Overlay layer provides three grayscale shapes (squares) that will be used for the menu's selected and activated states.

4 Switch back to DVD Studio Pro, and in the Graphical view, double-click the default menu item to open it in the Menu Editor.

5 From the Assets tab's Menus folder, drag the **standardMenu.psd** asset over the Menu Editor, but don't release the mouse button.

The Drop palette appears.

6 Choose Set Background, All Layers Visible.

The asset is assigned to the menu. But if you take a close look, you'll see that the Overlay layer is currently enabled, and the overlay graphics are displaying over the background graphics. The Overlay layer has to be specifically activated later, so let's turn it off in the Inspector's Background area.

7 In the Graphical view, select the Menu 1 item.

The Inspector updates to display the menu's properties.

8　In the Menu Inspector, select the Menu tab.

9　In the Background Layers area, deselect the Overlay layer.

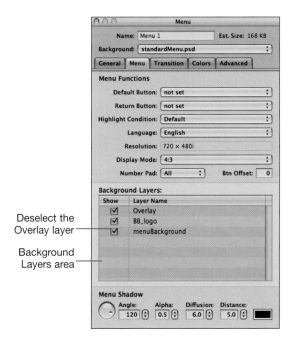

Deselect the
Overlay layer

Background
Layers area

In the Menu Editor, the Photoshop document's Overlay layer is no longer displayed.

10　While you're in the Menu Inspector, change the menu's name to *Main Menu*.

11 In the Menu Editor, drag hotspots around the menu's buttons, and give each button a name that reflects its target.

This menu is well on its way to being finished. Next you need to add the overlay layer to create the selected and activated button states.

Exploring the Overlay Layer

In the last exercise, you took a look at the overlay layer in the **standardMenu.psd** Photoshop document, and you saw that the overlay layer contained three squares. Furthermore, each square consisted of three grayscale colors. Let's take a moment to explore this overlay layer further.

First, those three grayscale colors are distinct shades of black—specifically, 100% black, 66% black, and 33% black. (There's also a fourth color in the overlay layer: 0% black, which is white.) The second thing to be aware of is that the shapes on the overlay layer exactly cover the black squares on the menu background. When properly configured in DVD Studio Pro, the shapes from the overlay layer provide a template used to map colored button states over the menu background. This theory may seem a bit esoteric at first, but a bit of practice shows exactly what's going on. Let's configure this overlay.

> **TIP** All transparent areas in an overlay image are mapped to 0% black (100% white).

100% black
66% black
33% black

1 Without releasing the mouse button, drag the **standardMenu.psd** item from the Assets container over the Menu Editor.

The Drop palette appears.

2 Choose Set Overlay.

In the Menu Inspector, at the very bottom of the General tab is an Overlay File pop-up menu. This menu now shows that the **standardMenu.psd** asset is used as the overlay file. Directly under the Overlay File menu is an Overlay Layer pop-up menu. It currently says menuBackground, but this is not the correct overlay layer. By default, this menu displays the first, or lowest, layer in the Photoshop document. The overlay layer in this document is a couple of layers up, so you'll need to select it from the Overlay Layer pop-up menu in the Inspector's General Tab.

3 In the Inspector, click General Tab

In the middle of the General Tab there is an overlay file area.

4 From the Overlay Layer pop-up menu, choose the layer named Overlay.

5 In the Menu Editor, select a menu button.

6 Use the button state controls at the bottom of the Menu Editor to preview your normal, selected, and activated button states.

The keyboard shortcut for toggling through button states is W.

TIP ▶ If you can't see the button state controls in the Menu Editor, your screen resolution might not have enough width. To fix this, make the Menu Editor wider, and the button state buttons will magically appear. You can also access the button state controls from the View menu.

Normal button state control

Selected button state control

Activated button state control

Presto! Colored buttons. As you can see, DVD Studio Pro is mapping colors onto the menu, based on the shapes in the overlay layer.

Using Advanced Overlays with Grayscale Color Mapping

In Lesson 11, you imported a four-color overlay from a Photoshop file to use in place of the simple overlay for the Tiger DVD's main menu. In this exercise, we'll go deeper by working with three grayscale colors defined for our Photoshop overlay image. As you'll see, grayscale mapping gives you lots of control over the look of your button states.

The grayscale colors in the overlay image are called *key colors*. They literally provide a key that tells DVD Studio Pro how to create colored button states.

However, DVD Studio Pro still needs to know what colors to map onto the overlay's key colors. You provide this information by configuring the key colors in Menu Inspector's Colors tab.

TIP ▶ Grayscale color mapping is sometimes called *luma mapping,* because it's actually the luminance, or brightness, of the grayscale colors that DVD Studio Pro reads.

1 In the Button Inspector, select the Colors tab.

2 From the Overlay Colors area, select Advanced.

Choose Advanced

Grayscale color key

3 Ensure that the Mapping Type is set to Grayscale.

The Inspector's Key area updates to display a grayscale color key. All of the grayscale values used in the overlay layer have their own color and opacity settings.

NOTE ▶ When you use grayscale mapping, you need a good monitor! If you are using a monitor with poor contrast reproduction, designing grayscale overlays is difficult because you will not see a noticeable difference between 100% black and 66% black. To solve this problem, you can use chroma (chrominance) mapping. Chroma mapping is available from the Colors tab's Mapping Type area, and it works exactly the same way as grayscale mapping, except instead of using 100% black, 66% black, and 33% black in your overlay image, you use 100% black, 100% red, and 100% blue. For more information, refer to Lesson 11.

4 Ensure that the Selection State is set to Selected.

You'll configure the selected state colors first. After they are set, you will move on to configure the activated colors.

5 Select different colors and opacity values for each of the grayscale values in the overlay, except for the 0% black (white) value.

Color patches ⎯⎯⎯
Opacity settings ⎯⎯⎯

6 Click the buttons you created in the Menu Editor, and see how the selected button's overlay changes to the chosen colors and opacity values.

7 In the Inspector, set the Selection State to Activated.

Notice that enabling the Activated Selection State causes two things to happen in the Menu Editor. First, the selected button updates to display the activated colors. Second, the button state controls along the bottom of the Menu Editor change to visually reinforce that you are currently looking at the menu's activated button states. As you can see, the Inspector's Selection State area lets you cycle through the display of button states in the Menu Editor in exactly the same way as clicking the Button State controls at the bottom of the Menu Editor. It's a handy little trick to know!

Activated button state Activated button state control

8 Select colors and opacity values for each of the activated state's grayscale colors.

9 Simulate the menu and check out your handiwork.

Customizing Button Colors

The color palette in the Inspector's Colors tab provides access to only 16 colors. That's a pretty limited selection, and you may need to change the default colors to something a bit more appropriate for your menu design.

Fortunately, DVD Studio Pro gives you access to full 16-bit color for your buttons. Use the following steps to choose any color you need to preserve the integrity of your presentation.

Only 16 colors are available from the Color palette

1 At the bottom of the Colors tab, click the Edit Palette button.

The Color palette drops down from the top of the Inspector.

2 Click the red color patch.

The Color Picker appears.

3 From the Color Picker, choose a color.

TIP ▶ Use the Color Picker's magnifying glass to sample colors from anywhere on your screen, including the Menu Editor! This is a great trick when you need to match your button states to existing colors on the menu.

Magnifying glass

4 Close the Color Picker.

The Color palette updates with the new color.

5 Click the Color palette's Close button.

The new color is now available from all of the Menu Inspector's color patches.

Saving New Default Colors

This project will use several menus by the time we're done with it. To preserve the continuity of your display, each menu should use button states that are the same color. Although you could hand-configure each new menu to use the proper colors, there's a better way.

Using the Inspector's Save As Default button, you can make the current color and opacity values the default color and opacity values for all newly created menus. (Menus that already exist in the project will not be changed to match the new colors.) This expedites your workflow, because when you create a new menu, all the effort that goes into specifying overlay colors will have already been done. At that point, it's just a simple matter of defining button hotspots for the new menu, and your work is almost finished.

1 In the bottom-right corner of the Inspector's Colors tab, click the Save As Default button.

The colors specified for the selected and activated button states are now saved as the default button state colors. This change is also reflected in DVD Studio Pro's Preferences.

2 Choose DVD Studio Pro > Preferences.

The Preferences window opens.

3 Select the Colors pane, and make sure the Show pop-up menu is set to Menu.

As you can see, the colors you selected in the Menu Inspector have now been saved as DVD Studio Pro's default colors. If need be, you can also change the default colors, including the colors in the button state Color palette, right here in the Preferences window.

4 Close the Preferences window.

Refreshing Assets

By now you've seen that DVD Studio Pro will happily work with layered Photoshop files. Although you *could* flatten all the finished menu's background layers into a single layer before bringing the document into DVD Studio Pro, it is usually best to leave your menu's layer structure intact. When you change a source asset, this change ripples into your DVD Studio Pro project, so leaving the menu's layer structure intact gives you a lot of flexibility to go back and make changes later, if necessary. This time-saving feature is quite powerful, so we suggest you use it!

In fact, we'll put it to practice right now. Take a close look at the menu you are currently working on, and notice that the drop shadow has disappeared from the Black Box logo. This is because the drop shadow was added to the logo as a layer style in Photoshop.

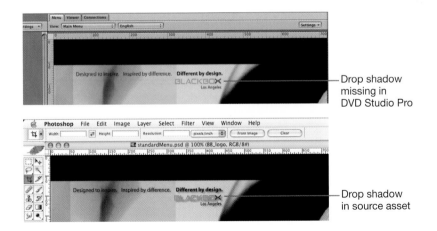

Drop shadow missing in DVD Studio Pro

Drop shadow in source asset

Photoshop uses a layer's alpha channel to create layer styles, which it generates in real time whenever the document is open. But note that these layer styles are not actually represented as pixels on the layer. DVD Studio Pro does not know how to generate these Photoshop layer styles, so if you want layer styles to be visible in your DVD-Video project, you'll need to turn all layer styles into actual pixels that DVD Studio Pro can see and display.

1 In the Assets tab, Ctrl-click the **standardMenu.psd** asset and choose Open in Editor from the shortcut menu.

The source asset opens in Photoshop. In the Layers palette, there is a small "f" symbol on the right side of the BB_logo layer. This is the Layer Style icon, which denotes that at least one layer style is attached to the layer.

Layer uses layer styles

TIP ▶ To add layer styles to a layer in a Photoshop document, simply double-click the layer in the Layers tab. A dialog, as shown in the next part of the exercise, will prompt you to select and edit the style you wish to apply to the layer.

2 In the Layers palette, double-click the Layer Style icon.

The Layer Style window opens. Currently there is a drop shadow applied to this layer, but you could also enable Bevel and Emboss, Outer Glow, or any other layer style that fits.

Drop Shadow layer style

3 Click OK to close the Layer Style window.

In the next few steps, you will render the layer style into actual pixels that DVD Studio Pro can see.

4 In the Layers palette, make sure the BB_logo layer is selected.

5 At the bottom of the Layers palette, click the Create New Layer icon (the one that looks like a turning page).

A new layer is added above the BB_logo layer, and this new layer is automatically selected.

6 In the Layers palette, select the BB_logo layer once again.

7 Link the new layer to the BB_logo layer by clicking its linking box.

Layer 1 is linked to BB_logo layer

BB_logo layer is selected

At the top-right corner of the Layers palette is a small button with a right-pointing triangle. When clicked, it reveals the Layers palette menu. This menu contains several options for working with layers, including a few options used to combine layers together. Let's do this now.

8 From the Layers palette menu, choose Merge Linked (or press Cmd-E).

The layer style is rendered, and the Layer Style icon no longer appears on the right edge of the BB_logo layer.

9 Save the document.

10 Return to DVD Studio Pro, and look at the menu in the Menu Editor.

DVD Studio Pro understands that you've resaved the file, and it updates to display the drop shadow under the BB_logo layer.

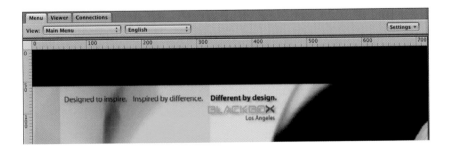

Advanced Menu Audio

Without audio, a menu is only half an experience. And with tools like Apple Soundtrack at your disposal, there's no reason not to add audio to your menus. (The menu audio in this project was created and mixed in Soundtrack.)

The DVD-Video specification includes only a few compliant digital audio formats. In this case, "compliant" simply means legal for use in DVD-Video. The compliant formats include the following:

▶ AC-3 (Dolby Digital)

▶ 16- or 24-bit, 48 or 96 kHz PCM (Pulse Code Modulated—AIFF, WAV, or SDII)

▶ MPEG1-Layer2

▶ DTS

If you include any of these audio formats in your project, DVD Studio Pro will use them in their native format. On the other hand, if you add files in non-compliant digital audio formats, such as MP3 or AAC, or 44.1 kHz PCM files ripped from an audio CD, DVD Studio Pro will happily accept them and let you add them to project items. However, when you build the project, DVD Studio Pro must first encode the files to 48 kHz, 16-bit DVD-Video–compliant files before it multiplexes the DVD-Video. With these rules in mind, let's add some audio to the menu.

> **TIP** ▶ DVD Studio Pro will let you import and work with any type of audio file that QuickTime understands. If you're unsure whether or not DVD Studio Pro will play a particular audio file, try opening and playing the file in QuickTime first.

NOTE ▶ DVD Studio Pro will accept DTS audio files, but the Simulator does not include a DTS decoder. If you add DTS files to your project, you will need to build a finished disc and test it in a DVD-Video player that supports DTS playback before you will be able to hear the DTS audio.

1 In the Assets tab, open the Audio folder and take a look inside.

This folder contains several audio files. If you take a close look at the Assets container's Type column, you can see there is a mix of AC-3 and PCM files.

NOTE ▶ If you can't see the Assets tab's Type column, grab the right edge of the Assets tab's quadrant and drag it right to make the Assets tab wider.

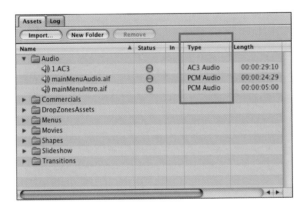

2 In the Graphical view, select the Main Menu tile.

The Inspector updates to display the menu's properties.

3 Click the Inspector's General tab.

Toward the bottom of the General tab is an audio area that is currently empty. Watch this area as you add audio files to the menu.

4 From the Assets tab, drag the **mainMenuIntro.aif** asset over the Menu Editor, and use the Drop palette to add the audio file to your menu.

In the Inspector, the Menu tab's Audio area updates to show that the **mainMenuIntro.aif** file has been added to the menu.

5 In the bottom-right corner of the Menu Editor, click the Motion button.

The audio plays.

6 Click the Motion button once again to stop audio playback.

Concatenating Audio Files

You can add multiple audio files to the same menu, and DVD Studio Pro will automatically concatenate them, or string them together, into one long audio stream. However, there is a small catch with concatenating audio—and, in fact, with menu audio in general:

Per the DVD-Video specification, all audio streams used in all project menus must be exactly the same format.

For example, you cannot mix AIFF with AC-3 files, and you also cannot mix 5.1 AC-3 files with 2.0 AC-3 files—"the same" means exactly the same! If you add different formats of audio streams to different project menus, DVD Studio Pro will stop and display the following warning dialog when you attempt to build your project.

MORE INFO ▶ There are several situations in which you might want to concatenate audio in a menu. For starters, you can easily add several audio streams together to make a standard still menu play longer. But there's an even better reason.

When a menu loops, the transition from the end of the menu to the beginning is not seamless, and you will always experience a short glitch (a pause) in audio playback. If you are using a background loop that is perfectly trimmed, such as a drum loop, this inherent glitch will make it impossible to create a continuous, seamless playback loop. However, if there's enough space on the disc, you can concatenate several copies of the same loop together, perhaps for several minutes or more! This makes it unlikely that the viewer will sit and watch the menu long enough to hear the glitch when the menu times out and replays.

1 From the Assets container, drag the **mainMenuAudio.aif** asset over the Menu Editor, and use the Drop palette's Add to Existing Audio option.

In the Menu Editor, the General tab's Audio area updates to show two different files.

TIP ▶ To delete an audio file from the menu, select it in the Menu Inspector's Audio area and press Delete.

Two audio files

Total duration of menu audio

While DVD Studio Pro has concatenated the audio files, it has not automat-
ically updated the duration of the menu. In the bottom-left corner of the
Inspector's Audio area, the total Audio duration is displayed (00:00:29:29).
Let's quickly update the menu's duration to match the duration of the audio
streams. To do that, we need to switch back to the General tab.

2 In the Inspector, click the General tab.

Halfway down the General tab's right edge there is a Duration setting.

3 Type *00:00:29:29* into the General tab's Duration field, and press Return.

4 In the bottom-right corner of the Menu Editor, click the Motion button.

The audio plays, and after the **mainMenuIntro.aif** file is finished, the **mainMenuAudio.aif** file begins to play.

5 Click the Motion button one more time to turn off the audio.

6 From the Assets tab, drag the **1.AC3** asset over the Menu Editor, and use the Drop palette's Add to Existing Audio option.

A warning dialog appears. This dialog says the audio file does not match the menu's existing audio file format, so DVD Studio Pro won't allow you to add it to the menu. Why? Because it's an AC-3 file, and the other files in the menu are AIFFs. Remember: All audio files in all project menus must be exactly the same format. When it comes to menu audio, you can't mix and match.

Using Motion Menus

It may surprise you to learn that in the end, all menus are basically motion menus. DVD-Video is designed to display only MPEG video streams. Consequently, all other graphics that go into your project—including Photoshop documents used in still menus and slideshows—must be converted to the MPEG format. When DVD Studio Pro builds your project, it encodes still menus, such as the standard menu you're working on, into MPEG stills (technically, I-frames, but more on that in Lesson 17). So the question must be asked: If still menus are turned into MPEG video, can you also use *moving* MPEG video in menus? The answer, of course, is yes. Doing so creates a *motion menu*, and it's a very easy process.

1 In the Assets tab, open the Menus folder and locate the
 MotionMainMenu.mov asset.

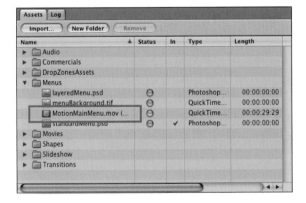

2 Double-click the **MotionMainMenu.mov** asset.

The movie opens in the Viewer and begins playing. It shows a sequence of fades that build the menu on the screen.

3 In the Graphical tab, double-click the Main Menu tile to open it in the Menu Editor.

4 From the Assets tab, drag the **MotionMainMenu.mov** file over to the Menu Editor, and choose Set Background.

The video asset is assigned as the menu's background. Note that the highlights you've created stick to the menu, so there's no need to alter your highlights after adding the new background asset.

5 In the bottom-right corner of the Menu Editor, click the Motion button.

Motion button

You've just created a motion menu. But there's currently a bit of a problem. For starters, the button overlays appear before the buttons fade onto the screen. Additionally, there are no normal button states. Problems indeed, but easy ones to solve.

No normal button states

Highlights appear before menu buttons fade in

Setting a Loop Point

The motion menu you're working on has a 5-second intro that consists of the button graphics fading onto the screen. Because the fade section acts as a transition into the menu, you need to ensure that the button overlays do not appear until after this transition has finished. In DVD Studio Pro, you can achieve this goal by setting a menu *loop point*.

As the name implies, the loop point setting tells the DVD player where to jump back to when the menu is set to loop. For example, at the end of this menu's video clip, the DVD-Video player will refocus its laser back to the beginning of the menu and play it all over again. However, you do not want viewers to see the intro transition every time the menu loops, so setting a loop point ensures that the laser jumps back to the point defined as the loop point, instead of to the beginning of the menu.

> **NOTE ▶** If you use DVD Studio Pro's menu-compositing features to add text or drop zones to a menu, you will *not* be able to set a loop point.

1 In the Menu Inspector, select the General tab.

At the top of the General tab are three display areas: one for the menu start, one for the menu loop point, and one for the menu end. You can use the Start and End settings to trim the beginning or end of the video used in your menu, but for the purpose at hand, you are going to adjust the Loop Point setting.

2 On the Loop Point setting, click the increment button.

Increment button

As you click the Increment button, a few things happen. First, the Menu Editor updates to display the video frame indicated by the Loop Point setting. This is important, because as you design motion menus, the Menu Editor, when not in motion, will always display the frame exactly at the loop point, not the beginning or end frames. Second, the timecode setting to the left of the Increment button jumps by 15 frames every time you click to increase the loop point position. As you'll come to see in Lesson 17, all MPEG streams are divided into groups of pictures, and each group of pictures is typically 15 frames in duration. Furthermore, each group of pictures has a single I-frame, and it's these I-frames that the loop point must latch on to. For this reason, you cannot create frame-accurate loop points inside DVD Studio Pro. Keep this in mind when designing your motion menus!

TIP ▶ If you need to set a loop point that is frame-accurate, there's a bit of extra work involved. First, open the source video asset in Final Cut Pro. Then set a chapter or compression marker on exactly the frame where you want the loop point to occur. Next, export an MPEG-2 stream directly from Final Cut Pro's Timeline, either using the File > Export > Using QuickTime Conversion option, or the File > Export > Using Compressor option. When the file is encoded to MPEG-2, the frame you tagged with the chapter marker will become an I-frame. Back in DVD Studio Pro, you can then set the loop point to this I-frame, and your menu will loop back to exactly the frame you require.

3 In the Loop Point timecode box, type *5.0* and press Return.

The loop point jumps to the frame at timecode value 00:00:05:00. Notice that you didn't have to type all of the zeros in the timecode value. DVD Studio Pro is smart, and it realizes that "5.0" means second number 5, frame number 00. It's a handy workflow feature!

4 Set the General tab's At End pop-up menu to Loop.

5 Simulate the menu.

OK, the overlays now display only after the button graphics fade onscreen. This menu is starting to look good. However, there are still no normal button states. You'll fix this in the next section.

6 Close the Simulator.

Advanced Overlay Tricks

Earlier in this lesson, you adjusted the selected and activated overlay colors for this menu, but you left the normal state overlays untouched. This was because the normal state for the buttons was already included in the background graphics, so there was no need to set up the normal state overlays—doing so would have obscured the graphics on the menu background below. However, the video you added as the menu background does not have normal button states on it, so let's use the normal state overlays to show viewers where to click.

1 In the Menu Inspector, choose the Colors tab.

2 In the Colors tab's Selection State area, select Normal.

All overlay key colors are set to 0% opacity

Notice that all the key colors in the normal state are assigned colors, but these colors use an opacity value of 0, which means they are currently completely transparent.

3 Increase the opacity values for the 33% black and 66% black key colors only.

Why 66% and 33% black? As you may recall, the overlay uses three different grayscale values. The areas covered by 33% and 66% black are exactly the same size as the black square from the original background graphics. If you look at the Menu Editor, you'll see that there are now multicolored squares exactly where the normal button states should be. However, these squares should be black, so let's adjust the color next.

4 Set both the 33% and 66% key colors to black.

5 Simulate the menu.

The overlays turn on only after the intro transition has finished, and the normal button states are now displayed. The menu now looks exactly as it should.

Creating Layered Menus

Layered menus are not often used in DVD-Video. They suffer from a few basic problems. For example, they are slow to respond when a user interacts with them on a computer, and they can't have audio or motion backgrounds. But don't stigmatize layered menus for what they can't do, because these menus have definite uses.

Layered menus use a separate layer in a Photoshop document for the menu background graphics, and additional layers for each button state. When a button is selected or activated, DVD Studio Pro enables the entire layer for that button state.

The advantage of layered menus is that selecting a button can "turn on" graphics outside of a button's hotspot. This is a common feature of the Internet, where, for example, selecting a button causes information elsewhere on the Web page to update. Corporate DVD-Videos are often based on concepts gleaned from the Internet, and these presentations sometimes have an information area on the menu that updates as product pictures are selected. Layered menus provide this type of interactivity, whereas standard menus can't.

Additionally, layered menus are not limited by the 16 colors in the overlay key color palette. Button states on a layered menu can be any color or design that you can create in Photoshop. With a bit of imagination, layered menus can be much more visually engaging than standard menus.

1 In the Assets tab's Menus folder, Ctrl-click the `layeredMenu.psd` asset and choose Open in Editor from the shortcut menu.

The menu opens in Photoshop.

Button state layers

Background layers

2 In the Layers palette, use the Eye icon to turn the layers on and off, and check out the graphics on each layer.

As you turn layers on and off, notice that each layer is named for the graphics of the button state it contains. Also notice the empty layers named with a dash (–). These layers are used to group button states together. As you'll come to see, these "dash layers" make it easier to identify which layer is which when you're creating button states in DVD Studio Pro.

Adding a Layered Menu

Follow these steps to add a layered menu to your project.

1 Back in DVD Studio Pro, click the Graphical tab; then Ctrl-click in an empty space in the Graphical view to bring up the contextual menu, and choose Add > Layered menu.

A layered menu item is added to the Graphical view, and the Menu Editor updates to display the new menu, which is currently empty. In the Graphical view, there's not much visual difference between the layered menu item and

the standard menu item you created earlier. Layered menus are a darker shade of blue, but that's all there is to visually differentiate the two. Don't confuse them with standard menus, because you can't make a layered menu in a standard menu item!

Standard menu Layered menu

NOTE ▶ In the Outline tab and in the toolbar, there is a bit of a visual difference between layered and standard menus. If you take a close look, you'll see that standard menus have a single layer in the icon, whereas layered menus have two layers.

Layered menu icon
 Standard menu icon

2 From the Assets tab, drag the **layeredMenu.psd** asset and hold it over the Menu Editor.

The Drop palette appears.

3 Choose Set Background, No Layers Visible.

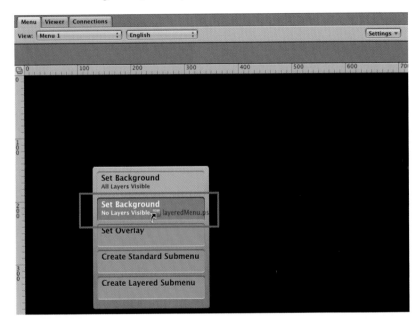

Why Set Background, No Layers Visible? Because layered menus commonly have lots of layers used for button states but only one or two layers used for the background. It's much easier to turn on one or two layers than to turn off dozens of button state layers. So when you add layered menu assets using the Menu Editor's Drop palette, it's easier to start with no layers visible.

4 In the Inspector, looking at the General tab's Background area, enable the bottom two layers in the list: BB_logo and menuBackground.

5 Drag out hotspots for all three of the menu's buttons.

6 Name the buttons *Before*, *After*, and *Main Menu*.

Creating Layered Menu Buttons

The trick to layered menus is the way you assign layers to button states. Each individual button on the menu will use unique layers from the Photoshop document. Let's start the process by configuring the Before button.

1 In the Menu Editor, select the Before button.

The Inspector updates to display the button's properties. Notice that in layered menus, the Button Inspector has a Layers tab, which isn't there when you're working with standard menus.

2 In the Inspector, choose the Layers tab.

The Layers tab is divided into four columns. There's a column each for the normal, selected, and activated states, and a final column displaying all the layers in the Photoshop document.

NOTE ▶ The layers named with a dash are those empty layers you saw in the Photoshop document a few pages ago. Notice how the "dash layers" help to visually group button states together.

3 In the Normal column, select the check box for the Before – Normal layer.

4 Finish this button by selecting the appropriate check boxes for the Before button's selected and activated states.

5 Repeat steps 1 through 4 to assign button states for the menu's After and Main Menu buttons.

6 Simulate the menu, and use the mouse to interact with the menu buttons.

Graphic updates as you interact with menu buttons

The graphic on the right side of the screen updates as you select each new button, giving you a preview of the item the button targets. Cool!

7 Save your project.

▶ Layered Menu Magic

Layered menus are not part of the DVD-Video specification. In fact, they are unique to DVD Studio Pro. When you build the project, DVD Studio Pro effectively makes a separate menu for each button state in the layered menu and uses auto actions to jump among this series of new, single-state menus. The reason you can't have audio in layered menus is directly related to this fact—it's because you can't have a single audio stream stretch across multiple menus.

Continues on next page

Additionally, every time the DVD-Video player's laser has to refocus on a different project item, you will always experience a short pause, sometimes up to a second or more. A layered menu is converted into a series of menus that the DVD-Video player must jump through as buttons are selected and activated. All of this jumping around means that layered menus are slow to respond to viewer interaction.

By the way, DVD Studio Pro is not doing anything here that you wouldn't be able to create manually in this program or other DVD authoring software. It takes time, but you can create your own series of *standard menus* and use the Auto Action function to have buttons automatically jump from menu to menu as they are selected. Remember, standard menus can use audio, so this is a great way to create the illusion of button sounds that trigger when a button is selected. Who said you couldn't have mouse-over sounds?

Standard menu Button Inspector

Advanced tab

Auto Action function

Lesson Review

1. DVD Studio Pro lets you create two types of menus. What are they?

2. The Square Pixel dimensions for creating menus in Photoshop are what?

3. An overlay can use three shades of black, which map to different colors and/or opacity values for your buttons in DVD Studio Pro. What are the types of shades of black?

4. The color pallet in DVD Studio Pro lets you choose from X number of different colors for you buttons. X equals what?

5. True or false: If you change a source asset on your hard drive, the change ripples into your DVD Studio Pro project.

6. Unless the motion button is enabled, the Menu editor always shows you which frame of a motion menu?

Answers

1. Standard overlay menus, and (Photoshop) layered menus.

2. 720 X 534 square pixels.

3. 100% Black, 66% Black, and 33% Black.

4. 16, though you can edit the pallet to make those 16 colors any color you desire.

5. True.

6. The frame directly under the Loop point, as set in the Menu Inspector's General tab.

Keyboard Shortcuts

| W | Toggles between button states |

15

Lesson Files	Lessons > 15_Creating_Menu_Elements-Start
Media	Media > Blackbox folder
Time	This lesson takes approximately 60 minutes to complete.
Goals	Convert a button to a drop zone
	Discover how to make your own DVD Studio Pro shapes
	Learn how to use styles to quickly create menu elements
	Import a LiveType project file (.ipr file) and make a round-trip from DVD Studio Pro to LiveType
	Create a custom menu template
	Explore special-purpose template buttons

Creating Menu Elements

With a little creativity you can do some fairly advanced menu composition right in DVD Studio Pro's Menu Editor. For example, in previous lessons you added text to a menu background, placed text and graphics directly in menu buttons, and experimented with adding graphics to drop zones. Indeed, DVD Studio Pro's menu composition features are incredibly advanced for a DVD-authoring program.

This lesson expands upon your previous experiments in menu compositing by showing you how to create some of the menu elements you've been working with and by teaching you some advanced menu design techniques. You'll learn how to make your own shapes, and then add those shapes to a menu background to create drop zones and buttons. You'll also get some practice creating styles—in this case, a button style—as a way to unify the look and functionality of your menus.

Midway through this lesson, you'll get to experiment with round-trips between LiveType and DVD Studio Pro—a technique that will change

the way you work with LiveType and advance the way you make menus in DVD Studio Pro. As the lesson progresses, you will complete a menu layout and then save the layout as a custom menu template that will be used in a later lesson. There's a lot of cool stuff to cover in this lesson, so let's begin.

Drop Zones vs. Buttons

Drop zones and buttons are extremely similar. Fundamentally, a drop zone is just a type of button that the user doesn't interact with. In fact, buttons and drop zones are so similar that you can actually convert a button to a drop zone, and vice versa.

To experience the close relationship between drop zones and buttons first-hand, let's quickly create a drop zone by transforming a button in the Menu Editor.

1 In DVD Studio Pro, open the file named **15_Creating_Menu_Elements-Start** (or keep working on the project from the last lesson).

2 In the Assets tab, open the Menus folder and locate the asset named **menuBackground.tif**.

3 From the Assets tab, drag the **menuBackground.tif** asset over the Graphical view and release it.

By default, dropping a still picture asset into the Graphical view creates a new standard menu. Additionally, the Menu Editor updates to show the still image, with all layers visible. Take a close look at the Menu Editor and note that this new menu is just an empty background.

4 In the Assets tab, open the DropZonesAssets folder and select the
BB_Logo.psd asset.

The Inspector updates to display the asset's properties. Notice that this
asset is a single-layered Photoshop document, 400 pixels wide and
60 pixels tall.

5 Drag the **BB_Logo.psd** asset over the Menu Editor, and choose Create
Button from the Drop palette.

DVD Studio Pro creates an odd shaped button. Certainly, this button is
not 400 pixels wide and 60 pixels tall. To allow the **BB_Logo.psd** asset to
fully display, you'll need to change the button's dimensions.

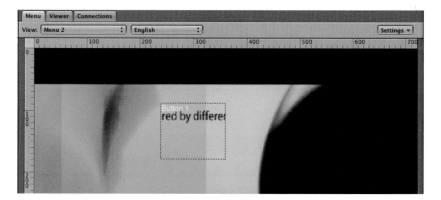

6 In the Menu Editor, select the new button.

The Inspector updates to display the button's properties.

7 Select the Button Inspector's Advanced tab.

At the bottom of the Advanced tab is a Coordinates & Size area.

8 Adjust the button's coordinates to the following:

Top = *60*

Bottom = *120*

Left = *50*

Right = *450*

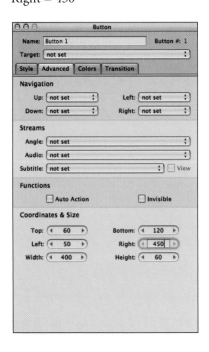

These coordinates alter the button's dimensions to 400 pixels wide by 60 pixels tall, and they also position the button correctly on the menu. You can now clearly see the **BB_Logo.psd** asset set in the button.

9 In the Menu Editor, Ctrl-click the new button and choose Convert Button to Drop Zone from the shortcut menu.

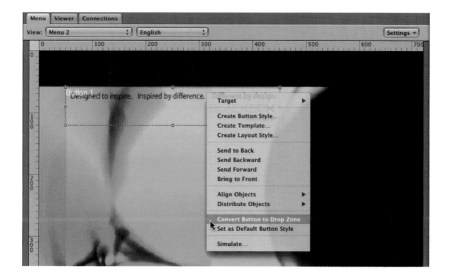

The button is converted to a drop zone. However, this drop zone isn't very complex. It simply displays a still image—in this case a corporate logo—on top of the menu background.

Introducing Shapes

Shapes are like little islands of graphical content that you can move around and reposition over a standard menu background. A shape may contain any graphical content that you can create on a Photoshop layer. You can even have transparent areas in a shape that allow the menu background and *set assets* to show through. A set asset is a still image or video that is "set" into the shape.

Shapes can be used as either drop zones or buttons. However, there are a few differences between the ways that drop zone and button shapes are created and used.

A *drop zone shape* is used to blend new graphical content with a pre-existing menu background. For example, video assets can be set in drop zones to quickly create a motion menu.

A *button shape* provides all the same functions as a drop zone, but it also contains information that DVD Studio Pro can use to create button highlights.

In the following exercise, you'll use one of DVD Studio Pro's default shapes to check out how shapes work.

1 In the Palette, click the Shapes tab.

At the top of the Shapes tab are three shape group buttons. The first button, Apple, displays the default shapes that come with DVD Studio Pro. The other two buttons, Custom and Project, are currently empty. But not for long, because you'll fill them with shapes over the course of this lesson.

NOTE ▶ Unlike DVD Studio Pro 3, where the shapes were stored inside the Application package itself, when you install DVD Studio Pro 4 your shapes are stored in the Startup Disk > Library > Application Support > DVD Studio Pro > Apple > Shapes folder.

2 Use the Palette's scroll bar to scroll down to the Frame Gold section.

3 Grab the FrameGold6 shape (or any of the Frame Gold shapes—for this experiment it doesn't matter which one you use) and drag it over the Menu Editor.

The Drop palette appears. Notice that the choices are Create Button and Create Drop Zone. Earlier in this lesson you saw how easy it is to convert buttons to drop zones and vice versa. Because buttons and drop zones are so similar, shapes can be used to create either.

4 Choose Create Drop Zone.

Because this is the second drop zone added to this menu, DVD Studio Pro creates a large drop zone named Drop Zone 2.

5 Use the handles around the edge of the drop zone to resize it so that it's smaller, with an aspect ratio that is roughly 4:3.

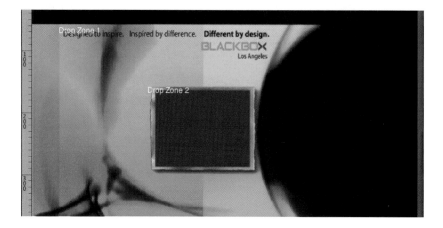

6 From the Asset container's DropZonesAssets folder, drag the **rusty.mov** asset over the drop zone, and choose Set Asset from the Drop palette.

The video asset is set in the button.

7 In the bottom-right corner of the Menu Editor, click the Motion button.

The set asset plays in the drop zone.

8 In the Menu Editor, select the drop zone and press Delete.

The drop zone is deleted.

Creating Drop Zone Shapes

A drop zone shape is like a small graphical program that is compiled by DVD Studio Pro. Like all programs, a shape must be carefully written by you, the graphical programmer. The output file for a shape is a Photoshop document. Concerning dimensions, the Photoshop document can be any size at all— 720 × 534, 242 × 242, 9 × 9, or whatever you require. You can always resize a shape inside DVD Studio Pro.

When it comes to the document's layer structure, however, there are strict conventions you must follow. Each shape should have four layers, and the content of each layer is rigidly defined.

The following exercise walks you through a typical shape file, demonstrating how shape layers are configured.

> **TIP** You can increase the size of a shape inside DVD Studio Pro, but doing so causes the shape to become blurry. To guard against this happening, always design shapes at the largest possible dimensions needed—you can then resize to make them smaller in DVD Studio Pro.

1 In the Assets tab's Shapes folder, Ctrl-click the **BB_Shape1.psd** asset and choose Open In Editor from the shortcut menu.

The **BB_Shape1.psd** asset opens in Photoshop. This file has four layers:

▶ The Icon layer, which is the top layer

▶ The Highlight layer, which is second from the top

▶ The Shape layer, which is second from the bottom

▶ The Mask layer, which is the bottom layer

The order of these layers is important to note because it determines how DVD Studio Pro compiles the shape. Layer names are not important, but the layer order and content is.

2 In the Layers palette, deselect the Eye icon to turn off visibility for every layer except the Mask layer.

Black: Set asset will be transparent

Grayscale: Set asset will have graduated transparency

White: Set asset will be opaque

Mask layer

This first layer defines which area of the shape will display set assets. For example, in the preceding exercise, you set a video clip into a drop zone. When the menu played, the video clip was visible through a rectangular portion of that drop zone. In that shape, the rectangle that the video played through was defined by a Mask layer similar to this one. The set asset will display only in the white and gray areas of the Mask layer.

The Mask layer itself uses grayscale to determine the transparency of areas in the set asset. Areas in the Mask layer that are 100% black create complete transparency in the set asset; areas of 100% white are completely opaque. Graduated transparency occurs wherever there are gray areas in the Mask layer. Light gray areas cause the set asset to appear less transparent than dark gray areas.

3 In the Layers palette, deselect the Eye icon for the Mask layer, and then select the Eye icon for the Shape layer.

Shape graphics

Graduated transparency

100% transparent

Shape layer

This is the second layer in the shape document, and this layer contains the graphics you will composite over the menu background. You can use graduated transparency in this layer to allow the menu background underneath to show through. And note that the Shape layer is rendered over the set asset when DVD Studio Pro compiles the project. With this in mind, make sure the Shape layer is transparent in any place you need the set asset to show through.

NOTE ▶ Graduated transparency is allowed in the Shape layer.

4 Skip the Highlight layer for a moment.

The Highlight layer is used for button shapes only. The shape you're look-ing at will be used as a custom drop zone; it's not a button shape, so it doesn't need any graphical content on this layer. (The Highlight layer is discussed in the upcoming section titled "Creating Button Shapes.") However, you still need the Highlight layer. Remember, DVD Studio Pro reads the order of layers in a shape file, so it's important that the third layer remain in the document, even if it's empty.

5 In the Layers palette, deselect the Eye icon for the Shape layer, and then select the Eye icon for the Icon layer.

The fourth layer serves as the thumbnail image assigned to the shape in DVD Studio Pro's Palette. The thumbnail lets you spot a shape at a glance, so make sure it properly represents the shape's visual content.

NOTE ▶ Make sure there is at least some graphic on the fourth layer, even if it doesn't represent the shape. If you leave this layer empty, no icon will appear in the Palette, which means there won't be anything to grab when you want to drag the shape into your project.

Importing Shapes

Once you've created a shape, you must import it into DVD Studio Pro's Palette before you can use it. The Palette's Shapes tab divides shapes into three different groups: Apple, Custom, and Project. Apple shapes are the default shapes installed with DVD Studio Pro; the Custom and Project groups are shapes that you make.

You determine whether to import shapes into the Custom or into the Project groups. The choice depends upon how you intend to use the shape in the future. If the shape should be available to all projects, whenever DVD Studio Pro is open, import the shape into the Custom group. If it's a shape designed for a particular project, and one you are unlikely to use in any other DVD-Video, import it into the Project group.

In the next exercise, you'll explore the differences between these two types of groups by importing a shape into both.

1 In the Palette, ensure that the Shapes tab is selected.

At the bottom of the Shapes tab is an Import button.

2 Click the Import button.

An Import window drops down from the Palette's title bar.

3 Use the Import window to locate the file named **BB_Shape1.psd**, and click Import.

4 Click the Custom group button.

The shape has been imported as a Custom shape. It is now available to all DVD Studio Pro projects. On your hard disk, you can now find this shape in the *Startup Disk* > Library > Application Support > DVD Studio Pro > Shapes folder. The path to the imported shape is traced in the following figure.

This shape has been designed explicitly for the Black Box DVD-Video, and you are unlikely to use it in any project other than the one you're currently working on. Why clutter up the Palette's Custom group with a shape you'll never use again? The Project group would be a far better home for this shape.

5 In the Palette, select the shape, and press the Delete key or click the Delete button at the bottom of the Palette.

A warning dialog tells you this shape will be permanently deleted from your hard disk. Keep this in mind, because when you clean up the Shapes tab, you clean the files right off your system.

6 Click OK to dismiss the warning dialog.

On your hard disk, the shape has been deleted from the *Startup Disk* > Library > Application Support > DVD Studio Pro > Shapes folder.

Shape has been deleted from the hard disk

Assets in the Assets tab cannot be imported as project-only Palette shapes in DVD Studio Pro 4. Therefore, you must delete **BB_Shape1.psd** so that you can import it into the Palette.

7 Ctrl-click the Palette's background, and choose Import from the shortcut menu.

The Import window drops down from the Palette's title bar.

8 Select the **BB_Shape1.psd** document, but don't import it just yet.

9 At the bottom of the Import window, select the "For this project only" check box, and then click the Import button.

10 Click the Palette's Project button.

The shape has been imported into the Project group.

Creating Drop Zones from Shapes

A few minutes ago you imported the **BB_Shape1.psd** shape into the shapes Project group. Let's add that shape to the project.

1 Drag the **BB_Shape1.psd** project shape over the Menu Editor, and choose Create Drop Zone.

The shape is added to the menu as a drop zone.

2 In the Menu Editor, select the drop zone and align it with the menu's right edge, in the center of the menu.

A horizontal yellow guide line will appear when the drop zone is exactly aligned to the middle of the menu, and you will not be able to differentiate between the edge of the drop zone and the menu background.

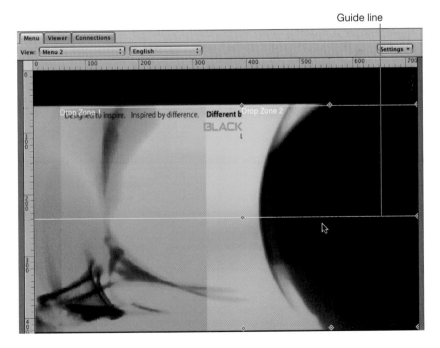

Guide line

3 From the Assets tab's DropZonesAssets folder, drag the **rusty.mov** file over the drop zone, and choose Set Asset.

4 In the bottom-right corner of the Menu Editor, click the Motion button.

Rusty the fish swims in the drop zone! What a clever little fish…

5 Click the Motion button once again to stop playback.

Changing Drop Zone Order

At the moment, there's a glaring problem with this menu. Drop Zone 2 is covering the right edge of Drop Zone 1. Fortunately, DVD Studio Pro lets you change the order of drop zones, which means you can composite drop zones on top of each other to build visually complex menus.

Drop Zone 2 is currently selected in the Menu Editor, so let's move it under Drop Zone 1.

1 In the bottom-left corner of the Menu Editor, click the Send Back One
Step button.

Drop Zone 2 is moved under Drop Zone 1, and you can now clearly see
the Black Box logo.

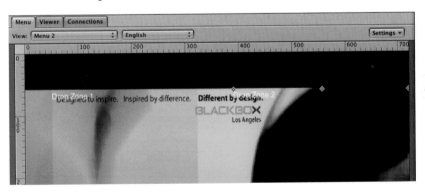

Creating Button Shapes

To create a button shape, you follow the same procedure you would for creating a drop zone shape, but with one important difference: You must create an overlay image on the shape's third layer.

1 In the Assets container's Shapes folder, Ctrl-click the **BB_ButtonShape1.psd** asset and choose Open In Editor from the shortcut menu.

Photoshop pops open to display the shape's source file.

2 Use the Layer palette's Eye icons to turn each layer on and off, and examine the contents of each layer.

Like the drop zone shape you explored earlier, this shape has exactly four layers. Unlike the drop zone shape, this shape has graphics on the Highlight layer. DVD Studio Pro will use these graphics to create button states. Let's take a moment to examine this layer, because its graphics have been configured in a very particular way.

3 Use the Layers palette's Eye icons to ensure that just the Highlight layer is visible.

4 Press Cmd-+ to zoom in on the image until it is large and easy to see.

Important: Note that you can see through certain portions of the graphics to the layers below!

When it comes to creating multicolored button states, shapes work differently from an overlay image. In the last lesson, you learned that an overlay image could use 100% black, 66% black, 33% black, and 0% black to create multicolored button states. Shapes, on the other hand, use opacity, not grayscale values, to create these multiple colors. Specifically, shapes use 100% opaque, 75% opaque, 50% opaque, and 0% opaque.

The following table shows how opacity maps to the four grayscale values you used in the last lesson.

Opacity Values in Shape Highlight Layers

Opacity Value	Equivalent Grayscale Value
100% opaque (0% transparent)	100% black
75% opaque	66% black
50% opaque	33% black
0% opaque (100% transparent)	0% black (100% white)

With these four opacity values in mind, let's import the button shape and see how these values translate into multicolored button states.

5 In DVD Studio Pro, import the shape into the Palette's Shapes tab (see "Importing Shapes," earlier in this lesson, for more information).

You can import the shape as either a custom or project shape. However, because this is a generic shape that could be used in many different types of projects, let's import it into the Custom shape group.

Shapes tab Custom group

Import shape button

6 Drag the new shape over the Menu Editor, and choose Create Button from
the Drop palette.

A new button is created on the menu.

7 Position the button as shown here.

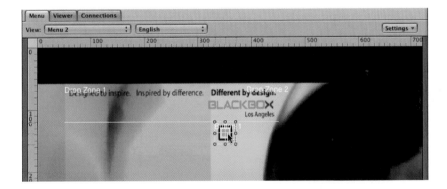

Notice that this button is a multicolored button. Furthermore, the key col-
ors assigned in the Inspector's Colors tab have been assigned using the
opacity values in the shape's third layer. Cool!

NOTE ▸ In Lesson 14 you changed DVD Studio Pro's default colors to a
custom set of colors. If you did not work through Lesson 14, your newly
created button might not display multiple colors.

Creating Styles

A *style* is a preconfigured menu element you can drag from the Palette to the Menu Editor to quickly unify the look and functionality of all your project's menus. Styles contain properties such as background graphics, button state colors, text fonts, and text color settings. In fact, styles will store any property that concerns the visual appearance of a menu element.

To create a style, you must first completely format a single menu element. The button you added in the last section is a menu element, and you are going to need several instantiations of this button later in the lesson. To save time later, let's finish formatting this button, and then save it as a button style.

1 In the Menu Editor, select the button.

The Inspector updates to display the button's properties. The first tab in the Button Inspector is the Style tab. This tab is used to format buttons, and all of the settings in this tab will be stored in the final button style.

2 In the Text area of the Inspector's Style tab, type *Button 1* and select the Shadow check box.

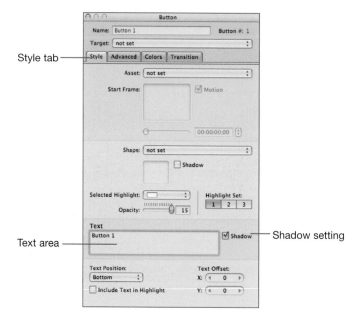

3 Use the Style tab's Position pop-up menu to align the text to the left of the button.

Position pop-up menu

4 Use the Style tab's Offset X adjustment to move the button text a bit farther left.

Offset X setting

There is a vertical line that splits this menu roughly in half. When the text is properly aligned, the distance between the text and this vertical line will be the same as the distance between the button graphics and the line.

Vertical line

5 Format the button text to 24-point Helvetica.

The button is styled correctly, and it looks pretty good! In the next section, you will save this button as a button style.

Saving Styles

Once a button is completely configured with all the necessary graphics and text, it's time to save it as a button style. Saved styles are added to the Palette's Styles tab. Similar to shapes, styles can be saved to one of two different groups: the Custom group and the Project group.

▶ Custom group styles are available to all DVD Studio Pro projects. These styles are saved in the *Startup Disk* > Library > Application Support > DVD Studio Pro > Apple > Styles folder.

▶ Project group styles are available only to the currently open project. The saved style will be stored in the project bundle itself, in the Contents > Resources > Styles folder.

> **TIP** ▶ To find a project style, Ctrl-click the project bundle (the file that DVD Studio Pro creates when you first save the project) and choose Show Package Contents from the shortcut menu.

The following steps demonstrate how to save this style into the Project group.

1 In the Menu Editor, Ctrl-click the newly styled button and choose Create Button Style from the shortcut menu.

A Save dialog drops down from the Palette's title bar.

2 Name your style *BB_Button_Style*.

Under the Save dialog's name text box are two check boxes: Project and Self-Contained.

▶ Select the Project check box if you want the style to be imported into the Project styles group. If you leave the check box unselected, the style will be imported into the Custom styles group.

▶ Select the Self-Contained check box if you'd like to move a copy of all the menu element's graphical content into the style. For example, all background graphics, shape elements, and set assets will be moved into the final, saved style.

TIP▶ You should always choose the Self-Contained check box when saving styles. Self-contained styles have all of the graphics necessary to re-create a menu element, whereas styles that are not self-contained continue to reference the original graphics files on your hard disk(s). If you delete those original graphics files, your style will no longer work.

3 Select the Project and the Self-Contained check boxes, and click Save.

NOTE ▶ Selecting the Project and Self-Contained check boxes will make your project file bigger, because all of the style's graphical elements will be copied into the project bundle.

4 In the Palette, select the Styles tab, then click the Project button, and finally click the Buttons button (for button styles).

The newly saved button style is now in the Project group.

NOTE ▶ If you did not select the Project check box when you saved the button style, the style will be located in the Custom group.

5 Drag the style from the Palette to the Menu Editor.

A new button is created.

6 Drag the style onto the menu four more times, for a total of six buttons.

7 Position the buttons as shown here.

Saving Default Styles

In the last exercise, you saw how easy it is to create new buttons from a button style. If you'd like to avoid a trip to the Inspector every time you need a new button, you can save a style as a default button style. Our menu needs a few more buttons. Specifically, it needs Back, Main Menu, and Next buttons. Let's add them now.

1 In the Menu Editor, Ctrl-click any button and choose Set as Default Button Style from the shortcut menu.

2 Draw three new buttons on the menu, and place them as shown here:

Each new button uses the new default button style and looks exactly the same as the other buttons on the menu.

3 Change the text on these three new buttons to *Back, Main Menu,* and *Next.*

Round-Trips to LiveType

LiveType is a titling and text animation tool that comes with Final Cut Pro. Little did anyone realize that LiveType would become the darling of DVD authors everywhere, because LiveType lets you quickly construct engaging motion menus.

DVD Studio Pro 4 contains several features that enhance its interaction with LiveType, including the following of particular note:

▶ Premultiplied alpha channels—The Menu Editor recognizes premultiplied alpha channels. LiveType creates movies with premultiplied alpha channels. This presents an excellent synergy, because if you set a rendered LiveType movie into a button or drop zone, you can see through transparent parts of the LiveType movie to the menu background below.

▶ Direct importing of .ipr files—An .ipr file is a LiveType project file. DVD Studio Pro lets you import .ipr files directly into your project and use them just as you would any other imported movie clip. This saves you time and disk space, because you no longer need to render finished LiveType movies. Just add the LiveType project file to your menu.

▶ Round-trips—Importing .ipr files has second distinct advantage: the round-trip. If you add an .ipr file to your DVD Studio Pro project, you can edit and resave the .ipr file, and the change will ripple into your DVD Studio Pro project.

Round-trips are an important workflow technique, so let's perform one to see how they work.

1 In the Assets container's DropZonesAssets folder, locate the **PlaceHolderText.ipr** asset.

This is a LiveType project file.

2 Drag the **PlaceHolderText.ipr** asset over drop zone 1, and choose Set Asset.

The .ipr file replaces the Black Box logo in drop zone 1. More to the point, the .ipr file perfectly fits the drop zone. Earlier you set this drop zone to be exactly 400 × 60 pixels, and the new .ipr file fits snugly in the drop zone.

The .ipr's current text tells us very little about the menu—it is placeholder text. Let's do a quick round-trip and change the text to *Chapter Menu.*

3 In the Assets tab, Ctrl-click the **PlaceHolderText.ipr** asset and choose Open In Editor from the shortcut menu.

The .ipr file opens in LiveType. This .ipr file has a single text track that says "Place-Holder Text." At first glance, you'll notice that this file is not 720 × 480 pixels. Indeed, it uses a custom project size. Let's check out the project's properties to discover this file's dimensions.

4 Choose Edit > Project Properties.

The Project Properties window opens. Notice that the file uses a width of 400 pixels and a height of 60 pixels. This is exactly the same size as the drop zone this asset is set in.

Width ⎯⎯⎯⎯

Height ⎯⎯⎯⎯

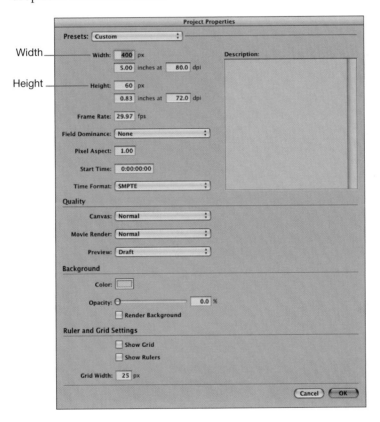

5 Click OK to close the Project Properties window.

6 In the LiveType Inspector, change the track's text to *Chapter Menu*.

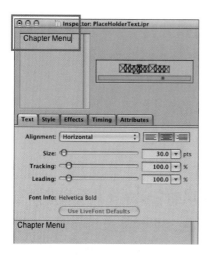

On LiveType's Canvas, the text updates to say "Chapter Menu."

7 Press Cmd-S (or choose File > Save).

LiveType resaves the project.

8 Switch back to DVD Studio Pro.

A few things have happened. First, the text in drop zone 1 has updated to say "Chapter Menu." Second, the Asset Refresh alert dialog informs you that the **PlaceHolderText.ipr** file has changed.

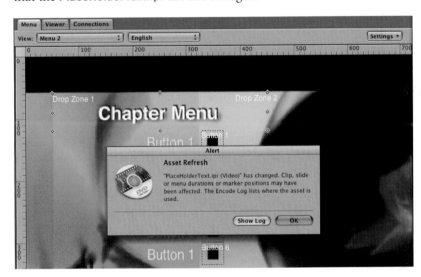

9 Click OK.

You've completed the round-trip. As you can see, it's now easier than ever to update LiveType project files that you add as drop zones, button text, or even complete menu backgrounds. Creating DVD-Video just got easier.

Creating a Menu Template

Our menu template is nearly complete. All buttons and drop zones have been added, but there are still a few tasks left. This menu will be used as a chapter menu, and you must ensure that its buttons are correctly named.

Creating Special-Purpose Template Buttons

All template buttons fall into one of two categories: general-purpose and special-purpose buttons.

General-purpose buttons use the default DVD Studio Pro naming structure, starting at Button 1. If a general-purpose button has a text element, as the buttons in our menu do, this text element will be changed to a marker's name when the template is assigned as a chapter menu.

> **NOTE** ▶ If a template button has an asset set into it, this asset will be changed to the marker's video when the template is assigned as a chapter menu.

Three special-purpose buttons are designed especially for chapter menus. To distinguish these buttons from their general-purpose counterparts, special-purpose buttons use an underscore before and after the button name. The special-purpose buttons are named _PREV_, _UP_, and _NEXT_. The _UP_ button links the chapter menu to the original menu (if applicable). If there are more chapters in the track than there are general-purpose buttons on the template, DVD Studio Pro will create a series of submenus until all chapters have been assigned to a menu button. With multiple menus created, viewers need a way to navigate forward and backward between the new chapter submenus. The _PREV_ and _NEXT_ buttons serve this purpose.

The menu you are working on has six general-purpose buttons, named Button 1 through Button 6. These buttons are correctly named. However, the

three special-purpose buttons at the bottom of the menu need to be renamed to match their functions. Let's do that now.

1 Name the template's Back button _PREV_.

2 Name the Main Menu button _UP_.

3 Name the Next button _NEXT_.

Saving a Template

Once a menu is completely configured with all the necessary graphics, text, and buttons, it's time to save it as a menu template. Saved templates are added to the Palette's Templates tab. As with styles and shapes, templates can be saved to one of two different groups: the Custom and Project groups.

▶ Custom group templates are available to all DVD Studio Pro projects. These templates are saved in the *Startup Disk* > Library > Application Support > DVD Studio Pro > Apple > Templates folder.

▶ Project group templates are available only to the currently open project. The saved template will be stored in the Project Bundle itself, in the Contents > Resources > Templates folder.

NOTE ▶ There is also a third templates group, called the Apple group. You cannot save a template into the Apple group, because this group stores only the templates that came with DVD Studio Pro. To access these templates, navigate to your Startup Disk > Library > Application Support > DVD Studio Pro > Apple > Templates folder.

When properly designed, templates are a very valuable commodity because you can use them to quickly create menus for any project. For example, you can use the template you're working on in other projects with only slight modifications to the graphics set in its drop zones. Each new template you build adds to your arsenal and provides expanded choices for future DVD designs. Consequently, it's typically best to save templates into the Custom group, as you'll do in the following steps, so that the templates are available to all future DVD Studio Pro projects.

1 Ctrl-click the Menu Editor's background, and choose Create Template from the shortcut menu.

A save dialog drops down from the top of the Palette.

2 Name the template *BB_Template.*

Under the Save dialog's name text box are two check boxes:

▶ Project—Select this check box if you want the template to be imported into the Project templates group. If you leave the check box unselected, the template will be imported into the Custom templates group.

▶ Self-Contained—Select this check box if you'd like to move a copy of all the graphical content for menu elements into the template. For example, all background graphics, shape elements, and set assets will be moved into the final, saved template.

TIP ▶ You should always select the Self-Contained check box when saving templates. Self-Contained templates have all of the graphics necessary to re-create the template, whereas templates that are not self-contained continue to reference the original graphics files on your hard disk(s). If you delete those original graphics files, your template will no longer work.

3 Select the Self-Contained check box.

4 Click Save.

5 In the Palette, select the Templates tab, and then click the Custom group button.

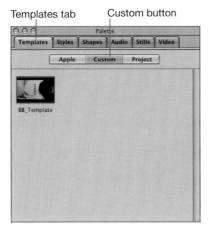

There's your template!

The menu you created the template from is still in your project. Because the template is complete and saved, you no longer need this original menu, so let's delete it right out of the project.

6 In the Graphical view, Ctrl-click the menu you've been working on, and choose Delete from the shortcut menu.

The menu is deleted.

Applying the Template

You've used templates at several points in previous lessons, and by now you should be familiar with how they work. In the following steps, you will apply your new template as a chapter index menu that links to ten slides in a slideshow.

There's one important thing to note, however. Because the slideshow has ten slides, but the template you created has only six general-purpose buttons, DVD Studio Pro will need to create two separate chapter menus. One will link to the slideshow's first six slides; the second will link to the slideshow's remaining four slides.

Ten slides

1 From the Assets tab, grab the entire Slideshow folder, drag it over the Graphical view, and drop it.

 DVD Studio Pro is smart, and it realizes that because the folder contains still images, it should create a slideshow. Consequently, a slideshow is automatically created and populated with the still images in the Slideshow folder.

2 In the Graphical view, select the main menu item.

The Menu Editor updates to display the main menu.

3 From the Graphical view, hold down the Option key and drag the new
slideshow over the main menu's Gallery button.

A Drop palette appears.

4 Choose Create Chapter Index.

The Choose Template or Layout Style window appears.

5 Select the Templates tab and then click the Custom button.

Your newly saved template appears.

6 Select the template and click OK.

In the Graphical view, DVD Studio Pro creates two new submenus—chapter menus!

7 Ctrl-click the Main Menu item, and choose Simulate from the shortcut menu.

8 In the Simulator, activate the main menu's Gallery button.

The first of the two new chapter submenus comes onscreen. Note that this menu is missing one special-purpose button—the button named _PREV_ (the Back button). When DVD Studio Pro creates the chapter menu, it understands there is no chapter submenu before this one, so it automatically removes the Back button.

No Back button

9 In the Simulator, click the menu's Next button.

The Simulator jumps to the next chapter submenu. Notice that this submenu does not have a Next button, but it does have a Back button. When DVD Studio Pro creates the chapter submenu, it understands there is no chapter submenu after this one, so it automatically removes the special-purpose button named _NEXT_.

No Next button

10 In the Simulator, click the main menu button.

Because this special-purpose button is named _UP_, the Simulator jumps to the main menu.

11 Save the project file to the My_Projects folder on your hard drive.

Lesson Review

1. To adjust a button's pixel dimensions accurately, you must do what?

2. A button shape is made up of how many layers?

3. True or false: When you import a shape as a custom shape, it's only available to the project you are currently working on.

4. Shape files can have multicolor highlights. What three opacity values map to the different colors?

5. What happens when you make a style self-contained?

6. True or false: If you import a LiveType project file (a .ipr file), you can open it in Livetype, change it, and resave it, and the changes will ripple into your DVD Studio Pro project?

Answers

1. Select the button, then visit the Button inspector's Advanced tab > Coordinates and Size area.

2. Four: the Icon, Highlight, Shape, and Mask layer.

3. False. It's available to all projects.

4. 100% opaque, 75% opaque, and 50% opaque.

5. All of the assets needed to recreate the style are stored with the style.

6. True. This is called a round trip.

16

Lesson Files	Lessons > 16_Creating_Transitions-Start
Media	Media > Blackbox folder
Time	This lesson takes approximately 60 minutes to complete.
Goals	Learn how to apply and configure transitions in DVD Studio Pro
	Explore video transitions in menus
	Learn how to create and install custom alpha transitions

Lesson 16
Creating Transitions

A transition provides a segue from one project item to another, via a short video clip. For example, it's common practice to insert a dissolve between a menu button and the item it targets. When the viewer clicks the button, the DVD-Video fades to black, and then the target item fades onto the screen. This provides a less jarring display than having the menu just pop offscreen when a button is activated.

In the olden days of DVD-Video authoring, you had to composite all transitions by hand using an application like Final Cut Pro or Motion, and then add the transition clips as individual tracks or menus in DVD Studio Pro. It took a lot of time and effort. Now, using DVD Studio Pro's transition features you can create transitions with the click of a button. DVD Studio Pro 4 does all the heavy lifting by compositing the transitions for you, behind the scenes.

DVD Studio Pro 4 transitions come in three varieties:

▶ *Standard transitions* use special effects such as blurs, ripples, or dissolves to transform the exiting project item into the entering project item.

▶ *Video transitions* use a premade QuickTime movie to transition from a menu to a targeted project item.

▶ *Alpha transitions* use a set of specially designed QuickTime movies to transition from one project item to the next.

This lesson will show you how to use and configure all three types of transitions. If you're working in the video market, or if you're a video enthusiast looking to take your DVD authoring to the next level, you'll find that this lesson makes an important addition to your DVD-Video skills. In the DVD authoring world it's all about having a leg up on the competition, and at this point in time no other DVD-Video authoring application provides such handy, timesaving, and advanced transition features as DVD Studio Pro 4.

Applying a Transition

Transitions can be applied to menus, menu buttons, slideshows, individual slides, tracks, and still image clips added to a track. All transitions start with a frame from the exiting item and end with the first frame from the entering item. When the exiting item is a menu, the transition start frame will be one of the following:

▶ If the menu uses a still background, the start frame will be the menu with all buttons in their normal state.

▶ If the menu uses a motion background, the start frame will be the first frame of the background video clip, with all buttons in their normal states and all drop zones displaying the first frame of their set assets.

NOTE ▶ All transitions are rendered into video clips and then encoded to MPEG-2 when you build the project. This means transitions add to the file size of your finished DVD-Video. This is particularly significant for transitions added to menu items, because the encoded menu transition clips are stored in the same physical domain on the finished DVD as the menus (VTS_01_0.VOB). According to the DVD-Video specification, this domain must be less than 1 GB in size. Because DVD Studio Pro must render a separate transition clip for every button on every menu with a transition applied, it's quite easy to fill this domain past its bursting point.

1 Open the project named **16_Creating_Transitions-Start**, or keep working on the project you finished in Lesson 15.

2 In the Graphical view, select the Main Menu item.

The Inspector updates to display the menu's properties. The third tab in the Menu Inspector is the Transition tab.

3 In the Menu Inspector, select the Transition tab.

4 In the Transition tab, click and hold the Transition pop-up menu.

The Transition menu lists all of DVD Studio Pro's default transitions, including 19 standard and 14 alpha transitions.

NOTE ▶ DVD Studio Pro's default alpha transitions use names that begin with an alpha sign (α). These transitions are located in the Startup Disk > Library > Application Support > DVD Studio Pro > Apple > Transitions folder.

Standard transitions

Alpha transitions

Video transition

5 From the Transition menu, choose Fade Through Color.

NOTE ▶ In the Graphical view a small triangle appears in the bottom-right corner of the item the transition is applied to.

In the Inspector, the transition parameters area updates to display new settings. The settings on display vary depending on which type of standard transition you choose. For Fade Through Color, you'll see a Duration slider and color patch.

Transition parameters area

6 Click the color patch.

The Color Picker opens.

> **TIP** ▶ Use the Color Picker's color sampler (the magnifying glass) to match colors from anywhere on the screen, including the Menu Editor.

Color sampler Color Picker Color patch

7 Choose an orange color similar to the menu background.

8 Close the Color Picker.

9 In the Inspector's Transition tab, click the Preview button.

The Transition thumbnail displays a preview of the Fade Through Color transition.

Start thumbnail ——— ——— End thumbnail

Transition thumbnail

10 Simulate the menu.

11 In the Simulator, activate the Gallery button.

The Simulator fades from the main menu, through the orange color you selected in step 7, and into the chapter menu.

Using a Video Transition

Menu transitions offer an option not found in slideshow and track transitions—the capability to use a video clip. If you've used a video compositing application such as Final Cut Pro or Motion to create your own custom transitions, you'll love not having to jump to a new track that holds the video transition.

Additionally, DVD Studio Pro projects can have a maximum of 99 tracks. When you use the video transition option, the transition is tacked onto the end of the menu domain on the final DVD (VTS_01_0.VOB). As a result, no extra tracks are used for the transition clip.

> **NOTE ▶** The menu domain VTS_01_0.VOB must be less than 1 GB in size, so be careful that your video transitions are not too big for this domain on the final DVD-Video disc.

1 In the Assets container's Transitions folder, double-click the video named **MotionMenuTransition.mov**.

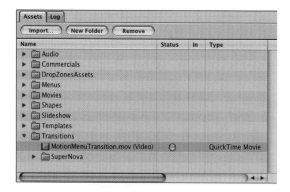

The clip plays in the Viewer. Notice that the clip is a transition that shows the main menu's text floating away. Let's return to the Menu Editor to assign this clip as a transition for the main menu's Gallery button.

2 Open the main menu in the Menu Editor, and select the Gallery button.

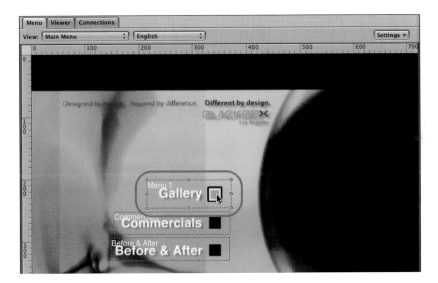

The Inspector updates to show the Gallery button's properties. Among the four tabs displayed in the Button Inspector is a Transition tab.

3 In the Button Inspector, select the Transition tab.

This tab is used to set a transition that is specific to the selected menu button. The Transition pop-up menu in this tab is currently set to Same as Menu, which means the button will use the same Fade Through Color transition that you specified in the last exercise.

4 Choose Video Transition from the Transition pop-up menu.

The transition parameters area updates to display an Asset menu. This is a hierarchical menu that lists all of the source files from the Assets tab that can be used as a video transition.

5 From the Asset pop-up menu, choose Transitions > **MotionMenu-Transition.mov**.

6 Simulate the main menu.

7 In the Simulator, activate the main menu's Gallery button.

The video transition segues from the main menu to the chapter menu.

NOTE ► You may see a small pause of black screen after the video transition ends and before the chapter menu comes onscreen. This occurs because the Simulator cannot composite the chapter menu fast enough to show it onscreen directly after the video transition has finished playing. Rest assured that on the final DVD-Video disc, the transition will play into the next menu without the black screen occurring.

8 Close the Simulator.

Using Alpha Transitions

An alpha transition is like a supercharged video transition. Similar to video transitions, alpha transitions use a video clip to segue from one project item to another. Unlike video transitions, the video clip in an alpha transition can have transparency, allowing you to see both the exiting and entering project items onscreen as the transition clip plays.

Because of this increased complexity, alpha transitions are composed of one to three different QuickTime videos, depending on the effect you wish to achieve with the alpha transition. Each of these videos serves a distinct purpose:

▸ The *asset movie* contains the video element that appears as the transition occurs. The asset video may have a premultiplied alpha channel that lets you see through to the exiting and/or entering project item(s).

▸ The *asset matte movie* is used to define which areas of the asset movie will be transparent when the asset movie does not have a premultiplied alpha channel.

▸ The *background matte movie* is used to blend the exiting and entering movies onscreen, at the same time.

The Transition Asset Folder

All of the videos that comprise a single alpha transition must be grouped into the same *transition asset folder*. The transition asset folder's name is used as the name for the alpha transition, and you must take care to ensure that all of the movies it contains are named in a very particular way. For example, if the transition asset folder is named SuperNova, the asset movie must be named *SuperNova.mov*, the asset matte movie must be named *SuperNova-matte.mov,* and the background matte movie must be named *SuperNova-backgroundMatte.mov*. If you name the movies in any other way, DVD Studio Pro will not recognize them.

NOTE ▸ The movies that comprise an alpha transition must be named using the conventions listed in the paragraph above, including the hyphen and capitalization. This is extremely important!

Transition asset folder Background matte movie

Asset movie Asset matte movie

Installing an Alpha Transition

Before you can use an alpha transition, you must install it. Alpha transitions can be installed in two different places on your system:

▸ At the root of your disk: *Startup Disk*/Library/Application Support/DVD Studio Pro/Transitions/

▸ In your home folder: *user*/Library/Application Support/DVD Studio Pro/Transitions/

DVD Studio Pro initializes all alpha transitions when it opens. Consequently, if you want to use an alpha transition, you must install it before you launch DVD Studio Pro.

NOTE ▸ When DVD Studio Pro opens, it automatically checks the vertical resolution of the movies in the transition assets folders. Movies that have vertical resolutions of 480, 486, 534, or 540 are assumed to be NTSC movies, and they will be available only to NTSC projects. All other vertical resolutions are considered to be PAL.

1 Save your project and quit DVD Studio Pro.

2 From this book's companion files, locate the folder named Media > Blackbox > Transitions > Supernova.

This folder is pictured in the preceding figure, and it contains all of the movies needed to create the SuperNova transition.

NOTE ▶ The SuperNova transition was constructed from the LiveType SuperNova object.

3 Copy the Supernova transition asset folder to your *Startup Disk*/Library/Application Support/DVD Studio Pro/Apple/Transitions folder.

4 Leave the Application Support/DVD Studio Pro/Apple/Transitions folder open on your Desktop.

In the next several sections of this lesson, you will be examining the assets in this folder, so leave it open on your screen so you can access it quickly.

5 Open the project you saved in step 1.

Let's assign the SuperNova alpha transition to the project's slideshow.

6 In the Graphical view, select the Slideshow item.

The Inspector updates to display the Slideshow's properties.

7 In the Slideshow Inspector, select the Transition tab.

8 In the Transition tab, click the Transition pop-up menu and choose the SuperNova transition.

> **NOTE ▶** Unlike DVD Studio Pro's stock alpha transitions, custom alpha transitions do not have alpha signs (α) at the beginning of their names. The alpha sign appears only in front of alpha transitions that are installed inside the DVD Studio Pro application package.

9 Simulate the Slideshow.

The SuperNova transition is placed between every slide.

NOTE ▸ Depending on the speed of your computer, the Simulator may drop frames during transition simulation. This is normal, and the final DVD-Video will play smoothly.

Exploring the Asset Movie

As you saw in the preceding section, the SuperNova alpha transition uses a video of a star going supernova to disguise a changing project item behind it. The video part of the supernova (the explosion you see during the transition) is contained in the **SuperNova.mov** asset movie. In the last exercise, you left the Application Support/DVD Studio Pro/Apple/Transitions/SuperNova folder

open onscreen, and the **SuperNova.mov** asset movie is in this folder. Let's open this asset movie in QuickTime and see what it looks like.

1 In the Finder, double-click the **SuperNova.mov** file.

The file opens in QuickTime.

2 Play the file.

It's a video clip of a star going supernova, over a black background. Let's see what happens if *only* this movie is available to the alpha transition.

3 Leave the **SuperNova.mov** file open in QuickTime.

You'll come back to this file in few minutes, so leave it open for now.

4 Make sure your Finder window is in Column view.

5 From the SuperNova folder, move the **SuperNova-backgroundMatte.mov** and **SuperNova-matte.mov** files two directories up (place them under the Transitions folder).

6 In DVD Studio Pro, simulate the slideshow again.

This time you see the asset movie during the transition, but you cannot see through the asset movie to the switching slides below. What happened? The short answer is that the **SuperNova.mov** asset movie does not have an alpha channel. To learn the long answer, read the next section.

Working with Alpha Channels

Earlier, you previewed the SuperNova transition attached to the slideshow, and you could see the slides changing behind the SuperNova transition. This is the "alpha" part of the alpha transition—in other words, you could see through the asset movie to the action below. To achieve this effect, you can include a premultiplied alpha channel directly into the asset movie. In fact, you *should* include an alpha channel in the asset movie, because it makes creating alpha transitions easier.

If the asset movie does not have an alpha channel (such as the one used in this transition), you can include an asset matte movie. The asset matte movie's sole purpose is to provide information used to create an alpha channel for the asset movie.

> **NOTE ▶** Although rare, there are situations where it's difficult to include a premultiplied alpha channel in your asset movie. For example, you may need to share your alpha transitions with a friend in a far-off country. It's very difficult to email that friend an animation codec movie with an alpha channel because the movie will be very large. If you compress the asset movie using a codec such as Sorenson 3, you'll make the movie's file size very small and easy to email, but the movie will not include an alpha channel. Fortunately, you can achieve the same effect by including an asset matte movie.

1 In the Finder, double-click the **SuperNova-matte.mov** file.

The movie opens in QuickTime.

2 Play the **SuperNova-matte.mov** file and take a close look.

Where the asset matte movie is black, the asset movie will be transparent. Where the asset matte movie is white, the asset movie will be opaque. Shades of gray in the asset matte movie will be varying degrees of transparent, depending on how gray they are.

Grayscale: Asset movie will have graduated transparency

White: Asset movie will be opaque

Black: Asset movie will be transparent

3 In QuickTime, close the **SuperNova-matte.mov**.

4 In the Finder, move the **SuperNova-matte.mov** file back into the SuperNova transition assets folder.

5 In DVD Studio Pro, simulate the slideshow again.

The graphics in the asset matte movie are now being used to provide alpha channel information for the asset movie. You can see through the transition to the changing slides below.

TIP ▸ DVD-Video is usually interlaced, which means there are 30 frames and 60 fields per second. For smoother transitions, render your asset matte movie at 60 progressive frames per second (*progressive* means "not interlaced"). DVD Studio Pro will automatically apply information from the correct frame in the asset matte movie to the correct field in the asset movie when it compiles the transitions.

Working with a Transition Switch Point

The transition switch point determines where the transition switches from the exiting item to the entering item. The transition switch point is used only if you do not include a background matte movie, and it follows a very particular set of rules:

▸ If the asset movie contains a marker named TransitionSwitchPoint, DVD Studio Pro will switch between the exiting and entering items at the frame indicated by the marker.

▶ If the asset movie does not contain a marker named TransitionSwitch-Point but does contain markers, DVD Studio Pro will switch between the exiting and entering items at the frame indicated by the first marker.

▶ If the asset movie does not contain any markers, the transition switch point will be directly in the middle of the asset movie.

1 If it is not already open, open the **SuperNova.mov** file in QuickTime.

Note that this asset movie has a marker named TransitionSwitchPoint.

2 Select the TransitionSwitchPoint marker.

QuickTime jumps to the marker. This is the frame where the exiting item will be replaced by the entering item as the alpha transition plays.

3 In QuickTime, close the **SuperNova.mov** file.

Exploring the Background Matte Movie

As you saw in the last section, DVD Studio Pro uses a transition switch point to determine where the exiting item is replaced by the entering item. However, this happens only if there is no background matte movie included with the alpha transition. If a background matte movie is included, it takes precedence over the transition switch point.

The background matte movie itself is very similar to the asset matte movie. It uses grayscale values to determine how the exiting and entering items will be blended during the transition.

1 In the Finder, double-click the **SuperNova-backgroundMatte.mov** file.

 The movie opens in QuickTime.

2 Play the **SuperNova-backgroundMatte.mov** file and take a close look.

 Where the background matte movie is white, the exiting item appears completely opaque. Where the background matte movie is black, the entering item will be opaque. Shades of gray in the background matte movie will create a blend of the exiting and entering items.

 NOTE ▶ In general, the background matte movie will begin with a completely white frame (the exiting item) and end with a completely black frame (the entering item). This appropriately reflects a transition from the exiting item to the entering one. How you get from white to black determines how the exiting and entering items are blended during the transition.

 To see exactly how this background matte movie works, let's look at it all by itself. Let's place *only* the background matte movie in the SuperNova transition assets folder, and then see what the transition looks like.

Black: Entering item
is 100 percent opaque

Grayscale: Exiting
and entering items
are blended

White: Exiting item
is 100 percent opaque

TIP For smoother transitions, render your background matte movie at 60 progressive frames per second.

3 From the SuperNova transition assets folder, move the **SuperNova.mov** and **SuperNova-matte.mov** files one directory up (to the main Transitions folder).

4 In the Finder, move the **SuperNova-backgroundMatte.mov** file back into the SuperNova transition assets folder.

5 In DVD Studio Pro, simulate the slideshow again.

This time you do not see the asset movie during the transition, because the asset movie is not in the SuperNova transition assets folder. However, you do see a smooth blend between the exiting and entering project items! This blend is created by the white, black, and gray areas in the **SuperNova-backgroundMatte.mov**.

6 In the Finder, move the **SuperNova.mov** and **SuperNova-matte.mov** files back into the SuperNova transition assets folder.

7 In DVD Studio Pro, simulate the slideshow again.

The SuperNova alpha transition displays an explosion, and the exiting item blends into the entering item. Perfect.

Feel free to apply this alpha transition to other project items.

> **TIP** ▶ The SuperNova alpha transition is now installed on your system and is available to any NTSC project you author.

8 Save the project file to the My_Projects folder on your hard drive.

Lesson Review

1. What's a transition?
2. True or false: An Alpha Transition must be installed before DVD Studio Pro is launched, or it will not be available to your project.
3. To install a transition, you must place it in which folder on your hard disk?
4. The transition asset movie contains what?
5. True or false: A custom alpha transition must have an asset movie, a matte movie, and a background matte movie.
6. What does the Transition switch point in the Asset movie do?

Answers

1. A smooth segue from one project item to the next.
2. True.
3. Startup Disk > Library > Application Support > DVD Studio Pro > Apple > Transitions.
4. The video that plays as the transition proceeds.
5. False, though if you want to ensure your transition has an alpha channel, it helps to have all three.
6. It tells DVD Studio Pro when to switch between displaying the outgoing item and the incoming item.

17

Lesson Files	Lessons > 17-Advanced_MPEG_Encoding_Start
Media	Media > Blackbox
Time	This lesson takes approximately 45 minutes to complete.
Goals	Learn how motion estimation facilitates temporal compression in MPEG-2 video streams
	Explore groups of pictures (GOPs), including the three types of frames they contain
	Use the Preview window to see how the final MPEG-2 stream will look, before the stream is encoded
	Set compression and chapter markers directly into the MPEG-2 stream
	Crop standard definition video (720 × 486) so that it fits in the 720 × 480 DVD-Video frame

Lesson 17
Advanced MPEG Encoding

DVD-Video is a delivery format not just for video, as its name implies, but for high-quality, crisp, beautiful digital MPEG-2 video. However, the video that goes onto that DVD is only as good as the encoder that produces it. Fortunately, we have Compressor.

In Lesson 10, you took Compressor for a test drive and learned how to produce MPEG-2 streams for use in DVD Studio Pro. This lesson builds upon that base by introducing you to some of Compressor's advanced MPEG-2 encoding features, including the following:

▶ Previewing encoding settings

▶ Setting chapter markers inside Compressor

▶ Cropping standard definition video (720 × 486) so that it fits into the 720 × 480 pixels of the DVD-Video frame

As this lesson progresses, we'll spelunk deep into the theory behind MPEG-2, exploring how motion estimation and groups of pictures (GOPs) conspire to strip redundancy out of the video stream, allowing up to two hours of high-quality video on a single DVD-5 disc. To encode MPEG-2 correctly, you have to know the theory. Sharpen those pencils, we're going in…

Setting Up

In this lesson you will encode a QuickTime movie called **Commercials.mov**.
This movie is currently in the Assets container of the project you've been
working on. Let's import the movie into Compressor.

1 In DVD Studio Pro, open the file named **17-Advanced_MPEG_Encoding_
 Start**, or continue working on the project from Lesson 16.

2 In the Assets tab's Commercials folder, Ctrl-click the **Commercials.mov**
 asset, and from the contextual menu choose Reveal In Finder.

A Finder window pops open to display the **Commercials.mov** file.

3 Launch Compressor (*Startup disk* > Applications > Compressor).

4 From the Finder, drag the **Commercials.mov** file into Compressor's Batch
 window.

 NOTE ▶ Leave the Finder window open onscreen. You'll come back to
 this window later in the lesson.

Choosing Quality Settings

In Lesson 10, you learned that the Quality setting is important because it affects both the look of the encoded MPEG-2 file and also the stream's resultant file size. In general, as you lower the quality, you also lower the file size. In fact, if you encode at Compressor's minimum quality setting of a mere 2 megabits per second (Mbps), you can squeeze nearly three hours of video onto a DVD-5 disc. If there's not much motion in the video, and you take time to create an appropriately configured preset, it will even look good. Compressor's a very advanced MPEG-2 encoder!

To prove how good Compressor is, we are going to encode the **Commercials.mov** movie at the lowest possible quality setting. By the end of this lesson, you'll know just how low you can push Compressor. You'll also see that cranking Compressor up to the highest possible setting is not just a waste of disc space, but also a waste of time for many projects.

1 Create a new Compressor preset and name it *LowQualityMPEG-2*.

2 In the Inspector window's Encoder pane, click the Quality tab.

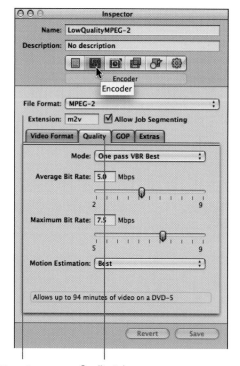

Encoder pane Quality tab

3 From the Mode pop-up menu, choose "One pass."

4 Set the Average Bit Rate slider to the lowest possible setting: 2 Mbps.

NOTE ▶ In general, you should *never* encode MPEG streams with a max bit rate higher than 8 Mbps. The DVD-Video specification requires DVD-Video players to stream a maximum of 10.08 Mbps off a DVD disc. If you set your max bit rate to 8 Mbps, that leaves only 2.08 Mbps for the audio and subtitle streams. A 48 kHz, 16-bit stereo PCM stream has a data rate of approximately 1.5 Mbps. Add that to the 8 Mbps for the video stream, and your DVD-Video will stream at a max bit rate of 9.5 Mbps—that's only 0.58 Mbps under the maximum allowed by the DVD-Video specification! When in doubt, a bit rate of 4.5 Mbps is always a good place to start, because 4.5 Mbps generally provides great balance between quality and file size.

About Motion Estimation

When an MPEG encoder creates an MPEG-2 stream, it divides each source frame into a matrix of 16-pixel-by-16-pixel squares called *macro-blocks*. As the encoder progresses from frame to frame, it can determine the color information in each macro-block, and then calculate how far blocks of color have moved within the frame.

For example, if you have a tripod shot of a balloon drifting across the sky, the blocks of color in the balloon never change—they simply float from left to right. Using motion estimation, Compressor can determine how far these blocks of color have moved, and then encode a *motion vector* to define this change of position. As a result, a tiny algorithm is all that's used to define the motion of these blocks of color over time; the individual pixels inside the blocks do not need to be re-encoded! It's sort of like MPEG-2's version of the sprite animation techniques found in Macromedia Flash or Totally Hip LiveStage Professional.

Compressor has three levels of motion estimation: Good, Better, and Best. The only difference between the three is that the Best setting searches farther afield in the frame to find macro-blocks that have moved than the Better setting, which in turn searches farther than the Good setting. But all of that extra searching takes an increased amount of time, so if you choose Best motion estimation, be prepared to wait.

For us, time is critical, since we have so many other things to learn in this lesson. Let's set motion estimation as low as it will go.

1 From the Motion Estimation pop-up menu, choose Good.

NOTE ▶ To see how motion estimation works, you need Digigami's MPressionist.X, which allows you to view macro-blocks in an encoded MPEG stream, and even to see how these macro-blocks move from frame to frame. For more information, visit www.digigami.com.

Digigami's MPressionist.X allows you to inspect motion vectors in MPEG streams.

Examining GOP Structures

Let's take a moment to dive deep into the science behind MPEG-2 encoding. MPEG-2 streams achieve such incredibly low data rates because they employ both *spatial* and *temporal compression*. Spatial compression occurs within the video frame, similarly to how the JPEG file format spatially compresses still images. Temporal compression, on the other hand, occurs between frames in the video stream. For example, the motion vectors described in the last section are a form of temporal compression, because they help to encode moving blocks of color, between video frames, over time.

All MPEG encoders begin the compression process by dividing the video stream into small units called *groups of pictures (GOPs)*. A GOP can have three different types of frames: I-frames, P-frames, and B-frames. Of the three, both I- and P-frames are considered *reference frames* because they can be used as the base from which to derive other frames in the GOP. With that in mind, let's take a closer look at these three frame types.

About I-Frames, P-Frames, and B-Frames

I-frame stands for *intra-frame*. I-frames are spatially encoded, within the video frame, in a way that is similar to encoding for JPEG still images. You can consider an I-frame to be the GOP's keyframe. It is the highest quality frame in the GOP, but it's also the one that takes the most bits to encode because the I-frame is not mathematically derived from any other frame. Rather, it contains all of the data needed to completely reproduce the frame, independent of any other frame in the GOP. As you'll come to see later in this lesson, I-frames are very important to the MPEG stream, because all chapter markers are locked onto I-frames.

P-frame stands for *predicted frame*. A P-frame is derived mathematically from content within the reference frame immediately preceding it. This could be an I-frame or another P-frame. Remember, both are considered reference frames.

For example, if a macro-block is black in the preceding reference frame, and also exactly the same shade of black in the current P-frame, the encoder doesn't need to re-encode that macro-block's color information. Rather, it can record a small motion vector that simply says, leave the macro-block the same color and in the same place as it was in the last frame.

NOTE ► Portions of the P-frame that aren't covered by motion vectors are encoded the same way as an I-frame.

A B-frame is a *bi-directional frame*. Although B-frames are similar to P-frames, they differ in being derived from information in both the previous and next reference frames. B-frames are the most efficient of the three types of GOP frames.

1 In the Inspector window's Encoder pane, click the GOP tab.

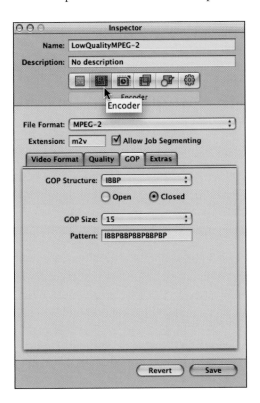

The GOP pane holds settings used to configure GOP structure and size. Of particular note, the Pattern field displays the GOP's sequence of I-frames, P-frames, and B-frames.

2 From the GOP Structure pop-up menu, choose IBP, and from the GOP Size pop-up menu, choose 7.

GOP Structure menu

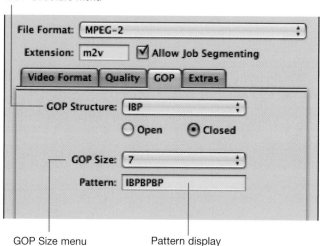

GOP Size menu Pattern display

The Pattern display updates to show the new GOP structure. The GOP Structure and GOP Size menus combine to determine how many I-, P-, and B- frames there will be in each GOP. As you can see, this new GOP has only seven frames, and only three of them are B-frames.

The GOP structure you select determines how far apart P-frames are in the stream. If the stream has a low amount of motion, P-frames can be spaced further apart because there is less change between successive pixels, over time. However, if the stream contains a lot of motion (as, for example, the car commercials in this stream do), moving the P-frames closer together provides enhanced image quality because there are fewer B-frames between the P-frames. This means the encoder does not have to span extra B-frames as it encodes successive P-frames, which makes it easier to create motion vectors.

Adjusting the GOP structure and size can result in higher quality MPEG-2 streams, but your file size will also go up, even if just marginally. By adjusting the GOP structure, you can create streams with more P-frames and fewer B-frames. P-frames more accurately reproduce the source image than B-frames, but that extra quality means P-frames also have a larger file size than B-frames. Consequently, if you add more P-frames to each GOP, you increase the size of each GOP.

NOTE ▶ There are no hard and fast rules about the GOP structure and size you should use. Your choices about structure and size depend upon the content of the stream you are encoding. In general, a GOP size of 15 frames for NTSC (12 frames for PAL) and an IBBP structure provide sufficient quality for most MPEG streams.

In the end, however, nothing beats experience. If you have a moment, encode the same source file with several different GOP structures and sizes. Then watch each encoded stream to see if there is a difference in quality. Make sure you also pay attention to the file size of each stream!

3 Ensure that the Closed GOP radio button is selected.

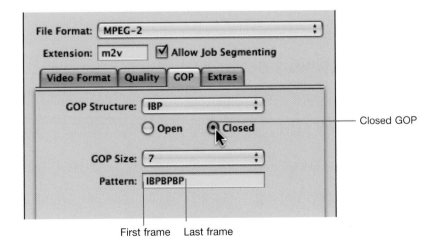

GOPs can be either open or closed. When Closed is selected, notice how the GOP begins with an I-frame and ends with a P-frame. An I-frame is self-contained and does not refer to any other frame in the GOP. A P-frame, on the other hand, refers to the previous reference frame to derive its image data. Consequently, a closed GOP is a self-contained unit in the final MPEG stream, because a closed GOP contains all of the information necessary to re-create every frame in the GOP.

NOTE ▶ If you are creating multi-angle or mixed-angle tracks, you *must* use closed GOPs. Multi-angle or mixed-angle tracks use I-frames as the bridge between video streams. In a closed GOP, the I-frame is always the first frame in the GOP. Consequently, if both streams use closed GOPs and the same GOP size and structure, all I-frames will align throughout the multi- or mixed-angle stream, which means the DVD-Video player can easily switch from one stream to another.

4 Select the Open GOP radio button.

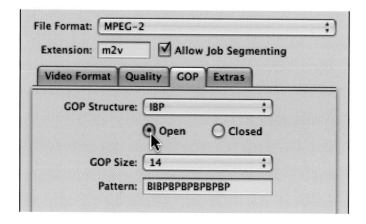

When Open is selected, the GOP Size updates to 14 frames. Additionally, the open GOP begins with a B-frame and ends with a P-frame. A B-frame refers to both the preceding and following reference frames. In other words, in order to derive its image data, the B-frame at the front of the open GOP refers to the P-frame at the end of the previous GOP. Thus, in contrast to a closed, self-contained GOP, an open GOP does not contain all of the information needed to fully re-create every frame in the GOP.

So why use open GOPs? The quick answer is file size. Open GOPs tend to have one fewer P-frame and one more B-frame than a closed GOP. B-frames are smaller than P-frames, so an open GOP structure will enjoy a smaller file size than a closed GOP, even if only a few kilobytes smaller. However, there are a lot of GOPs in an MPEG stream, so all those kilobytes add up!

NOTE ▶ DVD Studio Pro will accept both open and closed GOP streams, but open GOP streams cannot be used for mixed- or multi-angle tracks.

5 Close the Presets window and save your changed preset.

6 In the Batch window, assign the LowQualityMPEG-2 preset to the **Commercials.mov** file.

This file is ready for encoding. But before you click the Submit button, let's take a moment to preview the Encode settings, using Compressor's Preview window.

Previewing Compression Settings

Up to this point in the lesson, you've created the lowest quality MPEG compression setting possible. How do you think it looks? Although there's no substitute for actually encoding the video and taking a look, you can use Compressor's Preview window to quickly preview compression settings without outputting any video at all. The Preview window provides a real-time simulation of your encoder settings. Let's open the Preview window now and take a look at the quality of this yet-to-be encoded stream.

> **NOTE ▶** It's no secret that quality MPEG encoding takes a long, long time. Encoding with Compressor is no exception. If you choose the best possible settings for your encoding preset, it will take hours to encode an hourlong file. The Preview window will provide a good simulation of how the final file will look, but keep in mind that it really is just a simulation: The only way to truly test encode settings is to actually encode the file.
>
> To get around this problem, try encoding a 10-second clip trimmed out of the source footage. Pick a clip that represents a hard-to-encode section of the footage, such as a scene with lots of motion or visual complexity. If the encode settings look good in 10 seconds of a visually complex scene, they'll look good throughout the entire MPEG stream.

1 In the Batch window's toolbar, click the Preview button.

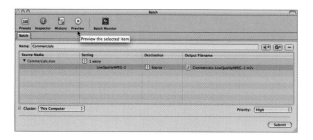

The Preview window opens.

Batch Item
selection Batch Item
buttons pop-up menu Source view Output view

Timeline Playback controls

2 To ensure that you're viewing the LowQualityMPEG-2 preset, select it from the Batch Item pop-up menu.

With a preset selected from the Batch Item pop-up menu, the Preview window lets you do A/B comparisons of your source and output video. At the top of the Preview window's display area is a slider, and a thin line extends vertically from this slider to bisect the display area. To the left of this line, the Preview window displays the source video; to the right, it displays a simulation of the output video.

3 Click the Preview window's Play button to start playback.

4 Drag the slider left and right to preview encoding.

As you can see, at the lowest possible MPEG-2 compression settings the video still looks pretty good. You will notice a small loss of detail in fine features. In addition, some colors might look a bit dull, particularly in high-motion parts of the stream. Otherwise, this low-quality setting is quite satisfactory.

5 Leave the Preview window open.

Setting Markers in Compressor

While exploring chapter markers in Lesson 12, you learned that markers can only be assigned to I-frames in the MPEG stream. A typical NTSC MPEG-2 stream uses a GOP size of 15 frames (12 frames for PAL), which means there will be one I-frame for every 15 frames, or two I-frames per second. This makes it very difficult to frame-accurately position markers inside DVD Studio Pro. You learned that to get around this you can insert chapter markers on individual frames in Final Cut Pro, and then export those markers into the final MPEG-2 stream.

In addition to using Final Cut Pro to insert chapter markers frame-accurately, you can do so in Compressor. In fact, Compressor allows you to insert two types of markers: compression markers and chapter markers. This is accomplished using Compressor's Preview window.

The source file you are about to examine was exported from Final Cut Pro as a self-contained movie, and several chapter and compression markers have been embedded into it. In the following steps you'll examine these markers in Compressor, and then add a couple of your own.

Compression Chapter marker Marker pop-up menu
marker (blue) (purple)

1 From the Marker pop-up menu in the bottom-right corner of the Preview window, deselect the "show compression markers" option.

The Preview window's timeline shows chapter markers only.

2 From the Marker pop-up menu, deselect the "show chapter markers" option and select the "show compression markers" option.

Only the single compression marker is displayed in the Preview window's timeline.

Setting Compression Markers

Compression markers force an I-frame at an exact frame in the MPEG stream. A compression marker, as its name implies, is meant to enhance compression by forcing an I-frame at any abrupt change in the scene. For example, if a sudden change in the scene, such as a cut or a quick fade, occurs in the middle of a GOP, it's very difficult for the encoder to use motion vectors and algorithms to encode that change. As a result, you might see a subtle breakup of your picture until the next I-frame comes along. By placing a compression marker at the beginning of that scene change, you force an I-frame, giving the MPEG encoder a clean slate to start the new scene from.

NOTE ▶ The GOP before the compression/chapter marker will be shorter than your specified GOP size. Compressor will cap off the shorter GOP with a P-frame, and then begin creating new GOPs from the frame tagged by the marker. After the compression/chapter marker, the MPEG stream continues with the specified GOP size and structure.

1 In the Preview window's Timecode text box, type *01:00:30:00*.

The playhead jumps to 30 seconds and 0 frames into the video. This frame marks a sudden scene transition.

2 Press the left arrow key.

The playhead jumps back one frame, and the screen goes black.

3 Press the right arrow key to move the playhead back to the first frame of the scene transition.

4 From the Marker pop-up menu choose "Add marker."

TIP ▸ In Compressor's Preview window, you can press the M key to add a marker, just as you can in Final Cut Pro and DVD Studio Pro.

A blue compression marker is added at the playhead's current position.

This demonstrates an important point:

By default, all new markers added to the Preview window are compression markers.

To make a chapter marker, you must transform a compression marker, as you'll see in the next exercise.

Setting Chapter Markers

Chapter markers work the same way as compression markers, with the advantage that you can name them. The name is encoded with the MPEG-2 stream, and the marker will be visible inside DVD Studio Pro's timeline-based Track Editor.

To make a chapter marker, you transform a compression marker by giving it a name. The playhead is currently parked over the compression marker at 30 seconds, 0 frames. Let's transform it.

1 From the Preview window's Marker pop-up menu, choose Edit.

A dialog drops down from the Preview window's title bar. This dialog prompts you to enter a name for the marker.

2 Name the marker *Mini – Carbo*, and click OK.

The compression marker is transformed into a chapter marker. Because the timeline is currently set to display only compression markers, the marker dissappears from the timeline. There is still one final compression marker in the timeline. Let's turn that one into a chapter marker, too.

3 Move the playhead to 01:01:00:00.

The playhead is parked over the final compression marker.

4 Name the compression marker *Honda – City*.

5 From the Marker pop-up menu, choose "show chapter markers."

All of the markers are now chapter markers, as displayed in the timeline.

Cropping Video

There are two types of video that are commonly used as source assets for DVD: standard definition video (SD) and DV video (DV). DV video uses the same frame dimension as DVD-Video: 720 × 480. Standard definition video, on the other hand, uses a frame dimension of 720 × 486—that's six extra vertical lines of resolution. The video you are currently working on is SD. If you take a quick look at the bottom-left corner of the Preview window, you'll see a display that shows the source video's frame dimension is 720 × 486—in other words, SD.

Before you can encode an SD video, you need to crop those extra six lines off. *Crop* is an important word here, because if you simply resize SD video to 720 × 480, your video will look mushy and blurred in the final MPEG stream, instead of retaining its sharp, crisp digital appearance.

By default, Compressor automatically crops four lines from the top and two lines from the bottom of SD video that is assigned an MPEG-2 preset. In the Preview window, a thin red outline surrounds the cropping area of the final MPEG stream. Areas of the video outside the red outline will be cropped off. To set your own custom cropping area, you need to visit the Geometry pane of your MPEG-2 Preset.

TIP ▸ In the Preview window, you can drag the red outlined cropping area to quickly change the way your video is cropped.

1 Open the Presets window and select the LowQualityMPEG-2 preset.

2 Select the Geometry button.

Selected MPEG-2 preset Geometry button

The Geometry pane includes a Source inset (Cropping) area that lets you define how many pixels will be cropped off the left, right, top, and bottom of your MPEG-2 stream.

3 For the Bottom setting, enter the value 6.

Six lines will now be cropped off the bottom of the video before it is encoded to MPEG-2.

TIP ▶ Remember, there are two fields in every frame! When cropping interlaced SD video, always use even numbers, or you may accidentally encode the MPEG stream using the wrong field order. For example, you can crop six lines off the top, or two lines off the top and four lines off the bottom, and your MPEG stream will look fine. However, if you crop three lines off both the top and bottom, you may run into interlacing problems in the final MPEG stream.

4 Close the Presets window and save the changed LowQualityMPEG-2 preset.

Adding the Encoded File to Your Project

With the encoding settings made and chapter markers set, encoding the file is all that remains. Let's do so now, and then import the file into DVD Studio Pro.

1 Set the Destination to the Source folder.

The Source folder should still be open on your Desktop. Choosing this folder as the destination makes it easy to find the file after it's encoded.

NOTE ▶ If you use Final Cut Pro's Export > Using Compressor option, choosing Source as the destination causes the encoded files to be placed at the root of your hard disk.

2 In the Batch window's Output Filename column, change the output file's name to *Commercials.m2v*.

A few steps from now, you will add this file to your DVD Studio Pro project, and it's very important that the name is exactly **Commercials.m2v**, so take care as you type.

3 In the bottom-right corner of the Batch window, click Submit.

The Batch Monitor opens, and the file is encoded. Once the file has finished encoding, you can drag it into DVD Studio Pro.

4 In the Finder, locate the encoded file.

5 Drag the file directly from the Finder into DVD Studio Pro's Graphical view.

A track item is added to the Graphical view.

6 Double-click the new Commercials track item to open it in the Track Editor.

There are a few important things to note. First, all of your named chapter markers are present in the Track Editor. Second, DVD Studio Pro has automatically added an audio track to the A1 audio stream. There's no audio stream in the MPEG-2 file that Compressor encoded, so where did this audio come from?

As we saw in Lesson 10, if you add a movie or MPEG-2 file to a track, DVD Studio Pro automatically looks in the asset's folder on the hard disk and checks to see if there's an audio file with exactly the same name as the video asset. If there is, DVD Studio Pro assumes the audio file is an audio stream that corresponds to the video and thus automatically adds it to the track! How cool is that?

NOTE ▶ DVD Studio Pro's Track Preferences pane contains an option called "Find matching audio when dragging." This option must be selected for DVD Studio Pro to automatically add matching audio streams to tracks.

Track Preferences pane

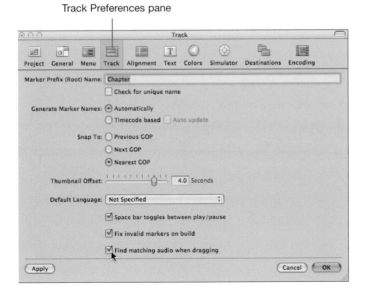

7 In the Track Editor, select the start marker.

The inspector updates to show the marker's properties. At the very top of the Marker Inspector there is a Name setting.

8 Rename the Start marker *Mini – Breeze*.

You are almost done. Let's finish this lesson by adding a chapter menu for this track.

9 In the Graphical view, double-click the Main Menu tile to open it in the Menu Editor.

10 From the Graphical view, hold down the Option key and drag the Commercials track over the main menu's Commercials button.

A Drop palette appears.

11 From the Drop palette choose Create Chapter Index, Make Connections.

The Choose Template or Layout Style window opens.

12 Click the Templates tab, click the Custom button, and select BB_Template. Click OK.

DVD Studio Pro adds a chapter menu for the Commercials track and links the chapter menu to the main menu's Commercials button.

13 Save your project.

14 Simulate the project to test the new chapter menu and the encoded MPEG-2 stream.

The chapter menu works great. But more important, the encoded track also looks pretty good, and it was encoded at 2 Mbps, which is a low data rate. Remember: There's rarely a need to encode your MPEG-2 streams at the highest possible data rate setting. Typically, a target data rate of between 4 and 6 Mbps is more than adequate to preserve the visual quality of the stream.

Lesson Review

1. What is a macroblock?
2. What is a Motion Vector?
3. What is a GOP?
4. What is a common GOP size for NTSC video?
5. What is an I-Frame?
6. In a Closed GOP, where is the I-Frame?

Answers

1. A macroblock is a 16-pixel by 16-pixel block inside the MPEG-2 video frame.

2. A motion vector is used to determine how far macroblocks have moved from frame to frame inside the MPEG-2 stream.

3. A GOP is a Group Of Pictures inside the MPEG-2 stream.

4. 15 frames (12 frames for PAL video).

5. An I-Frame is an Intra Frame, or keyframe.

6. In a closed GOP, the I-Frame is always the first frame in the GOP.

18

Lesson Files
Lessons > 18_Alternate_Angles-Start

Media
Media > Blackbox

Time
This lesson takes approximately 30 minutes to complete.

Goals
Learn the difference between multi-angle and mixed-angle tracks

Discover how to encode MPEG streams for alternate angles

Learn how to target alternate angles from menu buttons

Simulate alternate angles

Explore Final Cut Pro cut markers

Learn how to encode alternate angle streams directly from Final Cut Pro

Lesson **18**

Using Alternate Angles

The DVD-Video specification allows for up to nine video streams in each track. This includes the main video stream, along with up to eight alternate video streams.

Alternate angles give you a great deal of creative potential, because you can serve up all sorts of interesting extra content in these extra video streams. For example, 3D animators sending demos to clients can add the main animation to a track's first video stream, and a wireframe view of the same animation as an alternate angle. Or you could record a sports event with eight different cameras placed strategically around a field. Along with the main edit of the event, you may also include each camera angle as an alternate angle on the final DVD (for a total of nine separate angles). Using the remote control's Angle button, viewers can cycle from stream to stream, seeing the action the way they want to see it.

The possibilities for alternate angles are immense, but interestingly, they are one of the least used features of the DVD-Video specification. If you're looking for that extra edge to set your productions apart, this lesson will move you in the right direction.

Setting Up the Project

Blackbox is a film effects house in Santa Monica, California. To show interested parties the caliber of its work, we will add a "Before & After" track to this project. The Before & After track will display a "before" angle of a green-screened actor, and an "after" angle that is the same shot with various effects applied.

Let's check out these shots now. We'll also take a moment to set up this project so that it's ready to accept alternate angle streams.

1 Open the file named **18_Alternate_Angles-Start**, or continue working on the project from Lesson 17 in the My_Projects folder.

2 In the Assets tab's Movies folder, double-click the **ai-before.m2v** video.

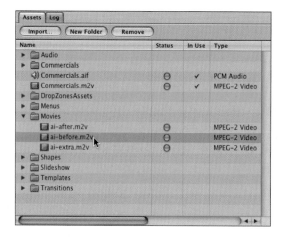

The **ai-before.m2v** video plays in DVD Studio Pro's Viewer. It shows an actor in front of a green screen.

3 Double-click the **ai-after.m2v** video.

The **ai-after.m2v** video plays in DVD Studio Pro's Viewer. It shows the actor after various effects have been applied to the shot.

The **ai-before.m2v** and **ai-after.m2v** videos will link to this project's Before & After layered menu. This menu is currently not connected into the project's navigational hierarchy. In the next steps you'll fix this problem by connecting the Before & After layered menu to the main menu.

4 In the Graphical view, double-click the Main Menu tile.

The main menu opens in the Menu Editor.

5 Position your pointer over the main menu's Before & After button.

A tooltip appears. It shows you the name of the button, followed by its target. Currently, the Before & After button's target is not set.

6 Ctrl-click the Before & After button, and choose Target > Menus > Layered Menu > Main Menu.

7 In the Menu Editor, double-click the main menu's Before & After button.

The Layered Menu opens in the Menu Editor. The Main Menu button currently has no target. It needs to link back to the main menu's Before & After button.

8 Ctrl-click the Layered Menu's Main Menu button, and choose Target > Menus > Main Menu > Before&After.

All items are now connected and ready to go. It's time to make the alternate angle track.

About Alternate Angles

DVD Studio Pro lets you create two different types of alternate angle tracks:

▶ **Multi-angle tracks**, in which each angle is exactly the same length as the main video stream.

▶ **Mixed-angle tracks**, which include alternate video streams that are shorter in duration than the main video stream. Where there's a space in the mixed-angle stream, DVD players revert to the main video stream, which they play until the mixed angle appears again. Mixed angles save disc space for alternate angle streams that do not need to run the length of the entire track. Technically, all angles in the mixed-angle track must be sandwiched by markers—one marker at the front, and one marker at the back.

Encoding Alternate Angle Streams

Whether you use multi-angle streams or mixed angle, creating alternate angles in DVD Studio Pro is remarkably easy—as long as the MPEG streams are correctly prepared before you import them into DVD Studio Pro. The DVD-Video specification requires alternate angle tracks to be multiplexed in a particular way, and you must encode your MPEG streams with several rules in mind.

For starters, DVD players use I-frames as bridges for jumping between alternate video streams, so all I-frames must be aligned across all alternate angle streams. This means all alternate angle streams must be encoded using the exact same GOP structure. If the MPEG in the V1 stream uses a 15-frame GOP, then all other alternate angle streams must use a 15-frame GOP. Furthermore, only closed GOPs will work for alternate angles in DVD Studio Pro, because only closed GOPs guarantee that an I-frame will appear at the exact same place in each GOP.

You must also pay close attention to the maximum bit rate used in each alternate angle. This is determined by the number of alternate angles in the track:

▶ For two to five angles, encode each video stream at a maximum bit rate of no higher than 8 Mbps.

▶ For six to eight angles, encode each video stream at a maximum bit rate of no higher than 7.5 Mbps.

▶ For nine angles, encode each video stream at a maximum bit rate of no higher than 7 Mbps.

> **NOTE ▶** The maximum allowable bit rate for alternate angle streams is also affected by the number of audio and subtitle streams in the track. The above numbers assume that the track will use a single AC-3 encoded audio stream. If you add alternate audio streams to the track, you will need to lower the maximum bit rate used for the alternate angle video streams. In general, it's best to use a maximum bit rate of no higher than 7 Mbps, even if your track has fewer than five alternate angles.

With these rules in mind, let's move on to creating multi-angle tracks.

Creating Multi-Angle Tracks

Now that you know the theory behind multi-angle streams, let's create one.

1 In the Graphical view, create a track, name it *Before & After*, and place it to the right of the Layered Menu item.

2 In the Graphical view, double-click the Before & After tile.

The track opens in the Track Editor. As you've seen in previous lessons, the Track Editor is divided into three sets of streams: At the top there are 9 video streams, in the middle there are 8 audio streams, and at the bottom there are 32 subtitle streams.

We are only working with alternate angles, so let's filter the Track Editor so that it displays only video streams. To filter the Track Editor, we'll use the Track Editor's stream configuration buttons.

3 In the top-left corner of the Track Editor, click the video stream configuration button.

The Track Editor updates to display all of the track's available video streams, V1 through V9. Notice that the V1 stream is separated from all potential alternate streams by a thin horizontal divider. The V1 stream is the most important stream in any track. All alternate video, audio, and subtitle streams run parallel to the V1 stream.

NOTE ▶ You can click more than one stream configuration button, and the Track Editor will split the available display area between the streams you choose to view.

4 From the Assets tab, drag the **ai-before.m2v** asset and drop it into the V1 stream.

That takes care of the V1 stream. Next, let's add an alternate angle to the V2 stream.

5 From the Assets tab, drag the **ai-after.m2v** asset and drop it into the V2 stream.

Voilà! A multi-angle track!

NOTE ▶ Alternate angle streams can be composed of many different clips arranged in sequence, as long as the sequence of clips has no gaps and is exactly the same length as the V1 stream. And of course, GOP structure and maximum data rate constraints are still in effect.

Previewing Multi-Angle Tracks in the Viewer

At the left edge of each stream in the Track Editor there is a Viewer Stream Selection button. This button determines which stream plays when you preview the track in the Viewer. Let's use the Viewer Stream Selection buttons on the V1 and V2 streams to preview this multi-angle track.

1 In the Viewer, play the Before & After track.

2 In the Track Editor, use the Viewer Stream Selection buttons to toggle the Viewer's display between stream 1 and stream 2.

As you toggle the display, the Viewer updates to show you the selected stream.

3 In the Viewer, click the Stop button to halt playback.

Creating Mixed-Angle Tracks

One disadvantage of alternate angles is that they consume a lot of disc space. For example, if you encoded the video tightly, you could squeeze up to 2 hours of video onto a single track on a DVD-5 disc. However, if that track has two angles, then the maximum duration of that track decreases to about an hour because you are effectively combining two different video streams into a single track. If you add three video streams, the total run time decreases to about 40 minutes. Put nine angles on a disc, and the maximum duration of the project decreases to just over 10 minutes.

To save disc space, DVD Studio Pro allows you to create mixed angles. In contrast to multi-angle tracks, where each angle is exactly the same length as the main video in the V1 stream, mixed-angle tracks can use video streams that are shorter than the main video stream, which means that there can be empty spaces in the alternate angle streams. Where there's an empty space in the stream, DVD players will default to playing the V1 stream. As soon as there's content to play in the alternate angle stream, DVD players will instantly and seamlessly switch back to displaying the alternate angle.

In some respects, mixed angles work exactly the same as multi-angles. They must be encoded using the exact same GOP structure as the main video in the V1 stream, and you still must keep the maximum bit rate limits in mind. But there is one additional technical concept to keep in mind when creating mixed-angle tracks: *In a mixed-angle track, all alternate angle streams must be enclosed by a marker at the front and a marker at the back.*

You'll learn more about this later in this lesson. For now, let's start by shortening the clip in the Before & After track's V2 stream.

Resizing Video Clips

DVD Studio Pro's Track Editor lets you resize clips by dragging their left and right edges, just as you would in Final Cut Pro. Accuracy is extremely important when editing mixed-angle streams. As a result, it's a good idea to keep an eye on the Track Editor's various timecode displays while resizing mixed-angle clips. The following exercise gives you some practice using the timecode controls when editing.

1 Position the mouse pointer over the front of the V2 stream.

The pointer turns into a resize icon.

As you perform the next task, watch the Start timecode box in the top-right corner of the Track Editor. This timecode box displays the start time of any clip selected in the Track Editor, relative to the start time of the track itself.

2 Drag the front of the clip until the Start timecode box says 00:00:02:00
(2 seconds into the track).

3 In the End timecode box, type *00:00:15:00*, and press Return.

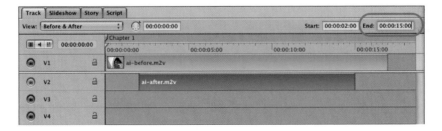

The clip in stream V2 is now only 13 seconds long. It starts later and ends
earlier than stream V1.

This mixed-angle track is close to complete. But there's one final step left:
adding sandwich markers.

Adding Sandwich Markers

Mixed-angle tracks must have markers sandwiching all mixed-angle clips. For the track you're working on, there must be a marker at the start, and a marker at the end of the clip in stream V2. To achieve this goal, you'll use DVD Studio Pro *cell markers*.

Every track can have a maximum of 255 markers. Of those markers, only 99 can be chapter markers. You could sandwich a mixed-angle clip with chapter markers, but doing so uses up two of these valuable marker types. Additionally, sandwiching mixed-angle clips with chapter markers allows viewers to jump back and forth to the beginning and end of the mixed angle by pressing the DVD player's Next Program and Previous Program remote control buttons. This is not necessarily a bad thing—it all depends on the presentation you're after. However, for the sake of demonstration, we'll conserve our chapter markers and use cell markers instead.

1 Create a marker at 00:00:02:00.

DVD Studio Pro creates a purple chapter marker, and the Inspector updates to display the marker's properties. The Inspector includes a marker Type area. In this area the Chapter check box is selected, indicating that this marker is a chapter marker. The other choices in the Type area include Button Highlight and Dual-Layer Break Point markers. If you disable all of the Type check boxes, you create a fourth type of marker—a cell marker.

Purple chapter marker at 00:00:02:00

Marker Inspector's Type area

2 In the Inspector's Type area, deselect the Chapter check box.

Green cell marker

No marker type selected

In the Track Editor, the marker turns green. It is now a cell marker.

You've inserted a cell marker at the beginning of the mixed-angle clip. Let's finish this mixed-angle track by adding a cell marker to the clip's end.

3 Ctrl-click the V2 stream's clip and choose Add Marker to Clip End.

A cell marker is added to the end of the clip, at 00:00:15:00.

4 Click the Viewer Stream Selection button for stream V2.

5 In the Viewer, play the track from the beginning.

As the track plays, keep an eye on the Track Editor's playhead. Where there's no clip in stream V2, the Viewer defaults to play the clip in stream V1. As soon as the playhead moves over the clip in stream V2, the Viewer displays stream V2. As you can see, in a mixed-angle track, playback always defaults to the V1 stream whenever the alternate angle streams do not contain a clip.

NOTE ▶ In mixed-angle tracks that need more than one alternate angle, parallel alternate angles must be exactly the same length, as shown in the figure below.

Targeting Alternate Angle Streams

One of the biggest challenges with using alternate angle streams is letting viewers know they're there. While it's a simple matter to switch between angles using the DVD player's Angle remote control button, if viewers don't know that a track has alternate angles, they are unlikely to ever see your alternate presentation.

To alert viewers, you can add a note to the DVD-Video's liner or even to a menu that targets the alternate angle track. Better still, you can make a menu with buttons that specifically target each alternate angle.

This is the approach we'll take in our project, and it's the reason we have Before and After buttons on the layered menu. Let's target this menu's buttons to the appropriate streams in the Before & After track.

1 In the Graphical view, double-click the Layered Menu tile.

The menu opens in the Menu Editor.

2 In the Menu Editor, select the Before button.

The Inspector updates to display the button's properties.

3 From the Inspector's Target menu, choose Tracks and Stories > Before & After > [Track].

Clicking the button now targets the correct track, but you still need to specify the video stream that should display when the track plays. To do so, you'll use the Inspector's Streams area. The Streams area provides an Angle menu that lets you select individual video streams in the targeted track. The Before & After track has the **ai-before.m2v** video in stream V1, so you need to select the first video stream from the Angle menu.

NOTE ▶ In layered menus, the Streams area is located on the Inspector's Button tab. In standard menus, the Streams area is located on the Inspector's Advanced tab.

4 In the Inspector's Streams area, click the Angle pop-up menu and select 1 (video stream 1).

When this menu's Before button is activated, the Before & After track will play stream V1, which contains the **ai-before.m2v** video.

Now let's set up the menu's After button.

5 From the Graphical view, hold down the Option key and drag the Before & After track tile over the menu's After button.

A Drop palette appears.

6 Choose Connect to Track.

The button is now targeted to the correct track. To finish the button, you need to select stream 2 as the display stream.

7 In the Menu Editor, select the After button.

The Inspector updates to display the button's properties.

8 In the Inspector's Streams area, click the Angle pop-up menu and choose 2 (video stream 2).

Does it work? Let's find out by simulating the menu.

Simulating Alternate Angle Streams

When viewers watch an alternate angle stream, they can use the Angle button on the DVD player's remote control to cycle through a track's alternate angle streams. Let's do the same in our Simulator.

1 In the Graphical view, Ctrl-click the Layered Menu tile and choose Simulate Menu.

The Simulator opens and displays the layered menu.

2 Click the After button.

The Simulator jumps to the Before & After track and plays video stream 2. Notice that the first 2 seconds of the track displays the Before video, but then at exactly 2 seconds into the track, it switches to the After video.

As viewers watch the DVD, they can use the Angle button to cycle through the track's angles. To mimic this behavior, the Simulator has an Angle menu.

3 Use the Simulator's Angle menu to switch to the first video stream.

4 Close the Simulator.

About Alternate Angle Errors

When creating multi- or mixed-angle tracks in the future, you may experience the dreaded "Cannot add entire video asset" error. This error occurs primarily if you have encoded your alternate angle MPEG streams with GOP structures that don't match. If this error occurs, there's only one thing to do—re-encode your MPEG streams!

Surprisingly, this error is very common if you encode MPEG streams directly from Final Cut Pro using Compressor. It's easy to fix, and you'll learn how in the following exercise. First, though, let's take a look at what happens when this error gets generated.

1 From the Assets tab, drag the **ai-extra.m2v** asset and drop it into the V3 stream, directly after the first cell marker.

A warning dialog appears. This dialog says the **ai-after.m2v** clip is only usable up to the timecode value of 00:00:02:00.

2 Click Use Anyway, and dismiss the GOP Alert dialog that appears by clicking OK..

Only the first 2 seconds of the **ai-after.m2v** clip are added to the track's V3 stream. What's going on here?

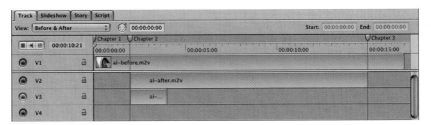

The main video stream in this track uses a 15-frame, closed GOP struc-
ture. As it turns out, only the first 2 seconds of the **ai-extra.m2v** asset has
GOPs that are 15 frames long. The next GOP is shorter, so DVD Studio
Pro must truncate the clip at the point where its GOP structure begins to
differ from the main video stream.

This problem was created by encoding the stream from Final Cut Pro
directly to MPEG video using Compressor. You'll see why this can be
problematic in the next section, but first let's delete this short clip from
the V3 stream.

3 In the Track Editor, select the clip in the V3 stream, and press the Delete key.

The clip is deleted from the V3 stream.

Exploring Final Cut Pro Cut Markers

The **ai-extra.m2v** clip was edited in Final Cut Pro. To avoid the time and disk
space required to render a final reference movie and then encode it, the clip
was encoded to MPEG-2 using Final Cut Pro's Export Using Compressor
option. This is a great time-saving and disk-space-saving feature, because you
can avoid rendering out a finished QuickTime movie before encoding, but it
has unexpected consequences when encoding MPEG-2 streams that will be
used for alternate angle tracks.

To facilitate higher quality encoding, Final Cut Pro automatically inserts com-
pression markers at every edit point in the sequence. These automatically
inserted markers are called *cut markers*. This ensures that every new scene
begins with a brand new I-frame, which improves the overall look of your
MPEG streams by making sure that a scene transition does not happen in the
middle of a GOP. However, with cut markers automatically inserted, you lose
the ability to control where I-frames will be placed in the MPEG stream, and
therefore wind up with very little control over the final MPEG stream's GOP
structure.

Fortunately, there's an easy way to fix this problem when you encode using
Compressor, as the following steps demonstrate.

NOTE ▶ This exercise assumes that you have Final Cut Pro installed on your system. If you do not have Final Cut Pro, skip ahead to "What You've Learned."

1 In the Assets tab, Ctrl-click the **ai-extra.m2v** asset and choose Reveal in Finder from the menu.

A Finder window opens. Next to the **ai-extra.m2v** asset there is an **ai-extra_FCP** project.

NOTE ▶ If your Finder window opens in column view, it may take a few seconds for the Finder to display the MPEG stream. Don't worry—the Finder is just thinking hard.

2 Double-click the **ai-extra_FCP** project file to open the project in Final Cut Pro.

The sequence's Timeline has three cut edits, including one at 00:00:02:03.

3 In Final Cut Pro, choose File > Export > Using Compressor.

Compressor opens, and the sequence is automatically added as a file in the Batch window.

4 In Compressor's Batch window, select the file and click the Preview button.

The Preview window opens.

5 From the Preview window's Marker menu, choose "show edit/cut markers."

Three green cut markers appear in the timeline, one for each of the cut edits in the Final Cut Pro sequence.

Unless further action is taken, Compressor will automatically insert I-frames at each of these cut markers when it encodes the MPEG stream. To avoid this, let's tell Compressor to ignore these cut edits.

6 Create a new Compressor MPEG-2 preset.

NOTE ▶ When you create the new MPEG preset, keep the maximum bit rate limitations for alternate angle streams in mind. To learn more, see "Encoding Alternate Angle Streams," earlier in this lesson.

7 In the new preset, click the Encoder button and then click the Extras button.

At the bottom of the Extras pane, you'll see the option "Include chapter markers only." With this option selected, Compressor will filter out all markers *except* chapter markers. A cut marker is not a chapter marker, so with this option selected, Compressor will remove cut markers (and any manually set compression markers) before it encodes the MPEG stream.

8 Click the "Include chapter markers only" check box.

9 Apply the preset to the file in the Batch window.

10 Encode the file.

11 Import the file into DVD Studio Pro.

12 In DVD Studio Pro, add the newly encoded file to the Before & After
track's V3 stream.

13 Edit the V3 stream so that it's exactly the same length as the V2 stream.

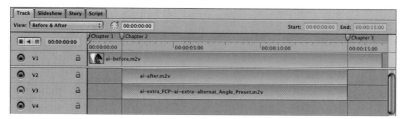

Nothing beats the sweet feeling of mixed-angle success!

14 Save the project file to the My_Projects folder on your hard drive.

Lesson Review

1. Each track in your project can have how many angles?

2. True or false: Each angle in a multi-angle track must use exactly the same GOP structure.

3. What's the Difference between multi-angle tracks and mixed-angle tracks?

4. Mixed-angle tracks must use markers, but where should you put them?

5. True or false: If you export using compressor from Final Cut Pro, each hard cut in your timeline is automatically turned into an I-Frame in the final MPEG stream.

Answers

1. One main angle, plus eight alternate angles for a total of nine different angles.

2. True. If not, DVD Studio Pro will only add the angle up to the point where the GOP structure differs.

3. In a multi angle track, all angles must be exactly the same length as the main angle, whereas in a mixed-angle track the alternate angles do not have to be the same length as the main angle.

4. Markers must "sandwich" the mixed-angles, with one at the front of the angle, and one at the back.

5. True. To avoid this, open your Compressor MPEG preset, visit the Extras tab, and enable the Include Chapter Markers only option.

19

Lesson Files	None
Media	Media > Advanced Authoring > Lesson 19
Time	This lesson takes approximately 60 minutes to complete.
Goals	Learn what formats of digital audio are compatible with DVD Studio Pro
	Explore AC-3 files and discover how they produce such tiny yet great-sounding audio streams
	Discover how to choose data rates for your AC-3 streams
	Explore dialog normalization
	Learn about dynamic range compression profiles
	Use downmix settings to turn a 5.1 surround stream into an appropriate stream for stereo playback

Audio Encoding

There's an old saying in the video world: Video is two-thirds audio. You can spend a great deal of time encoding perfect MPEG-2 streams, and your menus might be fun and engaging, but if your title's audio constantly peaks into distortion, or if you improperly encode an AC-3 (Dolby Digital) file so that its volume levels surge up and down (gain pumping), your carefully authored DVD will end up as a drink coaster. Audio is vital part of your project, and consequently it's incredibly important to get it right.

Fortunately, producing great-sounding audio streams is easy. It just takes a little practice. To help you on your way, this chapter details how to use Compressor to produce professional-quality, tightly compressed audio streams for use in your DVD Studio Pro projects. But be forewarned—creating AC-3 files takes practice, and also a practiced ear. Still, if you follow a few basic rules, much of the mystery behind Dolby Digital files will fade away, leaving you with audio that sparkles time after time.

Audio Formats for DVD-Video

DVD Studio Pro supports all of the following DVD-Video-compliant digital audio formats. *DVD-Video-compliant* means they are part of the DVD-Video specification, and are thus legal for use in DVD-Video titles:

▶ PCM—PCM stands for pulse code modulated, or uncompressed, digital audio. For example, AIFF, WAV, and SDII (Sound Designer 2) files all fall into the PCM category. For DVD-Video, PCM files must use a sampling rate of 48 or 96 kHz, at a bit depth of 16-bit, 20-bit, or 24-bit. PCM is a mandatory audio format for DVD-Video.

▶ AC-3—Also called Dolby Digital, AC-3 is a common 5.1 surround sound format. Like PCM, AC-3 is a mandatory audio format for DVD-Video, and every DVD player manufactured for the Western world must support this format. So if you deliver nothing but Dolby Digital audio streams on your discs, you can be sure your viewers will hear them.

▶ MPEG1-Layer 2—MPEG1-Layer 2 is a format of audio compression common on PAL DVDs. MPEG1-Layer 2 supports 5.1 surround sound and data rate compression but is not a mandatory audio format for DVD-Video.

▶ DTS—DTS is a high-quality surround format that offers higher data rate settings than AC-3, but DVD players are not required to have a DTS decoder. DTS streams are typically included as "optional" sound tracks, along with an AC-3 or PCM stream.

> **NOTE** ▶ The DVD Studio Pro Simulator does not have a DTS decoder. If you need to hear how a DTS audio stream sounds, you must burn a DVD disc and play it in a DVD player that supports DTS playback.

Of the formats just discussed, DVD Studio Pro comes with all the tools necessary to work with PCM and AC-3 files. If you want to use MPEG1-Layer 2 or DTS files, you'll have to look elsewhere for encoders.

The remainder of this chapter focuses on PCM and AC-3 digital audio.

Using Digital Audio Files in DVD Studio Pro

You just learned about all of the DVD-Video-compliant digital audio formats that DVD Studio Pro supports, but what about noncompliant formats such as MP3, AAC, or even 44.1 kHz PCM files ripped from an audio CD?

Well, guess what? DVD Studio Pro will actually let you work with noncompliant as well as compliant digital audio. In fact, DVD Studio Pro has a great built-in encoder that can transfer any format of audio that QuickTime understands into 48 kHz, 16-bit stereo PCM files (AIFF) that are DVD-Video-compliant.

1 In DVD Studio Pro, create a new, empty project.

2 From this book's companion DVD-ROM files, locate the Media > Advanced Authoring > Lesson 19 > MP3_Audio folder.

This folder has a single MP3 file in it: **trailer.mp3**.

TIP ▶ To open a Finder window over DVD Studio Pro, click the Finder icon in the Dock.

3 Drag **trailer.mp3** from the MP3_Audio folder directly into the Assets container.

DVD Studio Pro imports the file and converts it to a 48 kHz AIFF. Take a look at the MP3_Audio folder, and notice the new folder inside it, called MPEG.

New MPEG folder

4 Open the new MPEG folder and take a peek inside.

Notice the new AIFF file in this folder. This is the converted, 48 kHz, 16-bit stereo PCM file that DVD Studio Pro will use when it builds the project. As you can see, DVD Studio Pro quite handily converts any type of audio that you drag into the Assets container, including MP3, AAC, IMA 4:1, and even 44.1 kHz audio files ripped from audio CDs. Basically, if QuickTime can play the file, DVD Studio Pro will import and convert it.

TIP ▶ If you need to convert several audio files to 48 kHz from another format, use DVD Studio Pro. Just drag the files into the Assets container, go to the new MPEG folder, and harvest your converted audio files. This works great when, for example, you need to convert a few audio streams for editing in a 48 kHz Timeline in Final Cut Pro.

Note that by default, DVD Studio Pro encodes new files to the same folder as the source file, but you can change this functionality by using the Destinations pane in the Preferences window. Here you can choose to encode to the same folder as the source asset, to the project bundle itself, or to a specified or fallback folder.

Encoded file location

Destinations pane

When you select the Project Bundle option, DVD Studio Pro sends all encoded files into the *project bundle*—that is, to the file created when you first saved the project you're currently working on. You may access these files by Ctrl-clicking the project bundle and choosing Show Package Contents from the shortcut menu to tunnel into the project bundle.

Saving to the project bundle is a good way of consolidating all encoded assets to the same place on your hard disk(s), which is great for backing up projects but can result in huge project bundles. Additionally, if you select the project bundle as your encode destination, make sure you save your project before importing any files that need to be converted. Why? DVD Studio Pro needs to know where to place the encoded files, and if you haven't saved the project, there's no project bundle to store the encoded files. However, this problem isn't a show-stopper, because if the project is not saved, all encoded files will be sent to the fallback folder until you press Cmd-S to save that project.

About AC-3 Files

You just learned that AC-3 files are a mandatory digital audio format for DVD. In other words, all DVD players must support AC-3 playback. But AC-3 goes far beyond being just a standard. It also includes playback controls not available to the other formats. For example, AC-3 files incorporate a dynamic range control setting, as well as a volume control circuit (dialog normalization) that is designed to automatically adjust dialog levels between different audio streams.

Encoded Data and Control Parameter Settings

When an AC-3 file is created, two different types of data are wrapped into the package: *encoded data* and *control parameters.*

Encoded data settings control things like the number of channels in the file or the data rate—parameters that are "hardwired" with the file and cannot be changed after encoding is finished.

Control parameter settings are simply playback hints sent with the AC-3 file that tell the playback device how to play the encoded data. For example, the file's compression preset and downmix settings are all included as control parameters with the file, and they are interpreted by the playback device when the disc is played. Most control parameters can be overridden or altered by the playback device.

The following table lists encoded data settings and control parameters settings:

Encoded Data vs. Control Parameter Settings

Encoded Data	Control Parameters
Audio coding mode	Dialog normalization
Data rate	Bit stream mode
Apply Lowpass filter	Downmix settings
Apply DC filter	Copyright information
Apply 90° phase shift	Audio production information
	Compression preset
	RF overmodulation protection
	Apply digital de-emphasis

NOTE ► In the Disc Setup pane of the Apple DVD Player Preferences window, you can choose to disable Dolby dynamic range compression. This option overrides the included compression profile control parameters to help you avoid gain pumping—dramatic and unexpected fluctuations in volume—as a result of incorrectly encoded AC-3 streams.

Disk Setup pane

Frequency Masking

AC-3 files gain significant data reduction through a process of perceptual coding algorithms that selectively remove frequencies we can't hear from the final AC-3 stream. This process is based on *frequency masking.*

To get a sense of what this means, consider the following example. You're talking to a client on your cell phone, and a cement truck drives by. The rumble of the cement truck is loud, and it overrides your client's voice on the cell phone. Even though the client's voice is in a much higher frequency range than the rumble of the truck, loud sounds in one frequency range tend to override quieter sounds in adjoining frequency ranges. This phenomenon is called *masking*, and it lies at the heart of the AC-3 encoder.

When the AC-3 encoder creates a stream, it begins by separating the audio frequency spectrum into thousands of tiny bands. It then searches these bands to find which ones are relatively loud, compared with their neighbors. Bands that are so quiet they will not be heard are entirely removed from the stream. Consequently, AC-3 is a *lossy* compression process, because you can never get back the bits of audio—or the frequency ranges—that are thrown away.

Creating AC-3 Files with Compressor

The built-in encoder in DVD Studio Pro does not itself create AC-3 files. In other words, it will not transfer a PCM file to an AC-3 file. However, DVD Studio Pro does come with Compressor, and Compressor is more than up to the job of transcoding Dolby Digital files.

Let's start Compressor now and set up to make an AC-3 file:

1 Choose *Startup Disk* > Applications > Compressor.

> **TIP** ▶ If you haven't already added the Compressor icon to your Dock, do so now. With Compressor open, go to the Dock, Ctrl-click the Compressor icon, and choose Keep In Dock from the shortcut menu. Compressor will now be available right in the Dock, whenever you need it.

Compressor's Batch window appears on the screen.

2 In the Batch window, click the Import Surround Sound Group button (or choose File > Import Surround Group, or press Shift-Cmd-I).

A Channel Assignment sheet drops down from the Compressor title bar.

Okay, now you're ready to assign channels from a source digital audio file to be encoded. You'll learn how this works in the next section.

Assigning Source Audio Channels

Compressor is a versatile encoder, and it can create files of one (mono) to six channels (5.1 surround). Your first decision after opening Compressor is, "How many channels will my final AC-3 file have?" Once you've decided, you set the *audio coding mode*—AC-3 terminology for the number and arrangement of the channels in the stream.

Right now, Compressor is displaying the *input channel matrix*, which is where you assign audio channels to be encoded. By default, the input channel matrix is arranged to reflect the speaker positions of a 5.1 surround sound speaker system. But don't be fooled—you can encode any combination of audio channels, from 1 (mono), 2 (stereo), right up to 5.1 (surround). To demonstrate this, you'll begin by using Compressor to encode a stereo file:

1 In the Channel Assignment sheet, click the L button (Left Front Channel).

A selection dialog opens and prompts you to locate the file to use for the AC-3 stream's left channel.

2 Locate the file named Media > Advanced Authoring > Lesson 19 > AudioSlugs > –12TestTone.aif, and click Open.

The left channel of the file is assigned to the input channel matrix Front Left Channel button.

You can also drag and drop audio files from the Finder, directly onto input matrix channel buttons.

3 Open a Finder window over Compressor, and navigate to the **–12TestTone.aif** file.

4 Drag the **–12TestTone.aif** file directly onto the Right Front Channel button.

Compressor assigns the right channel from the AIFF file to the input channel matrix Right Front Channel button.

5 Click OK.

A new Surround group is added to the Batch window.

Creating a Dolby Digital Preset

You have a file imported into Compressor's Batch window. That's step one. But, there's a massive step still ahead—you need to create a Dolby Digital preset to assign to this file, which is not a shallow task:

1 Press Cmd-2 to open the Presets window.

2 Click and hold the Create New Setting button, and then choose Dolby Digital Professional from the pop-up menu that appears.

A new Dolby Digital preset is added to the Custom settings group.

3 Double-click the new Dolby Digital preset.

The Inspector updates to show you the preset's properties. In the following sections, you'll use the Inspector almost exclusively as you learn about all of the important settings required to create proper, professionally encoded AC-3 streams. With that in mind, focus your attention now on this very important Compressor window.

Assigning the Audio Coding Mode

The first step in creating a preset is determining how many audio channels the preset will encode. You already imported a stereo file into Compressor as a surround sound group. To properly encode those two audio channels into a stereo file, you must tell the Dolby Digital preset to always encode only stereo files, which you'll accomplish by setting the preset's audio coding mode:

1 In the Name field, change the preset name to *My Stereo Dolby Digital Preset*.

2 Ensure that 2/0 (L,R) is selected in the Audio Coding Mode menu.

Notice there are many channel configurations, from 1 channel (mono) straight through to 5.1 (surround sound). This is an important consideration, because a preset using a stereo audio coding mode cannot be used to encode a surround file, and vice versa. In fact, other settings in the preset, including Data Rate and Downmix settings, depend upon the audio coding mode used. Consequently, you need to create different presets for each different type of audio you encode on your computer.

Choosing a Bit Rate

Dolby Digital's biggest virtue is its capability to compress digital audio to make the file size smaller, while still maintaining high-quality sound. Although you could encode all AC-3 streams at the maximum setting legal for DVD-Video (448 kbps), doing so would create AC-3 streams that have a far bigger file sizes than needed. Instead, you should learn how to clamp down Compressor's digital "vise" to squeeze the smallest possible file size out of your AC-3 files while still maintaining optimal sound quality.

You can accomplish this by adjusting Compressor's Data Rate setting. The *data rate* (or *bit rate*) you select will depend entirely upon the content of the source material you are encoding. For example, if you're encoding a mono stream of narration only, you can use a lower data rate than you would use for a complete main mix (music and vocals) stereo file and still maintain high quality. Similarly, 5.1 streams, which have six channels of audio, need a higher data rate than stereo streams. For reference, the following table lists common data rates used with three common audio coding modes.

> **NOTE ▶** There's no hard and fast rule about which data rate to use. When in doubt, you may need to encode the same file with two or three different data rates and then audition the final files to hear which one sounds the best, given the resulting file size.

Data Rates for Common Audio Coding Modes

Audio Coding Mode	Data Rate
Mono (1/0)	96 to 128 kbps
Stereo (2/0)	160 to 224 kbps
5.1 Surround (3/2)	448 kbps

In the following exercise, you'll try out some different data rate settings:

1 In the Audio tab, choose 192 kbps from the Data Rate pop-up menu.

You are encoding a stereo file, so 192 kbps is a good data rate that provides an optimum balance between file size and sound quality in the final AC-3 stream.

You may have noticed that several data rate options are dimmed in the Data Rate menu. Compressor is smart enough to show you only the legal data rates for your target delivery system. For example, in DVD-Video, only data rates from 64 to 448 kbps are legal for use.

Compressor uses the setting in the Target System pop-up menu to determine which data rates are legal for use.

2 Choose Generic AC-3 from the Target System pop-up menu.

3 Choose 640 kbps from the Data Rate pop-up menu.

Notice that with Generic AC-3 selected as the Target System, you have access to three data rates that are higher than the maximum AC-3 data rate of 448 kbps for DVD.

4 Choose DVD Video from the Target System pop-up menu.

A dialog opens to tell you that the specified data rate is out of range for your target delivery system. Compressor goes ahead and changes the data rate to the next-closest legal setting for use with DVD.

5 Set the Data Rate for this stereo file back to 192 kbps.

Encoding a File

With the audio coding mode and data rate set, you can now encode the file. But one warning—these are the bare minimum settings you should make. There's a lot more you can do to tweak the file and make it sound better, and you'll learn about that in a few moments. For now, you'll step through the process of actually encoding a file:

1 In the Inspector, click Save.

2 Assign the new Dolby Digital preset to the file in the Batch window, and
 set its Destination to your computer's Desktop (or some other folder
 where you can easily access the file).

3 Click Submit.

The Batch Monitor opens and encodes the file.

About Dialog Normalization

In the audio world, normalization is the process of matching the volume level between two different songs. For example, it's common to normalize the volume of CD-Audio so that peak volumes of all songs on the disc are close to 0 dB on the digital scale (also referred to as 0 dBFS, or 0 dB *full scale*).

In the video world, audio is normalized in a slightly different way. When you watch a video, your ear pays the most attention to the audio stream's dialog, because it's the dialog that provides most of the information. During the video, certain sounds, like explosions or chirping crickets, are either louder or quieter than the dialog. Nonetheless, it is the dialog that we focus on, so it's common practice to normalize the audio levels of our video so that all dialog reaches the viewer at the same volume level, across all programs. This is the reason why the news announcer on one television channel is at the same volume as the narrator in a documentary on the next channel: The audio streams have been normalized so that the dialog in each plays at exactly the same volume.

With CD-Audio discs, you are concerned only with peak volumes—specifically to get the audio as loud as possible without clipping by pushing it past 0 dBFS—but in the video world you'll usually look at average volume levels. Peak volumes are still important, because you still need to ensure that your audio stream doesn't clip. But you'll instead focus on average volume levels because dialog is not a steady sound—it fluctuates over time, and even in individual words, as the talent speaks. For example, if you say the word "peak," notice that your voice sounds louder on the "p" part than it does on the "eak" part.

The main point to keep in mind is that it's advantageous to judge dialog using average volume levels, not peak volume levels. For reference, the following table lists the average and peak volume levels commonly used for several different audio and video formats:

Average and Peak Dialog Level Comparison

Audio Format	Average Dialog Level	Peak Volume
Audio-CD	–6 dBFS	–0.1 dBFS
Broadcast television	–12 dBFS	–6 dBFS
Movie soundtrack	–31 dBFS	–6 dBFS
DVD-Video	–31 dBFS	–6 dBFS

TIP ▶ Properly encoded AC-3 files used on a DVD will always sound quieter than broadcast television. If you need your project's audio to sound as loud as broadcast television, use PCM audio files that have an average level of dialog of –12 dB and peak levels no higher than –6 dB.

If you compare the settings in the preceding table, you'll see that movie soundtracks and DVD-Videos both use the same average dialog level (–31 dBFS), as well as the same peak volume. This is because DVD-Video was designed as a delivery format for movies. Although DVD uses have grown far beyond Hollywood, AC-3 files were nonetheless designed with Hollywood in mind.

However, not all audio streams are created using an average dialog level of –31 dBFS. For example, if you're editing in Final Cut Pro, you will more often than not edit dialog so that it uses an average dialog level of –12 dB. You'll then need to lower the volume of this audio stream to –31 dB to create perfect audio for DVD-Video. This is the job of dialog normalization.

MORE INFO ▶ For a good discussion on creating audio in Final Cut Pro, see the book *Apple Pro Training Series: Advanced Editing and Finishing Techniques in Final Cut Pro 4* (Peachpit Press, 2003). This book has a few chapters on creating audio, including discussions of how to use test tones and the difference between average and peak levels in Final Cut Pro.

In fact, –31 is such a key number that you can't set a dialog normalization value that's lower. Follow these steps to see what happens if you try to enter –35 into the Dialog Normalization setting:

1 In the Inspector, type *–35* into the Audio tab's Dialog Normalization field, and press Return.

> **TIP** ▶ Always press Return when entering your Dialog Normalization setting. If you don't press Return, Compressor will not lock in the changed setting.

Compressor beeps at you. In fact, –31 dBFS is the lowest setting you can make in Compressor's Dialog Normalization setting (read on to find out why).

2 Set the Dialog Normalization setting to –31, and press Return.

The Dialog Normalization Formula

Before you get into Compressor, you need to determine the average level of the dialog in your audio stream. You can do this by watching Final Cut Pro's audio meter and taking an educated guess, or you can use sophisticated audio analyzing tools such as the Waves Paz Analyzer (www.waves.com) and Logic Pro. Whichever method you use, remember what the average level of your audio stream's dialog is, because this is exactly the value you will type into Compressor's Dialog Normalization setting.

PAZ Analyzer in Average Volume Level (RMS) mode Average volume level

The Waves PAZ Analyzer is great at displaying average volume levels, as well as the frequency distribution of sounds in your audio stream.

The dialog normalization value (DNV) is stored as control parameters in the encoded AC-3 stream, and it is applied at playback by the DVD player's AC-3 decoder according to the following formula:

At playback, your AC-3 stream will be attenuated, or lowered in volume, by (31 + DNV) dB.

So, if your source audio stream has dialog at an average level of –12 dB, and you set its DNV to –12 at the time of encoding, at playback this stream will be attenuated by (31 + (–12)) dB, or 19 dB. That's a lot of attenuation, but the result is that the stream plays with an average level of dialog of –31 dB.

Similarly, if a second audio stream on your DVD has an average level of dialog of –20 dB, at playback it will be attenuated (31 + (–20)) dB, or 11 dB. The result is that this audio stream will also play back with an average dialog level of –31 dB. The two audio streams have both been normalized to –31 dB.

Let's put this theory into action. In the following steps, you will use Compressor to create three AC-3 files. The first file has an average level of dialog of –12 dB, the second is –20 dB, and the third is –31 dB. These streams also have a test tone at the same level as the dialog, so you can really hear how the Dialog Normalization setting affects them.

1 In QuickTime Player, open the following files, located in the Media > Advanced Authoring > Lesson 19 > AudioSlugs folder:

–12TestTone.aif

–20TestTone.aif

–31TestTone.aif

2 Play each file.

Listen carefully to the difference in volume between the three files. The **–12TestTone.aif** file is the loudest of all three files. The **–31TestTone.aif** file is quietest, and the **–20TestTone.aif** file sits somewhere in the middle. Leave these files open in QuickTime throughout the following steps so that you can later return to QuickTime to hear what the original files sound like.

You need to encode three different files, which is a perfect job for Compressor.

3 Add the files to the Compressor Batch window.

4 In the Presets window, create a new Dolby Digital Professional preset.

5 Double-click the new preset to open it in the Inspector.

6 Name it *-12 Dialog Normalization.*

7 Set the Audio Coding Mode to 2/0 (L,R), Data Rate to 192 kbps, and
 Dialog Normalization to −12. Press Return.

8 Repeat Steps 4 through 7 to create two additional Dolby Digital presets.
 Name them *−20 Dialog Normalization* and *−31 Dialog Normalization.* And
 finally, set each file's Dialog Normalization value to −20 and −31, respec-
 tively

9 In the Batch window, assign the *–12 Dialog Normalization* preset to the
–12TestTone.aif file; assign the *–20 Dialog Normalization* preset to the
–20TestTone.aif file; and then assign the *–31 Dialog Normalization* preset
to the **–31TestTone.aif** file.

10 Set the destination of each file to your Desktop.

11 Click Submit.

The Batch Monitor opens, and the files are encoded to your Desktop.

Auditioning a File

The final step in producing an AC-3 file is auditioning it to judge the encoded sound quality. There's no need to wait for the final DVD, because you can audition AC-3 files directly inside DVD Studio Pro.

1 In the Finder, select the three Dolby Digital files you just encoded.

> **NOTE ▶** Hold the Command key to select multiple files.

2 Double-click one of the selected files.

The files are imported into DVD Studio Pro and appear in the Assets tab.

3 In the Assets tab, double-click the **–12TestTone–12 Dialog Normalization.ac3** file.

The AC-3 stream begins playing in the Viewer. Listen carefully to the volume of this file. (This works best through headphones.) Remember that the source file was louder than the **–20TestTone.aif** and **–31TestTone.aif** files.

4 In the Assets tab, double-click the **–20TestTone–20 Dialog Normalization.ac3** file.

Do you notice anything interesting about the file's volume? It's exactly the same as that of the **–12TestTone–12 Dialog Normalization.ac3** file.

5 In the Assets tab, double-click the **–31TestTone–31 Dialog Normalization.ac3** file.

Once again, this file's volume sounds exactly like the volume on the other two, because all three files have been normalized to –31 dBFS. They are all now the same volume, because the Dialog Normalization settings in Compressor were all appropriately set to the average volume level of the dialog in the source files.

6 Switch back to QuickTime and play the original source files. Then use DVD Studio Pro to audition the encoded files one more time.

Notice the difference between the volume levels of the source and encoded files.

Understanding Compression Profiles

AC-3 files contain special control parameters that control *dynamic range compression* at playback. Not to be confused with data rate compression, dynamic range compression does not lower the data rate of the final AC-3 file. Instead, it helps to even out the difference between the highest and lowest volumes in a single audio stream.

You can assign one of six compression profiles to AC-3 files through the Dolby Digital preset's Preprocessing tab. Each compression profile is descriptively named. For example, if your audio stream contains music, the Music Standard profile is the one to select. If the audio stream contains nothing but dialog, use the Speech profile.

> **NOTE** ▶ AC-3 compression profiles are designed by Dolby, and you can't change them or their sound.

So what do these compression profiles sound like? Well, it's hard to tell sound from numbers, but the following table lists the different profile qualities for your reference.

AC-3 Dynamic Range Compression Profiles

Profile	Film Standard	Film Light	Music Standard	Music Light	Speech Quality
Null band width	10 dB	20 dB	10 dB	20 dB	10 dB
Null band range (dB)	(–31 to –21)	(–41 to –21)	(–31 to –21)	(–41 to –21)	(–31 to –21)
Max boost	6 dB	6 dB	12 dB	12 dB	15 dB
Boost ratio	2:1	2:1	2:1	2:1	5:1
Max cut	24 dB	24 dB	24 dB	15 dB	24 dB
Cut ratio	20:1	20:1	20:1	2:1	20:1

Notice that the null band of each compression profile straddles –31 dB. The null band specifies a range in which no dynamic range compression is applied to the file. When the volume of the stream pumps above the top of the null range, dynamic range compression is applied to lower the volume of the sound. When the volume goes below the bottom of the null band range, dynamic range compression is applied to raise the volume of the sound. The result is that the sound is always pushed toward the volume levels at the top and bottom of the null band.

If you've properly set your dialog normalization value, your audio stream's dialog will play at –31 dB. This means that dynamic range compression will not often be applied to the file—another important reason to properly assign your dialog normalization value. In fact, there's one thing about dynamic range compression that you must keep in mind:

If you don't correctly set your dialog normalization value, you MUST disable dynamic range compression, or your AC-3 file will very likely exhibit gain pumping—that is, dramatic and unexpected volume fluctuations.

It's hard to describe sounds in words, so let's play with Compressor's Dynamic Range profiles and see how they work. The test file you will encode is a test tone along with an intermittent beat. The test tone is at −21 dB, while the beat peaks at −1 dB.

1 In the Presets window's Settings tab, double-click the My Stereo Dolby Digital Preset.

The Inspector updates to display the selected preset's properties.

2 In the Inspector's Audio tab, ensure the preset's Dialog Normalization value is set to −31, and press Return.

Remember the dialog normalization formula: At playback the AC-3 stream will be attenuated $(31 + DNV)$ dB. Thus, when Dialog Normalization is set to -31, no attenuation will be applied to the file at playback $(31 + (-31) = 0$ dB of attenuation). This is appropriate for this exercise, because now you will hear only the sound of the dynamic range compression.

3 In the Preprocessing tab, set the Compression Preset to Film Standard Compression.

4 From a Finder window, drag the Media > Advanced Authoring > Lesson 19 > AudioSlugs > **–21TestTone-Beats.aif** file and drop it into Compressor's Batch window.

5 In the Batch window, assign the My Stereo Dolby Digital Preset to the file.

6 Set the file's destination to your Desktop, and encode the file.

7 Find the file on your Desktop, and double-click it.

The file imports into the DVD Studio Pro Assets tab.

8 In the Assets tab, double-click the newly imported file.

Notice that as the beat plays, the volume of the test tone dips. This is gain pumping, and it happens because the AC-3 Monitor is applying dynamic range compression to the loud beat, causing the entire audio stream to dip in volume until the loud beat passes, at which time the stream once again rises in volume. The reason? According to the dynamic range profile, the AC-3 Monitor is attempting to push the volume down to the null band range (–21 dB at the top). Consequently, the AC-3 Monitor is pushing the beat part of the stream from –1 dB to –21 dB. It doesn't sound very good at all!

9 In the Inspector's Preprocessing tab, set the Compression Preset to None.

10 Click Save to lock in the changed compression profile.

11 Re-encode the **–21TestTone-Beats.aif** file with this modified preset.

Remember to set your Desktop as the file's destination. And don't worry if you replace the file you made a few steps back, because DVD Studio Pro will automatically update and play the newly encoded file.

12 Switch to DVD Studio Pro and audition the new file.

This new file, with no compression preset, sounds much louder than the first one. This is because no dynamic range compression is applied. This file is coming out of Compressor at exactly the same volume as it went in.

TIP ▶ If you want to preserve the volume level of your source audio streams, set Dialog Normalization to –31 dB, and set the Compression Preset to None. Now your AC-3 streams will play at exactly the same volume as the source audio stream.

Surround Sound and Downmixing

As programs like Logic Pro begin to appear on more and more video editing stations, 5.1 surround sound is becoming increasingly popular. And of course, DVD-Video in conjunction with AC-3 audio makes a perfect 5.1 surround delivery format, so there's no reason not to jump onto this next wave in audio design.

MORE INFO ▶ To find out how to mix surround sound in Logic Pro, check out the book *Apple Pro Training Series: Logic Pro 7 and Express 7* (Peachpit Press, 2005). This book has a lesson dedicated to surround mixing, and it even comes with a 30-day demo of Logic, so you can try it out for yourself!

Logic Pro's Surround Panner

AC-3 files enjoy a tremendous advantage when it comes to delivering 5.1 surround audio streams because they incorporate a downmix algorithm that can turn a 5.1 surround stream into a properly formatted audio stream for the playback device. For example, if the playback device has only stereo outputs, a 5.1 surround AC-3 stream will automatically be converted to a stereo stream. In Compressor, you can control how this downmixing occurs. For example, you can decide how the surround channels are mixed into the stereo channels, so that your viewer will never miss a second of your sound.

1 In the Presets window's Settings tab, double-click the My Stereo Dolby Digital Preset.

The Inspector updates to display the selected preset's properties.

2 In the Inspector, change the preset's name to *My Surround Dolby Digital Preset*.

3 In the Inspector's Audio tab, set the Audio Coding Mode to 3/2 (L, C, R, Ls, Rs).

An alert dialog appears, telling you one or more data rates have changed. Your preset's data rate *was* set to 192, and that's too low for 5.1 surround. Consequently, Compressor has automatically increased the data rate to 224 kbps. In fact, 224 kbps is acceptable if your soundtrack has only vocals and a few effects swirling through the background, but if it's a full mix with music, effects, and vocals coming out of all six channels, you should double the data rate to the maximum allowed for DVD-Video: 448 kbps.

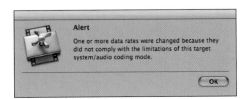

NOTE ▶ If your surround stream has a low-frequency effects channel, make sure that the Enable Low Frequency Effects check box is selected.

4 From the Data Rate pop-up menu, choose 448 kbps.

5 In the Preprocessing tab, make sure that the LFE Channel: Low-Pass Filter check box is selected.

This check box enables a brick-wall low-pass filter at 120 Hz. In general, 120 Hz is considered the highest frequency you should send to an LFE channel device, or subwoofer, so it's important to turn this filter on. With this filter disabled, you *could* encode a full frequency channel into the LFE channel, but no subwoofer would be able to accurately reproduce this sound. All those extra frequencies would be just a waste of bits in the final AC-3 stream.

6 In the Bitstream tab, choose a Center Downmix option.

The choices are –3.0, –4.5, and –6.0 dB. So which to choose? When you downmix the center channel, the sound in this channel is sent to both the left and right speakers to create the effect of a *phantom center channel.* Effectively, you are playing two mono streams of the exact same content, at the exact same time, through both the left and right speakers. The effect will be similar to having a center speaker.

There is an interesting phenomenon in audio: When you play the exact same sound twice, at the exact same time, the volume of the sound increases by 6 dB. When you downmix the center channel to both the left and right speakers, the sound of the center channel may increase by up to 6 dB relative to the other sounds in the AC-3 stream. To counteract this, you can choose to attenuate the downmixed center channel by up to 6 dB.

7 Choose a Surround Downmix option.

The choices are –3.0, –6.0, and – ∞ (infinity) dB. When you downmix the surround channels, the sound in the left surround speaker is sent to the front left speaker, and the sound in the right surround speaker is sent to the right front speaker. If you wish to ensure that the surround channels are not downmixed into the front channels, choose the – ∞ option.

NOTE ▶ The LFE channel is not downmixed into the left and right channels. Consequently, it's a good idea to mix some of your bass sounds into the left and right channels when you're creating your surround audio streams in an audio editor like Logic Pro.

8 In the Batch window, click the Import Surround Sound Group button.

The input channel matrix sheet appears.

9 In the Media > Advanced Authoring > Lesson 19 > SurroundStems folder, locate the six surround stems and assign each stem to the appropriate input channel button. Click OK.

Note that each stem has a hyphen and an abbreviation at the end of the filename. These abbreviations are the default abbreviations applied by Logic Pro, and they stand for the following:

- C: Center
- L: Left
- Sub: Low-frequency effects
- R: Right
- Ls: Rear left
- Rs: Rear right

10 Assign My Surround Dolby Digital Preset to the file and encode it.

Lesson Review

1. Can you import a 44.1 kHz AIFF file directly into DVD Studio Pro?

2. Is 44.1 kHz AIFF a digital audio format that is legal for use in DVD-Video (is it part of the DVD-Video specification)?

3. In a Dolby Digital file, what is the audio coding mode?

4. What is the most common data rate for stereo AC-3 files?

5. True or false: Dolby Digital files can automatically raise or lower in volume to ensure a uniform volume level across all programs on your DVD-Video.

6. What is the dialog normalization formula?

Answers

1. Yes. In fact, you can import any audio format that QuickTime understands directly into your project.

2. No. DVD Studio Pro must convert all nonlegal digital audio formats, including 44.1 kHz AIFFs, into 48 kHz AIFFs, which are legal for use in DVD-Video.

3. The audio coding mode determines how many channels the final AC-3 file will have, and also their position inside the surround sound spectrum.

4. 192 kbps. 448 kbps is a common data rate for 5.1 surround files.

5. True. But only if you set the dialog normalization formula correctly.

6. At playback, your AC-3 stream will be attenuated, or lowered in volume, by (31 + DNV) dB.

20

Lesson Files	Lessons > 20_Scripting-Start; 20_Scripting-Finished
Media	Media > Advanced Authoring > Lesson 20 folder
Time	This lesson takes approximately 60 minutes to complete.
Goals	Learn how to script with General Parameter Register Memories (GPRMs) and System Parameter Register Memories (SPRMs)
	Discover how to use compare commands to program your DVD-Video to make its own decisions
	Use the Simulator's Information Drawer to keep track of GPRM and SPRM values as you simulate scripts
	Discover how to use a prescript
	Learn how to check SPRM 1, which stores the current audio stream
	Learn how to check SPRM 14, which stores the DVD player's aspect ratio
	Learn how to check SPRM 13, which stores the DVD player's parental level

Lesson **20**
Scripting

There's a simple fact about DVD-Video: It's old technology. Because you're familiar with Macromedia Flash on the Internet, and Macromedia Director or Totally Hip Software's LiveStage Professional, you tend to expect DVD-Video to live up to today's standard of interactivity. But the truth is, DVD-Video, as a format, was finalized in 1994. In other words, DVD-Video reached full maturity when Macromedia Flash was in its infancy.

The good news is that you're not stuck with a 1994 view of what interactivity should be. Scripting is one of the best ways to make your DVDs much more interactive.

This chapter begins by introducing you to several of the important scripts you'll use day-to-day with DVD Studio Pro. These scripts form the base of most of the scripts you'll write in DVD Studio Pro. Of course, scripts are situation-dependent, and your scripting requirements will change from project to project. However, with a little effort you can adapt the techniques learned here to your own personal projects in the real world.

Getting Started

In this lesson, you will take a project that is close to complete, and add the finishing touches through five scripts that complete the navigational structure of the DVD-Video. In a moment, you'll open the project and take a look at where you're going. But first things first—this project uses a custom alpha transition that we've created for you. You must install this alpha transition before you can continue. (To learn more about alpha transitions, see Lesson 16, "Creating Transitions.")

> **NOTE ▶** If you do not install the custom alpha transition, DVD Studio Pro will substitute the default transition when it loads this project. However, installing the transition takes less time than it took to read this sentence, so why not install it?

1 Drag the Folder named APTS_Trans from the Media > Advanced Authoring > Lesson 20 > Transitions folder and drop it into your *Startup Disk* > Library > Application Support > DVD Studio Pro > Apple > Transitions folder.

> **TIP ▶** If you don't see a Transitions folder in the Application Support > DVD Studio Pro folder, just create a new folder and name it *Transitions*.

If you do not have permission to access the *Startup Disk* > Library > Application Support > DVD Studio Pro > Transitions folder, use the

Startup Disk > Users > *your user name* > Library > Application Support > DVD Studio Pro > Apple> Transitions folder. The only difference between the two is that transitions in the *Startup Disk* > Library > ... folder are available to every user on the computer, whereas transitions in the *your user name* > Library >... folder are available to just that user.

2 Start (or restart) DVD Studio Pro.

Alpha transitions are loaded when DVD Studio Pro launches, so you need to start, or restart, DVD Studio Pro before this custom alpha transition will become available.

3 Open the DVD Studio Pro Project file named **20_Scripting-Start**.

Menus Scripts

Track Sponsor Web link

This project has a series of menus, a track, and two script items that have already been created for you. Notice that script items are brown.

This is a 16:9 project, so you need to be sure you are simulating at the correct aspect ratio. To do so, take a quick trip to DVD Studio Pro's Preferences window.

4 Choose DVD Studio Pro > Preferences, and click the Simulator icon to open that pane. Change the aspect ratio to 16:9.

Simulator Preferences pane

16:9 aspect ratio

5 Click OK to close the Preferences window.

6 Simulate the project and explore the navigation of this title.

There are a few mistakes, to be sure. In fact, the aspectRatioTest and parentalLevelTest menus just plain don't work. That's because you need to do some scripting! Let's get started.

Scripting Basics

At its core, DVD-Video's interactivity is simply the capability to jump between project items. Whether you're using a track end jump to link to a menu, or a menu button to target a slide in a slideshow, DVD authoring is solely focused on building a navigational structure to display your items.

Scripting is a method for enhancing this kind of interactivity. When you write DVD scripts, you are essentially building complex and advanced project navigation structures—things you can't do using button targets or end jumps alone.

The climax of 95 percent of the scripts you'll write is a jump action that jumps the viewer out of the script to a different project item. You'll use jump actions a lot, so let's ease into scripting by checking one out.

1 Ctrl-click the Graphical view, and choose Add > Script from the shortcut menu.

A new script item is created.

2 Double-click the script to open it in the Script Editor.

By default each new script has a single Nop command. Nop stands for "no operation," or do nothing. When a DVD player runs into a scripted Nop command, it does exactly what the Nop command says to do—nothing! In other words, the DVD player will literally stop playback right at that point—usually displaying a black screen—because it has no further commands to follow. Because of this, you need to replace this default Nop command with a command that's a bit more useful.

NOTE ▶ If the Nop command is part of a pre-script, the Nop command acts as an exit command and the item that the pre-script is attached to will play.

3 In the Script Editor, select the Nop command.

The Inspector updates to display the selected command's properties. As you can see, there's not much to this script, because all of the Inspector's property areas currently say "Not Applicable."

Command menu

Let's turn this Nop command into a jump action.

4 From the Inspector's Command pop-up menu, choose Jump.

The Inspector updates to show you the jump command's unique properties. Back in the Script Editor, the command line changes to say "Jump not set." The next step is to set the project item that this command targets.

5 From the Inspector's Jump To pop-up menu, choose Menus > mainMenu > AudioStreamSelector.

This jump command now targets the AudioStreamSelector button on the main menu. But don't take our word for it—check it out for yourself.

6 In the Graphical view, Ctrl-click the new script tile, and choose Simulate Script from the shortcut menu.

The Simulator opens to display the main menu with the AudioStream-Selector button automatically selected. You've just programmed a jump action using a script!

7 Close the Simulator.

Using Variables

Scripting is powerful because it lets you program your DVD-Video to make its own decisions. These decisions can be based on viewer input, such as the order in which buttons are clicked, or they can be automatic decisions based on the order in which project items are played. In either situation, you will need to use variables to give your scripts maximum playback power.

In DVD-Video scripting, variables are called *General Parameter Register Memory*, or *GPRMs* for short. In DVD Studio Pro, you have access to eight GPRMs that you can use in your scripts.

> **NOTE** ▶ The DVD-Video Specification provides for 16 GPRMs. DVD Studio Pro gives you access to 8 of them, and reserves the other 8 GPRMs for "under-the-hood," or behind-the-scenes, calculations.

1 In the Graphical view, select the Script 1 item.

The Inspector updates to display the script's properties. These properties include all eight of the GPRMs available to your scripts. If you find it helps your workflow, you can rename these GPRMs to something more

descriptive than their default names. GPRMs are global to your entire proj-
ect, so it's often beneficial to use one GPRM in one script, a second GPRM
in the next script, and so on. Renaming a GPRM makes it less likely that
you will accidentally use the same GPRM in two conflicting scripts.

2 In the Inspector, double-click the text box to the left of GPRM 0 and type
 buttonSelector.

3 In the Script Editor, select the current command line.

 The Inspector updates to display the command's properties.

4 Change the selected command in the Inspector's Command pop-up menu from Jump to Set GPRM.

The Inspector updates to show the Set GPRM command's properties.

To experiment with variables, let's use the next few steps to store the value 1 in our newly named GPRM. In DVD Studio Pro methodology, you are going to move a value into the GPRM named buttonSelector. A quick look at the Inspector shows that DVD Studio Pro has already helped us along the way. The Operation menu says "mov," which means *move*, and the target for this move action is the buttonSelector GPRM. You're halfway there, but before you go any further, let's take a second to explore the Operation and Target pop-up menus.

5 Click and hold the Operation pop-up menu to open it.

The Operation pop-up menu shows all of the things you can do with this GPRM. For example, you can move a value into it (mov); perform addition (add), subtraction (sub), and several other mathematical operations; or even load a randomly generated number into the GPRM (ran).

6 Leave the Operation set to mov.

7 Click and hold the Target pop-up menu.

The Target pop-up menu displays all of the GPRMs, including the one you renamed to buttonSelector. As its name implies, the Target menu determines which GPRM you will move the value into in the next few steps.

8 Leave the Target pop-up menu set to buttonSelector.

9 From the Source Type pop-up menu, choose Immediate.

The Source Type pop-up menu determines the source of the info you will move into the target GPRM. There are several sources that you can use, and we'll cover each of them in later exercises. For now, let's concentrate on the Immediate source type. The Immediate source allows you, the DVD author, to state exactly what value should be loaded into the GPRM.

Once you've selected a source type, you need to define a source value.

10 In the Source Value text box, type *1*.

When the script executes, the value 1 will be moved into the GPRM named buttonSelector.

That was easy enough. Let's move on to the next section and put this script to action.

Using the Simulator's Information Drawer

The Simulator can show you GPRM settings, as well as other important script settings, as you preview your DVD. This information is displayed on the Simulator's Information Drawer. Let's use the Information Drawer now to check the value you moved into the buttonSelector GPRM.

1 In the Graphical view, Ctrl-click the Script 1 item, and choose Simulate.

The Simulator opens and plays Script 1. This script, of course, does not have a jump action, so the Simulator stops on a black screen after executing the script.

2 On the Simulator's remote control, click the Info button.

Info key

The Simulator's Information Drawer opens. The Information Drawer has two display areas: an Item Properties area and a Registers area.

Item Properties area Registers area

NOTE ► The Information Drawer can open on the top, bottom, left, or right side of the Simulator. Where it opens depends upon your screen resolution, and also on the Simulator's position on the screen. If the Simulator is close to the left edge of the screen, for example, the Information Drawer will most likely open on the Simulator's right side.

3 In the Information Drawer's Registers area, scroll down until you can see the GPRM settings.

Notice that the buttonSelector GPRM holds the value of 1. This confirms that you have just set the value for a variable in your DVD project. If you want to test this a bit further, close the Simulator, move a different immediate value into the buttonSelector, and then launch the Simulator once again to check out what the Information Drawer's GPRM settings say.

Programming the Title Button

One common rule of DVD navigation is that when the user returns to a menu, the button automatically selected should always be the one that corresponds to the last project item played. Using DVD Studio Pro's target menus, it's usually a simple matter to target jump actions directly to individual menu buttons. But in some situations, you can't control the way the user returns to a menu.

A classic example of this navigation problem is the Title button, which can only be set once for the whole project, in the Disc Property Inspector. In this section, you will program a script that looks at the last item played and then tells the DVD player which main menu button to select. You will then assign this script to the Title button, ensuring that the correct menu button is always correctly displayed, regardless of how the viewer returns to the main menu.

1 Ctrl-click the main menu item and choose Simulate Menu.

2 In the Simulator, click one of the main menu's buttons.

3 Now click the Simulator's Title button.

Title button Submenu

The Simulator jumps back to the main menu, and the top menu button highlights by default. To fix this navigation problem, you must use a script.

Top button selected

4 Close the Simulator.

Using the Last Item Command

To script the Title button, you need to solve this problem: How do I jump to specific menu buttons based on the last project item played? Fortunately, DVD Studio Pro has a special script command for just this purpose: the Last Item command. Every item in your project has a unique value assigned to it, and the DVD-Video player can use this value to keep track of the order in which items play. The last item command will always provide the value of the last project item played, whether it's the last track, the last menu, or even the last slideshow that played. Last item is a very versatile command.

To use the last item command, you do much the same thing as when you moved an immediate numerical value into the buttonSelector GPRM. But instead of moving a numerical value into the GPRM, you will now move the value of the last item played into the GPRM.

1 In the Graphical view, double-click the Script 1 item.

The script opens in the Script Editor, and the Inspector updates to display the script's properties. Let's take this opportunity to give this script a better name than "Script 1."

2 In the Inspector's Name text box, type *buttonSelectorScript.*

3 In the Script Editor, select the command line.

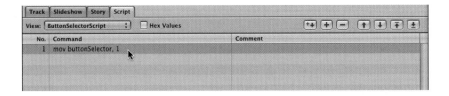

The Inspector updates to display the command line's properties. Right now this script is configured to move an immediate value of 1 into the GPRM named buttonSelector.

4 From the Inspector's Source Type pop-up menu, choose Special.

5 From the Source Value pop-up menu, choose Last Item.

Now the script says "move the value of the last item played into the GPRM named buttonSelector." This is a good start. But you need to check the value stored in the buttonSelector GPRM and then jump to the appropriate button on the main menu. To do so, you'll use a series of compare commands.

Using Compare Commands

In DVD Studio Pro, a compare command is similar to a conditional statement in other programming languages. Classically, a conditional statement has an "if, then" structure. In other words, a conditional statement might say, "*If* the last item that played was the AspectRatioTest menu, *then* play the Main Menu button named aspectRatioTest."

Compare commands in DVD Studio Pro work similarly, except the conditional statement is configured backward. So, in DVD Studio Pro, the conditional statement would say, "Play the Main Menu button named aspectRatioTest *if* the last item that played was the AspectRatioTest menu." It's a different sentence structure, but the result is the same.

As with all things in DVD Studio Pro, learning by example is the best way, so let's create a compare command and see how it works.

1 At the top of the Script Editor, click the Add Command button.

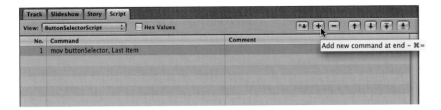

A new command line is added to the Script Editor, and by default this new command line is filled with an Nop command.

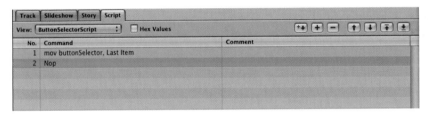

2 Create a jump command that targets the main menu button named aspectRatioTest.

For more information on creating jump commands, see the earlier section called "Scripting Basics."

3 In the Inspector, check the Compare Command check box.

Back in the Script Editor, an "if" section has been added to the jump com-
mand line. This is the compare command.

Compare command

4 In the Inspector's Compare Command area, set the "to" pop-up menu to
Jump Target.

5 In the Inspector's Compare Command area, set the "with value" pop-up menu to Menus > aspectRatioTest > [Menu].

The finished command line should look like the one in the following figure. Literally, this script now says

▶ Store the value of the last item played in the GPRM named buttonSelector.

▶ If the GPRM named buttonSelector has the value of the AspectRatioTest menu, play the main menu button named aspectRatioTest.

6 Repeat steps 2 through 5, creating a separate jump action and compare command for the project's two remaining submenus (parentalLevelTest and audioStreamChecker).

When you're finished, your Script Editor will look like this:

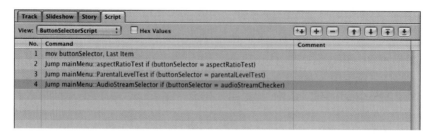

7 Click the Graphical view's background to select the disc itself.

The Disc Inspector updates to display the disc's properties. The Inspector's
General tab has a Remote Control area that display a Title button setting.

8 From the Remote Control area's Title setting, choose Scripts >
buttonSelectorScript.

9 Simulate the project, and use the Title button to jump from submenus back to the main menu.

Each time you return to the main menu, the proper button automatically highlights.

Using Escape Commands

DVD players execute scripts beginning at command line 1, and then progress to command line 2, command line 3, and so on. If a particular command line cannot be executed (for example, if a compare command is false), the player simply skips to the next command line, and it keeps going until it finds a command line that jumps it out of the script. But what happens if the script does not contain any command lines that the player can execute? The player continues to the end of the script and stops. Black screen…oh no!

To guard against this, you should place an escape command at the end of every script. An escape command is a jump action placed in a script's last command line. If by some chance the player works through every line in the script without executing, the escape command ensures that your DVD keeps playing. Typically, you'll use the escape command to jump the viewer back to an easily recognizable menu, such as the project's main menu, although the choice is up to you and depends on the particular situation.

Let's add an escape command to the buttonSelectorScript you've been working on.

1 Add a new command line to the end of the buttonSelectorScript.

2 Configure the new command as a jump command.

3 Use the Inspector's Jump To menu to target this jump command at the project's main menu.

Escape command line Jump command

Scripting Audio Streams

In earlier lessons you learned that it's possible to include up to eight alternate audio streams in every track. Projects that have alternate audio streams often include an *audio options* menu that allows users to choose which audio stream they'd like to hear. When you return to the audio options menu, it's a good idea to ensure that the correct button is automatically selected so that viewers know which audio stream they've been listening to. To achieve this, you will need to write a script.

In Lesson 18 you experimented with dialog normalization by encoding three AIFFs to AC-3. The source AIFFs each had a test tone, one at –12 dB, one at –20 dB, and the last at –31 dB. The project you're currently working on has a single track, and that track contains the three source AIFF streams as well as the three encoded AC-3 files. It also has an audioStreamChecker menu that allows viewers to choose which of these six audio streams they'd like to hear. However, when you return to the audioStreamChecker menu, the first menu button is selected by default, instead of the button that corresponds to the last

audio stream that played. In the following section you'll create a script to fix this navigational problem. But first, let's see how the problem affects this project.

Alternate audio streams Selected button Button targets audio stream

1 In the Graphical view, Ctrl-click the audioStreamChecker menu, and choose Simulate.

2 On the Simulator, click any button other than the −12 Test Tone (original) button.

The Simulator jumps to the audioStreamTrack and plays the correct audio stream.

3 Wait for the track to finish playing, or click the Simulator's Menu button to jump back to the audioStreamChecker menu.

The –12 Test Tone (original) button is automatically selected, instead of the button corresponding to the last audio stream you heard. To fix this navigational inaccuracy, you must use System Parameter Registers.

Using System Parameter Registers

Like General Parameter Register Memories (GPRMs), System Parameter Register Memories (SPRMs) are used to store data as the DVD plays. But unlike GPRMs, SPRMs are not programmable, and you cannot use them to store variables. Instead, SPRMs are used to store information about the playback device, or the system, that the DVD is playing on. For example, when users set up their DVD players, they can specify their preferred aspect ratios, language settings, and parental levels. Some SPRMs, like the region code, are hardwired into the playback device; other SPRMs are used to track the button, chapter, or audio stream that is currently playing. For reference, the table below lists all available SPRMs and their functions.

Because SPRMs return information about the way the DVD player is configured, and also about how the DVD is playing, they are like properties in other scripting languages. All scripting languages use a common technique in which you load the value of a property into a variable, and then check that variable to make a decision and perform an action. DVD Studio Pro works exactly the same way by using SPRMs in conjunction with GPRMs. For example, you can move the value of an SPRM into a GPRM, and then check that value to make navigational decisions.

The following exercise will move the value of SPRM 1 (the current audio stream) into GPRM 1. Later command lines will check GPRM 1 to see what the current audio stream is and then jump to the appropriate button on the audioStreamChecker menu.

System Parameter Register Memories

SPRM	Function
SPRM 0	Menu language description code; DVD player set up by user
SPRM 1	Current audio stream number; set by user or program
SPRM 2	Current subtitle stream number; set by user or program
SPRM 3	Current angle number; set by user or program
SPRM 4	Current playing title number (Title); set by DVD player
SPRM 5	Current Video Title Set (VTS) number; set by DVD player
SPRM 6	Current title PGC number; set by DVD player
SPRM 7	Current part of title number (chapter); set by DVD player
SPRM 8	Current highlighted button number; set by viewer in DVD player
SPRM 9	Navigation timer; set by program, then times out
SPRM 10	Timer target; DVD track to play when SPRM 9 times out
SPRM 11	Player audio mixing mode for karaoke; set by program or DVD player setup
SPRM 12	Country code for parental management
SPRM 13	Parental management level in effect
SPRM 14	Player video configuration (Aspect Ratio, Letterbox Mode)
SPRM 15	Player audio configuration (DTS, AC-3, MPEG, PCM, SDDS)
SPRM 16	Initial language code for audio, DVD player setup by user
SPRM 17	Initial language code extension for audio
SPRM 18	Initial language code for subtitle, DVD player setup by user

Continued on next page

System Parameter Register Memories (continued)

SPRM	Function
SPRM 19	Initial language code extension for subtitle
SPRM 20	Player region code
SPRM 21	Reserved
SPRM 22	Reserved
SPRM 23	Reserved

NOTE ▶ For a list of all possible SPRM values, see the DVD Studio Pro manual's section on scripting.

1 In the Graphical view, Ctrl-click the background just under the audioStreamChecker menu, and choose Add > Script.

2 Double-click the name of the new script, and rename it *audioButtonSelector.*

3 Double-click the new script's icon to open it in the Script Editor.

4 Change the default Nop command to a Set GPRM command.

5 From the Inspector's Source Type menu, choose SPRM.

6 From the Inspector's Source Value menu, choose SPRM 1 (the current audio stream SPRM).

7 From the Inspector's Target menu, choose GPRM 1.

The finished command line now says, "Move into GPRM 1, the value of SPRM 1." To continue this script, you need to know the potential values that may now be moved into GPRM 1. The following table lists all of SPRM 1's potential values.

SPRM 1 Values

Current Audio Stream	SPRM 1 Value
Audio Stream 1	0
Audio Stream 2	1
Audio Stream 3	2
Audio Stream 4	3
Audio Stream 5	4
Audio Stream 6	5
Audio Stream 7	6
Audio Stream 8	7

> **NOTE ►** In most scripting languages, numbering always starts at 0, and DVD Studio Pro is no exception. When it comes to audio streams, the first stream is number 0, the second is number 1, and so on. In essence, the numbering scheme is offset by –1.

8 Create a new line of code, with a compare command, that says the following:

"Jump to button 1 of the audioStreamChecker menu, if GPRM 1 equals the immediate value of 0."

> **NOTE ►** For more info on creating compare commands, see the "Using Compare Commands" section earlier in this lesson.

9 Now create a third line to your script, again with a compare command, that says the following:

"Jump to the button 2 of the audioStreamChecker menu, if GPRM 1 equals the immediate value of 1."

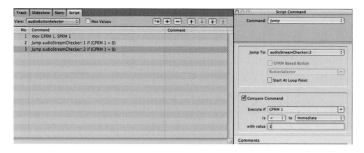

10 Create jump commands for the remaining four alternate audio streams. When you are done, you should have seven lines of code, as shown here:

This script is finished—sort of. You still need to ensure that the script executes at the appropriate time during your DVD's playback. In a moment, you'll do just this by assigning this script as a pre-script for the audioStreamChecker menu.

Targeting Scripts

When you programmed the remote control's Title button earlier in this lesson, you targeted the Title button directly at the buttonSelectorScript. In fact, you can directly link to any script from any of DVD Studio Pro's target menus. For example, using target menus, you can place a script between a track and a menu by targeting the script from the track's end jump setting.

1 In the Graphical view, select the audioStreamTrack.

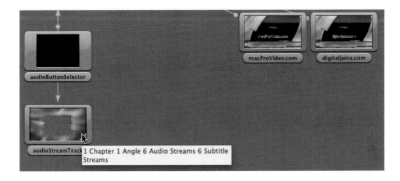

The Inspector updates to display the track's properties.

2 From the Inspector's End Jump menu, choose Scripts > audioButtonSelector.

Now, when the track finishes playing, it will jump to the audioButtonSelector script, and this script will check to see which audio stream the track was playing, before jumping to the audioStreamChecker menu.

But what if the user presses the remote control's Menu button while the track plays? In this situation, the DVD should jump back to the audio-StreamChecker menu, but before doing so, the audioButtonSelector script must be executed to choose the correct button. As you can see, you will also need to target the Menu button to the audioButtonSelector script if you want your DVD to navigate correctly. That's two individual settings. (Are there any others you've forgotten?) Wouldn't it be nice if you could just make one setting and ensure that your DVD will navigate correctly regardless of the path a viewer takes to get to the audioStreamChecker menu? Using pre-scripts, there is!

Using Pre-Scripts

A *pre-script* is a script that launches before the item it's assigned to, instead of after. In the following exercise, you'll assign the audioButtonSelector script as a pre-script to the audioStreamChecker menu. As a result, the audioButton-Selector script will always execute before the audioStreamChecker menu appears onscreen.

1 Select the audioStreamChecker menu.

The Inspector updates to display the menu's properties.

2 In the Inspector, choose the Advanced tab.

Advanced tab

Pre-Script menu

Halfway down the Advanced tab is a Pre-Script pop-up menu.

NOTE ▶ Pre-scripts can be attached to menus, slideshows, tracks, and stories.

3 From the Pre-Script pop-up menu, choose Scripts > audioButtonSelector.

This pre-script is now assigned, but there's one more important thing you must know about pre-scripts before you simulate the project to test this pre-script: Pre-scripts execute only when the DVD jumps to the root of the item to which the pre-script is assigned.

The root of an item is denoted in DVD Studio Pro's target menus by the item name in square brackets. For example, when targeting the root of a menu, you would choose the [Menu] option. If you target a button on the menu, the pre-script will not execute.

4 Select the audioStreamTrack item.

The Inspector updates to display the track's properties.

5 From the Inspector's End Jump pop-up menu, choose Menus > audioStreamChecker > [Menu].

6 To see the efforts of your labor, Ctrl-click the audioStreamChecker menu and choose Simulate Menu, click an audio stream button, and then click the menu key on the remote to return to the menu.

Now the correct audio stream button is always automatically selected.

NOTE ▶ You may notice that this script does not have an escape command on the last command line. There is a reason for this: Pre-scripts will not stop playback if no command line is executed, and instead the DVD player will just jump to the root element of the project item the pre-script is assigned to. Consequently, an escape command is unnecessary.

Checking Aspect Ratio

The project you're working on uses a 16:9 aspect ratio—in other words, it's a widescreen project. You've included just one set of 16:9 assets for this project, because it is unlikely you will ever build this example scripting project and watch it on a 4:3 television. In the real world, however, it's common to include both 16:9 and 4:3 assets on the same disc. For example, you could create two different sets of project menus—one set using a 16:9 aspect ratio and one set using a 4:3 aspect ratio. At playback, you can have the DVD-Video check the DVD player's aspect ratio setting and then jump to the matching set of menus. This ensures that viewers always see assets that are properly designed for their playback systems.

The DVD player's aspect ratio setting is stored in SPRM 14, and it can return the values listed in the table below. In the following example, you will write a script that checks SPRM 14 and then displays the correct button on the aspectRatioTest menu. Although you are not jumping to a completely different menu, you are still going to script a jump action to jump to the correct button on this menu.

SPRM 14 Values

Display Mode	Value
4:3	0
Pan-Scan	256
Letterbox	512
16:9	3072

1 In the Graphical view, add a new script under the aspectRatioTest menu, and call the new script *aspectRatioScript*.

2 With the new script still selected in the Graphical view, move over to the Inspector and name GPRM 2 *aspectRatioHolder*.

3 Double-click the script icon to open it in the Script Editor.

4 In the first command line, move the value of SPRM 14 into the GPRM named aspectRatioHolder.

5 On command line 2 of the script, create a new jump command that targets the aspectRatioTest menu's 4:3 button.

Next comes the part you have to think about. You are about to add a compare command to line 2 that checks the value of SPRM 14 that is currently stored in the GPRM named aspectRatioHolder. But first, refer to the table at the beginning of this exercise. Notice that every value less than 3072 is a 4:3 aspect ratio, and the value 3072 is the only one used for 16:9. Armed with that knowledge, you can write a compare command that jumps to the 4:3 button only if the value of the aspectRatioHolder GPRM is less than 3072.

6 Create the compare command that says: "Jump to the aspectRatioTest menu's 4:3 button *if* the aspectRatioHolder GPRM is less than the immediate value of 3072."

> **NOTE ▶** Be sure to choose a less-than operator (<) for your compare command. It's quite easy to accidentally select a greater-than operator (>), but that won't work at all well in this script.

Finished command line

7 On command line 3 of the script, create a new jump command that says: "Jump to the aspectRatioTest menu's 16:9 button."

We don't need a compare command here. Why? Because if line 2 is false, that means the DVD player is set to 16:9. The script will skip to line 3, and we will then jump to the 16:9 button. This script is done. Of course, you must still target the script from the menu's Test button, or there will be no way to execute the script.

NOTE ▶ In this script, command line 3 also acts as your escape command, because if no other command lines execute, line 3 will jump to the 16:9 button and the DVD will, at the very least, keep playing.

8 In the Graphical view, double-click the aspectRatioTest menu to open it in the Menu editor.

9 Ctrl-click the aspectRatioScript button (the Test button), and choose Target > Scripts > aspectRatioScript.

10 Ctrl-click the menu background, and choose Simulate.

11 Activate the Test button.

The 16:9 button is underlined.

12 Use the Simulator's Preferences pane to change the project's aspect ratio to 4:3 letterbox.

13 Simulate the menu, and activate the Test button once again.

The 4:3 button is now underlined.

14 Use the Simulator's Preferences pane to change the project's aspect ratio back to 16:9.

Checking Parental Level

Consider the following example: Your project contains content that some parents might find objectionable. Most DVD players allow viewers (such as parents) to set a parental level that is stored in SPRM 13. Armed with this knowledge, you can write a script that checks SPRM 13. If it's set to a low parental level, the DVD may then jump to a PG- or G-rated version of the content, instead of the R-rated version.

NOTE ▶ Some DVD-Video players do not correctly implement parental control options. Forewarned is forearmed!

SPRM 13 Values

Rating	SPRM 13 Value
G	1
PG	3
PG-13	4
R	6
NC-17	7

1 In the Graphical view, add a new script under the parentalLevelTest menu, and call the new script *parentalLevelScript*.

2 Double-click the new script to open it in the Script Editor.

3 On the first command line, move the value of SPRM 13 into GPRM 3.

Refer to the table at the beginning of the exercise and note that the General (G) rating has an SPRM 13 value of 1. GPRM 3 is now holding the value of SPRM 13, so you can write a command line that jumps to button G of the parentalLevelTest menu, if GPRM 3 equals 1.

4 Configure command line 2 to say: "Jump to the parentalLevelTest menu's button named G *if* GPRM 3 equals 1."

5 Create four additional command lines, one for each parental level setting listed in the table at the beginning of the exercise, and make sure each command targets the correct button on the parentalLevelTest menu.

> **TIP** ▶ In the Script Editor, you can copy (Cmd-C) and paste (Cmd-V) command lines. When writing repetitive command lines like the ones in this step, it's often useful to copy and paste the first line, then reconfigure the pasted command lines so that they target the correct project items.

When you're finished, the script should have six lines of code and should look like this:

6 At the bottom of the Script Editor, add a jump command that targets the Unspecified button of the parentalLevelTest menu.

> **NOTE** ▶ This last command line acts as the script's escape command.

7 In the Graphical view, double-click the parentalLevelTest menu.

The menu opens in the Menu Editor.

8 Ctrl-click the ParentalScript button (the Test Button), and choose Target > Scripts > parentalLevelScript.

9 Ctrl-click the background of the Menu Editor, and choose Simulate Menu.

10 Click the Test button.

The Simulator always highlights the Unspecified button! This is because there is no parental level setting preference for the Simulator. However, there *is* a trick you can use to simulate parental levels. You'll explore this in the next section, so leave the Simulator open and keep reading.

Simulating SPRMs

Earlier in this lesson you looked at the Simulator's Information Drawer. The Information Drawer lets you see the value of SPRMs and GPRMs as you simulate projects. Up to this point, you may have thought the Information Drawer was just a static display area, but it's not—the Information Drawer is interactive! In fact, you can change SPRM values in the Information Drawer, and see how these changes affect the playback of the project you're simulating.

1 In the Simulator's Information Drawer, locate SPRM 13.

2 Change SPRM 13 to the value of 1.

3 On the parentalLevelTest menu, click the Test button.

The G button highlights.

4 In the Information Drawer, change the value of SPRM 13 to 4.

5 On the parentalLevelTest menu, click the Test button.

The PG-13 button highlights.

6 Close the Simulator.

Using Jump Indirect

This project's menus all have two small buttons hidden in the action safe area, and these buttons link to DVD@ccess-enabled menus that take you to the sponsor's Web sites. Right now, you can jump to these DVD@ccess-enabled menus from any project menu. But when the DVD@ccess menus time out, they always return to the main menu. That is not correct navigation. Instead, they should return to the menu that jumped you to them in the first place. Fortunately, this is a very easy script to create, using DVD Studio Pro's jump indirect command.

Jump indirect will jump to a target value stored in a GPRM. As you saw earlier in this lesson, the last item command is used to store the target value of a project item in a GPRM. Does that give you any ideas?

In the following steps, you will use the Jump Indirect command in conjunction with the Last Item command to ensure that you always return to the correct menu after clicking one of the DVD@ccess buttons.

1 In the Graphical view, double-click the MPV-webSelector script.

The script opens in the Script Editor (the macProVideo.com button in each menu targets this script). Command line 1 of this script moves the value of the last item played into GPRM 7. Note that the last item to play will always be the menu that jumped you to this script. The next line jumps to the macProVideo.com DVD@ccess menu.

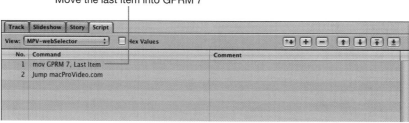

Move the last item into GPRM 7

2 From the Script Editor's View pop-up menu, choose the DJ-webSelector script.

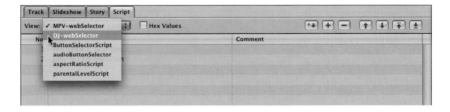

The DJ-webSelector script appears in the Script Editor (the digitalJuice.com button in each menu targets this script). Note that this script is very similar to the MPV-webSelector script. It still moves the value of the last item layed into GPRM 7, but it then jumps to the digitalJuice.com DVD@ccess menu.

The main point to take away from this is that in either script, GPRM 7 is filled with the value of the last item played. This is important, because you'll use the next script you create to check the value of GPRM 7.

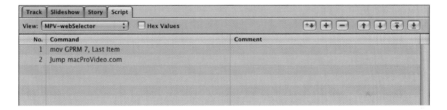

3 Add a script under the Web link menus, and name it *returnScript*.

4 Double-click the returnScript to open it in the Script Editor.

5 For command line 1, choose the Jump Indirect command.

6 From the Inspector's Set To pop-up menu, choose GPRM 7.

That's all there is to it. But before you test out this script, let's think about the script's logic. In the MPV-webSelector and DJ-webSelector scripts, you loaded the value of the last item played into GPRM 7. This value will stay in GPRM 7 until it is overwritten by another value, so you can use this new script's jump indirect command to check GPRM 7 and jump to whatever value GPRM 7 contains.

7 For safety's sake, create an escape command that jumps to the main menu.

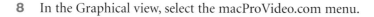

8 In the Graphical view, select the macProVideo.com menu.

The Inspector updates to display the macProVideo.com menu's properties.

9 From the General tab's Action pop-up menu, choose Scripts > returnScript.

Next you need to set the timeout action for the digitaljuice.com menu.

10 In the Graphical view, select the digitaljuice.com menu.

The Inspector updates to display the digitaljuice.com menu's properties.

11 From the General tab's Timeout Action menu, choose Scripts > returnScript.

12 Simulate the project, and use the Web link buttons at the bottom of each menu to jump to the Web link menus.

> **TIP** ▶ When the Web link menus time out, they return to the correct project menu.

> **NOTE** ▶ Why are the buttons to the sponsor Web link menus hidden in the action safe area? You cannot launch Web links on a television set, so viewers watching the project on a TV don't need to see the Web link buttons. This is a simple way to remove temptation, because on a TV, clicking these buttons does nothing. On a computer, however, these buttons will be visible and clickable.

Lesson Review

1. What does SPRM stand for?
2. What are SPRMs used for?
3. What does the Simulator's Information Drawer do?
4. What does the Last Item script command do?
5. What is a compare command?
6. How does a pre-script work?

Answers

1. System Parameter Register Memory.

2. System Parameter Register Memories (SPRMs) are like properties in other scripting languages; they return information about the way the DVD player is configured, as well as information about how the DVD is playing.

3. The Simulator's Information Drawer lets you check—and change—the value of GPRMs and SPRMs as you simulate projects.

4. The Last Item script command returns the value of the last item played in your project.

5. Compare commands are similar to conditional statements in other scripting languages, except they are written in reverse order. In other words, the"then"part of the statement comes before the "if"part.

6. If a script is assigned as a pre-script, it will execute before the item that it is attached to plays. However, a pre-script executes only when the DVD jumps to the root of the item it is attached to.

Appendix **A**

Creating a Motion Menu
in Final Cut Pro

Used extensively in most motion picture DVD releases, motion menus
add extra interest to your DVDs. DVD Studio Pro is not the only appli-
cation you can use to create a motion menu; depending on your work-
flow or the specific needs of the project, there may be times when you'd
prefer to create a motion menu using Final Cut Pro. This appendix,
presented in PDF format on the companion DVD, will show you
how to create a basic motion menu using Final Cut Pro. See Lessons >
Apdx_MotionMenu.

Bit Budgeting

There's one constant in the world of DVD-Video authoring—the size of your target DVD disc. Although the duration of your video may vary, in the end you have to squeeze that video onto a disc with finite space. This forces you to make some hard choices, because as video duration increases, you must decrease the encode quality in order to reduce the video's file size to make it fit on the target disc. This is where bit budgeting lends its talented hand.

If you have less than an hour of video on your disc, there's no need for a bit budget. An hour of video encoded at 9 Mbps will have a resultant file size of under 4 gigabytes (GB) (9 Mbps is the highest bit rate setting offered by the QuickTime MPEG encoder). In everyday authoring, you will use bit rates that are lower than 9 Mbps, so an hour of video, along with all associated audio streams and menus, will almost always fit on a DVD-5 disc.

But when the duration of your video passes 60 minutes, it's handy to know how to bit budget. Lesson 10 introduced you to bit budgeting. This appendix gives you an in-depth look at what it's all about.

How a Bit Budget Works

To make things easy, bit budgets are calculated in bytes, rather than kilobytes, megabytes, or gigabytes. This takes a lot of confusion out of the process, because you don't have to convert between kilobytes and megabytes, or compensate for the differences between computer and DVD storage conventions. Whether on a computer or on a DVD disc, a byte is always eight bits, which makes the calculations easier to handle.

You can't control the size of subtitle streams or menu images, and audio streams need to be encoded at very particular settings to maintain quality. In fact, of all the assets in your project, the video is the only one where large shifts in encode quality are acceptable. For example, there's not a terribly noticeable difference between video encoded at 6.5 Mbps and video encoded at 7.5 Mbps. Of course, a practiced eye can see the difference, but not as easily as any old ear can hear the difference between an AC-3 stream encoded at 96 kbps and one done at 192 kbps.

> **NOTE ▶** You may have read that DVDs can hold up to 4.7 GB of data. This number is misleading. In fact, DVDs can store up to 4.7 *DVD gigabytes* of data, which is not the same as a *computer gigabyte*. Confused? The 4.7 GB number you see on the label makes DVDs appear to store more information than they do. Here's how it works: A DVD actually holds 4.7 *billion bytes* of information. However, in computer terms, 1 kilobyte (KByte) is equal to 1024 bytes, 1 megabyte (MB) is equal to 1024 KBytes, and 1 GB is equal to 1024 MB. There's a lot of extra "24s" hanging around, and indeed, if you do the math, 4.7 billion bytes actually equals approximately 4.37 computer GB. The difference in data storage is over 300 MB!

Making a Bit Budget

To make a bit budget, you calculate the storage space you need for all the assets you have no control over. Then you subtract this amount from the total disc capacity of your target DVD, depending on the DVD-Video disc format you will be using (for instance, DVD-5 or DVD-9). Whatever is left over on the disc after you subtract the space you need for everything else is the room you have for the video.

Here is a summary of the steps for making a bit budget. Each step is explained later in this appendix.

1 Determine the storage capacity of your target DVD.

2 Reserve 5 percent of the target DVD disc as overhead for assets that may be added at a later point in the authoring process. Subtract this 5 percent reserve from the total capacity of the target DVD disc.

3 Calculate the storage space needed for your project's audio streams. Subtract this from the total capacity of the target DVD disc.

4 Calculate the storage space needed for all subtitle streams. Subtract this from the total capacity of the target DVD disc.

5 Calculate the storage space needed for highlight and Adobe Photoshop layer menus. Subtract this from the total capacity of the target DVD disc.

6 Calculate the storage space needed for any DVD-ROM content (on a hybrid DVD). Subtract this from the total capacity of the target DVD disc.

7 Use all remaining storage capacity for the project's video streams (including motion menus).

Determining Disc Capacity

You will usually decide upon a target DVD disc size before you start authoring the project. For example, if you intend to use your computer's SuperDrive to record a DVD-R, you know you'll be working with a DVD-5. If you are authoring a disc containing a feature-length movie, you may need to move up to a DVD-9. This makes the first step of creating a bit budget easy: Think of the type of DVD disc on which you'll distribute your project, and look at the following table to determine its available storage capacity:

DVD Storage Capacity

Media Type	Disc Capacity
DVD-5 (DVD-R)	4,700,000,000 bytes
DVD-9	8,540,000,000 bytes
DVD-10	9,400,000,000 bytes
DVD-18	17,080,000,000 bytes

Determining the Reserve

Multiplexing the project creates control data (.ifo files) and backup files (.bup files) that you will not be able to account for in advance. For this reason, leaving a bit of extra room on the disc is always a good idea. There will also be times when you unexpectedly need to add extra assets you didn't account for in the bit budget. Leaving a reserve gives you a margin of error that often provides the difference between a project that fits on a disc and one where you must go back and re-encode video assets at a lower rate.

For most situations, a reserve of 5 percent is adequate. The following table lists the reserve values to use with several different types of DVD discs:

Five Percent Reserve Values

Media Type	Reserve
DVD-5 (DVD-R)	235,000,000 bytes
DVD-9	427,000,000 bytes
DVD-10	470,000,000 bytes
DVD-18	854,000,000 bytes

Calculating Audio Storage

The total storage space needed for audio streams depends upon the length and bit rate of each stream. The following table lists common audio stream bit rates:

Audio Stream Bit Rates

Stream Type	Bit Rate
Stereo AC-3	192,000 bits/second (24,000 bytes/second)
5.1 AC-3	448,000 bits/second (56,000 bytes/second)
16-bit stereo PCM	1,536,000 bits/second (192,000 bytes/second)

To calculate how much (in bytes) of the target DVD disc your audio streams will consume, use the following formula:

Total audio minutes \times 60 \times audio bit rate \div 8 = Audio storage

(where 60 represents seconds per minute and 8 represents bits per byte).

If your project uses audio streams encoded using several different bit rates, you'll need to do some extra math. First you must calculate the size of each individual stream. Then you add the totals together to determine the storage space needed for all audio streams combined.

Calculating Subtitle Storage

Each individual subtitle within a subtitle stream uses around 4000 bytes; that's 4000 bytes for each group of letters that flicks across the screen. To calculate the storage space (in bytes) for subtitle streams, you must count each separate subtitle in every project subtitle stream, and then multiply that number by 4,000:

Number of subtitles × 4000 = Subtitle storage

Calculating Still Menu Storage

Just as with a JPEG still image, the amount of space needed to store a still menu varies with the menu's visual complexity. Despite this fact, it's rare for a still menu, no matter how visually complex, to take up more than 150,000 bytes on the final DVD disc.

Highlight menus turn a subpicture stream (the overlay) on and off over the top of a single background image, so each highlight menu uses approximately 150,000 bytes. Use the following formula to calculate the storage space (in bytes) needed for a project's highlight menus:

Number of highlight menus × 150,000 = Subpicture storage

Photoshop layer menus work differently. When DVD Studio Pro compiles your project, it creates a new I-frame for each button state of every button on the menu. When buttons are selected or activated, the DVD-Video player actually jumps between these separate I-frames to create a rollover effect. Use this formula to calculate the storage space (in bytes) needed for Photoshop layer menus:

Total number of buttons on all Photoshop layer menus × number of button states + 1 × 100,000 = Photoshop layer menu storage

(where the +1 represents the menu normal state).

Button states can be selected and activated. If your Photoshop layer menu uses selected and activated states, the *Number of button states* value equals 2. If only selected states are used, then the *Number of button states* value equals 1.

> **TIP** If your project uses a combination of highlight and Photoshop layer menus, calculate each group of menus separately and add the totals together to find the combined storage capacity needed for all of the project's menus.

Calculating Transition Storage

DVD Studio Pro 4 will automatically generate transitions for you. Because DVD Studio Pro generates the transitions when the project is built, it's nearly impossible to estimate exactly how much storage space your transitions will require. However, you can get close.

You will typically include transitions of no longer than 2 seconds in your projects. A 2-second transition absorbs approximately 1,000,000 bytes of storage space (slightly less than 1 MB). This provides a good best-guess estimate to use for transitions in your bit budget.

The next step is determining how many transitions your project uses. To do so, you must tally up each and every project item and element that uses a transition. This includes each menu, each button, each slide, and each track.

Number of required transitions × 1,000,000 = Transition storage

Calculating DVD-ROM Storage

To calculate the size of your project's DVD-ROM content, in the Finder select the folder containing the DVD-ROM content and press Cmd-I. An Info window opens and tells you how big the folder is. You must next convert the size of the folder into bytes using this formula:

Size of folder in MB × 1024 (KBytes) × 1024 (bytes) = DVD-ROM storage

> **TIP** In the Info window, the number in parentheses is the file size in bytes.

Calculating Video Bit Rates

In bit budget terms, this is the endgame! This step determines the bit rate to use when encoding MPEG-2 video streams for your project's tracks and motion menus. It's a two-step process. In the first step, you will calculate the amount of space left on the disc after all your audio, subtitle, menu, and DVD-ROM content is accounted for. This left-over space will be filled with video streams. Use the following formula to determine how much space is available for your project's video assets:

> DVD disc capacity
>
> – Reserve
>
> – Audio storage
>
> – Subtitle storage
>
> – Subpicture streams
>
> – Photoshop layer menu storage
>
> – Still menu data
>
> – Transition storage
>
> – DVD-ROM storage
>
> _____
>
> = Space available for video assets

A DVD disc is like an orange cut in half. The fuller the disc is with video content, the sweeter the images when the disc is squeezed by the DVD-Video player. You want to fill the disc to the brim with video, which means you must figure out the compression *sweet spot* for your video streams—that is, the bit rate that creates the highest quality of video that fits in the left-over space on the target DVD disc. After figuring out how much space is left on the disc, use this formula to determine the maximum bit rate for encoding project video streams:

> Space available for video
>
> ÷ Video minutes
>
> ÷ 60 (seconds per minute)
>
> × 8 (bits per byte)
>
> ÷ 1,000,000 (bits into Mbits)
>
> _____
>
> = Video data rate (in Mbps)

NOTE ▶ Don't forget that the total combined data rate for all assets in a single multiplexed DVD-Video stream is 10.08 Mbps. If your bit budget says you can use a high bit rate, take a moment to add up the bandwidth needed for each track in your project. Add the video stream's data rate with the combined sum of the track's audio and subtitle stream data rates. This final number should not exceed 10.08 Mpbs.

Final Cut Studio Workflows

Apple's family of professional audio and video applications are designed to work together seamlessly, even in the most demanding postproduction workflows. The Final Cut Studio product line—a comprehensive and integrated postproduction package—includes Final Cut Pro 5, Soundtrack Pro, Motion 2, DVD Studio Pro 4, Compressor 2, LiveType 2, Cinema Tools 3. These tools, in conjunction with Shake 4 and Logic Pro 7, provide professional editors with the most comprehensive toolkit in the industry. The appendix on the DVD accompanying this book details the roles of each application in the Final Cut Pro production process. You will also find a sample Final Cut Studio workflow, and information on "roundtripping," the ability to embed and open application project files while working in another application. See **Lessons>Apdx_Final Cut Studio Workflows**.

Glossary

4:3 The most common video aspect ratio, used for NTSC and PAL video standards. Also known as the 1.33 aspect ratio. See also *aspect ratio*.

16:9 The widescreen aspect ratio supported by the DVD-Video specification. Also known as the 1.78 aspect ratio. See also *aspect ratio*.

AC-3 audio Compressed audio format developed by Dolby Laboratories. Also known as Dolby Digital audio. Supports single-channel through 5.1 surround sound configurations.

action safe area An area close to the edges of the screen, which contains information that is not as important or may be cut off on some televisions.

active area Rectangular area that defines the part of the overlay graphic used for a button. Also defines a button's "hotspot" that can be clicked when viewing the title on a computer. See also *button*.

aspect ratio A video frame's width-to-height ratio on your viewing screen. The most common aspect ratio is 4:3 used for standard video. The DVD-Video specification also supports the 16:9 aspect ratio. See also *4:3*; *16:9*.

assets The audio, video, and still image files used by DVD-Video Studio Pro in authoring DVD projects.

AUDIO_TS folder One of two folders required on DVD-Video discs (the VIDEO_TS folder being the other). The AUDIO_TS folder is reserved for use on DVD-Audio titles, and is always created but left empty when building projects with DVD Studio Pro. See also *VIDEO_TS folder*.

authoring The process of creating a DVD. Authoring a DVD project requires you to use your sources to create elements, such as menus and tracks, connect the elements so that the viewer can get from one to the other, and then format the project into a DVD-compliant set of files, images, or DVD. See also *elements*.

B

background image All menus have a background image, over which the menu's buttons are placed. The background can be a still image or a motion video (creating a motion menu). See also *motion menu*.

bit rate The number of bits per second that make up a digital video or audio asset. The higher the bit rate, the better the quality. However, higher bit rates require larger file sizes and can cause playback problems if the DVD player is unable to keep up. The DVD-Video specification places bit rate limits on assets used in DVD titles.

build Compiles the project into its DVD-compliant format, creating the AUDIO_TS and VIDEO_TS folders. The streams that make up a track are multiplexed into a single video object file.

button Each DVD menu has from 1 up to 36 buttons that the viewer can activate to access areas within the DVD. You can also place buttons over a video track. DVD Studio Pro supports three button types: overlay-based using an overlay graphic, shape-based using supplied or custom shape graphics, and layer-based using layers in a Abode Photoshop format file. You can connect buttons to a wide variety of project elements, including buttons on other menus, tracks, stories, slideshows, and scripts. See also *button navigation*; *button states*; *motion button*.

button navigation Defines what happens when you press a remote control's arrow buttons. You can manually configure each button's navigation settings or use DVD Studio Pro's auto assign feature to automatically set the navigation of all buttons on a menu at once. It is important to set the navigation so that viewers can logically get from the current button to the desired one.

button states Each button on a menu can be in one of three states: normal, selected, and activated. In the normal state, the button displays its inactive condition. All buttons on a menu except one are in the normal state. A button enters the selected state when the viewer navigates to it. Only one button at a time can be in the selected state. The selected button enters the activated state when the viewer presses the remote control's Enter button. Depending on the button type, you use highlights or layers to indicate each button's state.

C

chapter Used to identify places in a track that you can connect to. Commonly used to identify scenes for a chapter index menu. You can assign up to 99 chapters in each track.

clip Term used to describe a video or audio asset, especially after they have been added to a track. See also *assets*.

color mapping When working with overlay graphics, the process of assigning a color and opacity setting to colors used in the overlay graphic. You assign separate colors and opacities for all three button states (normal, selected, and advanced). See also *overlay*.

compile See *build*.

Compressor The advanced compression tool that ships with DVD Studio Pro and Final Cut Pro.

constant bit rate (CBR) encoding A video MPEG encoding method that uses the same bit rate for the entire video file. Its primary advantage is that you can reliably predict the resulting file size. Its disadvantage is that all video scenes, whether still or with lots of motion, are treated the same. See also *variable bit rate (VBR) encoding*.

Dolby Digital See *AC-3 audio*.

D

droplets Active icons that provide a quick and easy way to convert video to a format such as MPEG-2 without having to open the Compressor application.

drop zone An element you can add to a menu's background. You can assign a still image or moving video asset to the drop zone. You can size, position, and rotate the drop zone. When you build the title, the drop zone is merged with the background. Drop zones cannot be linked to other elements in the project.

dual-layer disc A DVD with two layers on a single disc side, almost doubling a single-layer disc's capacity.

DVD-9 disc A dual layer disc that holds approximately 7.95 GB of information.

DVD@ccess A feature in DVD Studio Pro that allows you to add additional interactivity to your title when played on a computer. With DVD@ccess, you can add links to menus, tracks, and markers that can be used to open an application on the computer to display extra content. For example, you can open the system's Web browser and direct it to a specific URL.

DVD-ROM A DVD with files in addition to those included on a standard DVD-Video disc. These files are accessed when you play the title on a computer—they are ignored by standard set-top DVD players. The files can be almost anything you can write to a disc. Examples include additional graphics, such as brochures, or software.

E

elements A DVD project consists of elements, such as menus, tracks, stories, slideshow, and scripts. Authoring a project involves creating the elements and connecting them together. See also *authoring*.

encoding The process of converting video or audio into a different format. For DVD projects, this means converting the video into an MPEG-2 file, and the audio into one of several DVD-compliant formats.

F

first play The element of your project that appears when you start playing the title. You can assign any of your project's elements as the first play.

format The process of writing your build files to your output device, which can be a DVD-R drive, and DLT drive, or your system's hard disk.

L

letterbox A method for displaying 16:9 video on a 4:3 monitor. The entire frame appears, with black bars at the top and bottom. See also *pan and scan*.

line 21 support In NTSC systems, the video line that can contain special data. Most often used to contain closed caption information.

M

marker An element you can add to a track to identify specific parts of the track's content. There are several marker types, including chapter markers used to link chapter buttons, and button highlight markers used to control buttons over video. You can have up to chapter 99 markers in a track, and up to 255 total markers in a track.

menu An element of a project that provides buttons for the purpose of connecting to other elements in your project, such as tracks and slideshows. A menu can have a still or full motion background, and can have audio. See also *background image*; *drop zone*; *motion button*; *motion menu*.

motion button Button shapes that can display a thumbnail image of an assigned asset. The asset can be a still image or a video clip.

motion menu A menu that contains moving video content, either as the background, a motion button, or a drop zone. See also *background*; *drop zone*; *motion button*.

MPEG An group of encoding standards from the Motion Picture Encoding Group. They define the MPEG-1 and MPEG-2 encoding standards used by DVDs.

muxing The mixing of assets and building of your DVD.

NTSC NTSC stands for National Television Standards Committee, the organization that defines North American broadcast standards. The term "NTSC video" refers to the video standard defined by the committee, which has a specifically limited color gamut, is interlaced, and is approximately 720 × 480 pixels, 29.97 fps.

N

overlay A still graphic that provides the highlight information for the buttons when creating menus or buttons over video. Overlays can be simple, using a single color on a white background, or advanced, using up to four predefined colors. You use color mapping to assign highlight colors to those used in the overlay, setting different colors for each button.

O

P

PAL PAL stands for Phase Alternating Line. A 25 fps (720×576 pixels) inter-laced video format used by many European countries.

pan and scan A method for displaying 16:9 video on a 4:3 monitor. Content is cropped at each end so that the 4:3 monitor is filled. An MPEG-2 video clip with pan and scan can include vectors that dynamically change the part of the picture that is cropped. See also *letterbox*.

pixel aspect ratio The distance between a pixel, the one next to it, and the one below it defines its aspect ratio. A square pixel aspect ratio, as used on computer systems, has the same pixel distance in both directions. Video monitors do not have the same distance in both directions, and have rectangular pixels. NTSC and PAL video each have different pixel aspect ratios. This difference must be accounted for when creating graphics on a computer for use in a DVD project.

project When you author a DVD title with DVD Studio Pro, you create and work in a project.

S

scripts An advanced feature included in the DVD specifications, which uses a simple scripting language to provide interactivity and access to special functions available through a DVD player.

Simulator A tool in Digital Studio Pro that simulates a DVD player, enabling you to test your projects, or portions of your project.

slideshow An element in your project that contains up to 99 still images and accompanying audio. DVD Studio Pro allows you to convert a slideshow into a track so that you can add additional features to it, such as a subtitle or additional languages for the audio.

state (normal, selected, and activated) See also *color mapping*.

story An element in your project that is specific to a particular track, allowing you to create a customized playback of a track. These can be used to create alternative versions of a track that skip violent content or plays just the track's highlights.

subtitle The DVD-Video specification provides for up to 32 subtitle streams to be included in each track. These streams can contain plain text, similar to a closed caption function. They can also be used to provide buttons over video, allowing you to have buttons appear outside of the menus. You can create the subtitles within DVD Studio Pro or import them from outside sources.

timecode A method of associating each frame of video in a clip with a unique, sequential unit of time. The format is hours: minutes: seconds; frames.

T

title safe area The area containing important text and graphics that must remain intact when viewed on a television.

track The element of a DVD Studio Pro project that contains the video, audio, and subtitle streams that provide the primary content of the DVD. Each project can have a combination of up to 99 tracks, stories, and slideshows.

variable bit rate (VBR) encoding A video MPEG encoding method that varies the bit rate based on the video content. Scenes with little motion use low bit rates to reduce the disc space needed; scenes with lots of motion use higher bit rates for greater quality.

V

VIDEO_TS folder One of two folders required on DVD-Video discs (the AUDIO_TS folder being the other). DVD Studio Pro creates the VIDEO_TS folder when you build your project. It contains all of the video, audio, subtitle, menu, and navigation files that make up your DVD-Video title.

Index

H

I

W

Z

The Apple Pro Training Series

The official curriculum of the Apple Pro Training and Certification Program, the Apple Pro Training books are a comprehensive, self-paced courses written by acknowledged experts in the field.

- Focused lessons take you step-by-step through the process of creating real-world digital video or audio projects.
- All media and project files are included on the companion DVD.
- Ample illustrations help you master techniques fast.
- Lesson goals and time estimates help you plan your time.
- Chapter review questions summarize what you've learned.

Apple Pro Training Series:

0-321-33481-7

In this best-selling guide, Diana Weynand starts with basic video editing techniques and takes you all the way through Final Cut Pro's powerful advanced features. Using world-class documentary footage, you'll learn to mark and edit clips, color correct sequences, create transitions, apply filters and effects, add titles, work with audio, and more.

Apple Pro Training Series: Advanced Editing Techniques in Final Cut Pro 5
0-321-33549-X

Director and editor Michael Wohl shares must-know professional techniques for cutting dialogue scenes, action scenes, fight and chase scenes, documentaries, comedy, music videos, multi-camera projects, and more. Also covers Soundtrack Pro, audio finishing, managing clips and media, and working with film.

Apple Pro Training Series: Color Correction and Effects in Final Cut Pro 5
0-321-33548-1

This Apple-authorized guide delivers hard-to-find training in real-world color correction and effects techniques, including motion effects, keying and compositing, titling, scene-to-scene color matching, and correcting for broadcast specifications.

Apple Pro Training Series: Optimizing Your Final Cut Pro System
0-321-26871-7

Written and field-tested by industry pros Sean Cullen, Matthew Geller, Charles Roberts, and Adam Wilt, this is the ultimate guide for installing, configuring, optimizing, and trouble-shooting Final Cut Pro in real-world post-production environments.

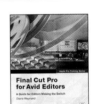

Apple Pro Training Series: Final Cut Pro for Avid Editors
0-321-24577-6

Master trainer Diana Weynand takes you through a comprehensive "translation course" designed for professional video and film editors who already know their way around Avid nonlinear systems.

The Apple Training Series:

Apple Training Series: iLife '05
0-321-33020-X
Apple Training Series: GarageBand 2
0-321-33019-6
Apple Training Series: Mac OS X Support Essentials
0-321-33547-3

Apple Training Series: Desktop and Portable Systems, Second Edition
0-321-33546-5
Apple Training Series: Mac OS X Server Essentials
0-321-36984-X

To order books or find out about the Apple Pro Training Series, visit: **www.peachpit.com/appleprotraining**